EXPLORING THE VIRTUAL FRONTIER: AN INTRODUCTORY GUIDE TO VIRTUAL AND AUGMENTED REALITIES

DR. AMOL PRAKASH BHAGAT, MILIND R. DHANDE, DR. SANDIP V. KENDRE, DR. PRITI A. KHODKE, DILIP R. UIKE

To the dreamers and innovators who dare to redefine reality,
To the pioneers who see possibilities beyond the tangible,
And to the curious minds exploring uncharted frontiers of technology—
This book is dedicated to you.

May your journey through the virtual and augmented realms inspire new horizons and infinite wonder.

Contents

Foreword

In the rapidly evolving landscape of technology, few innovations have captured the imagination of humanity like Virtual Reality (VR) and Augmented Reality (AR). These technologies are more than just tools—they are gateways to new dimensions of experience, creativity, and understanding. They offer us the ability to traverse fantastical landscapes, to see the unseen, and to engage with the world in ways once thought impossible.

The journey into the virtual frontier is as much about exploration as it is about discovery. It is a journey that demands an understanding of the principles underpinning VR and AR, the devices that enable these immersive experiences, and the architectures that make them possible. This book, *Exploring the Virtual Frontier: An Introductory Guide to Virtual and Augmented Realities,* serves as a comprehensive guide for anyone embarking on this exciting adventure.

Chapter 1 lays the foundation by delving into the concept of Virtual Reality—its introduction, evolution, and key elements. It challenges the reader to consider how "fooling" the brain with simulated environments impacts our perception and explores contemporary applications that demonstrate VR's transformative potential.

The exploration continues in Chapter 2 with an in-depth look at input and output devices that bring VR to life. From position trackers and navigation interfaces to gesture and haptic systems, this chapter offers a practical understanding of the tools that bridge the gap between the physical and the virtual.

Chapter 3 delves into the computing architectures that underpin VR experiences. The intricacies of rendering pipelines, workstation-based systems, and distributed architectures highlight the technological backbone supporting virtual worlds.

Transitioning to Augmented Reality, Chapter 4 introduces readers to the fascinating realm of AR, examining its defining characteristics, underlying technologies, and its relationship with other innovations. Chapters 5 and 6 expand on AR's hardware, software, and applications, offering insights into its transformative role across industries and its potential future trajectories.

This book is not merely an academic exploration; it is a call to embrace the opportunities presented by VR and AR. Whether you are a student, a developer, a researcher, or simply an enthusiast, this guide aims to provide you with the knowledge and tools to engage with these revolutionary technologies meaningfully.

As you turn the pages, may you find inspiration and guidance to navigate this frontier, pushing the boundaries of what is possible and shaping the realities of tomorrow.

Preface

In a world increasingly shaped by technological innovation, Virtual Reality (VR) and Augmented Reality (AR) stand as transformative forces, redefining how we perceive, interact with, and shape our environment. These technologies, once confined to the realms of science fiction, have matured into powerful tools that are reshaping industries, enriching entertainment, and expanding the boundaries of human creativity and knowledge.

Exploring the Virtual Frontier: An Introductory Guide to Virtual and Augmented Realities is designed to provide a foundational understanding of these emerging fields. It is a comprehensive resource for students, professionals, and enthusiasts eager to delve into the principles, technologies, and applications that make VR and AR possible.

The book begins with an exploration of Virtual Reality in Chapter 1, examining its evolution, foundational concepts, and the physiological underpinnings that make immersive experiences possible. Topics such as the key elements of VR, its contemporary applications, and its potential to challenge our perception of reality are discussed in detail.

In Chapter 2, we dive into the input and output devices that bridge human interaction with virtual environments. From position trackers and navigation interfaces to gesture and haptic systems, this chapter emphasizes the technological tools that create seamless and immersive experiences.

Chapter 3 tackles the complex computing architectures behind VR, shedding light on rendering pipelines, PC-based graphics systems, and distributed VR frameworks. These insights highlight the intricate technological backbone required for creating immersive virtual environments.

The focus shifts to Augmented Reality in Chapter 4, offering an introduction to this dynamic field, its defining features, and its historical evolution. The chapter explores AR's relationship with other technologies and sets the stage for understanding its potential.

Chapters 5 and 6 delve into the hardware, software, and applications of AR. From mobile AR's advantages and limitations to the diverse industries benefiting from AR solutions, these chapters provide practical insights into how AR is revolutionizing our world.

This book was conceived to empower readers with a blend of technical depth and practical relevance. Each chapter builds upon the last, creating a structured path through the complexities of VR and AR. It is our hope that this guide inspires curiosity, sparks innovation, and encourages readers to contribute to the ongoing evolution of these transformative technologies.

As you embark on this journey into the virtual frontier, remember that the limits of these technologies are only bounded by the extent of our imagination.

Acknowledgments

This book, *Exploring the Virtual Frontier: An Introductory Guide to Virtual and Augmented Realities,* would not have been possible without the support, guidance, and inspiration of many individuals and organizations.

First and foremost, we would like to express our deepest gratitude to the pioneers and visionaries in the fields of Virtual and Augmented Realities. Your groundbreaking work and relentless pursuit of innovation have provided the foundation for this guide.

To our mentors and colleagues in academia and industry, your insights, constructive feedback, and encouragement have been invaluable throughout the writing process. Your expertise and passion for advancing technology have profoundly influenced the direction and depth of this book.

A special thanks to the researchers, developers, and creators who continue to push the boundaries of VR and AR. Your commitment to shaping immersive and transformative experiences inspires the next generation of innovators.

To our friends and family, your unwavering support and patience have been a source of strength during this journey. Thank you for believing in the vision of this project and for always encouraging us to pursue our passion for technology and education.

We are also deeply grateful to our publisher and editorial team for their guidance, professionalism, and dedication. Your hard work and attention to detail have brought this book to life.

Finally, to the readers of this book—students, professionals, and enthusiasts alike—thank you for your curiosity and enthusiasm for exploring the virtual frontier. It is for you that this guide was written, and we hope it serves as a stepping stone toward your own discoveries and innovations.

About Authors

DR. AMOL P. BHAGAT completed his B.E. in Information Technology from Government College of Engineering, Amravati in the year 2005; with Master's degree in Computer Science and Engineering from Walchand College of Engineering, Sangli in the year 2009 and Ph.D. in Information Technology in year 2016 from Sant Gadge Baba University, Amravati. He is with Prof Ram Meghe College of Engineering & Management, Badnera- Amravati since the year 2010. He also completed his LL.B. from Dr. Panjabrao Deshmukh Law College Amravati. He has to his credit: 7 Granted Patents, 24 Patents filed, 100 Research papers published in National and International Journals and 8 books and 25 book chapters published. He received national and international awards of repute. He served as Resource Person in more than 130 programmes such as Workshops, STTPs, FDPs sponsored and funded by IETE, ISTE, IEI, AICTE, DST, CSI, NABARD, Ministry of Agriculture, etc. He has a vast experience in various domains like Medical Image Processing, Signal Processing, Soft Computing, Machine Learning, Deep Learning, Big Data Analytics, Quantum Computing, and Data Science.

MILIND R. DHANDE completed his B.E. in Computer Science and Engineering from Prof Ram Meghe Institute of Technology & Research, Badnera, Amravati in the year 1992. He has vast experience of 32 years. He is Assistant Director of Industry-Institute Interaction Cell Prof Ram Meghe Institute of Technology & Research, Badnera, Amravati. He is working as Associate Professor in Prof Ram Meghe Institute of Technology & Research, Badnera, Amravati.

DR. SANDIP V. KENDRE completed his B.E. in Information Technology form M. S. Bidve Engineering College, Latur in the year 2005; with Master's degree in Computer Science and Engineering from Walchand College of Engineering, Sangli in the year 2009 and Ph.D. in Computer Science of Engineering in year 2024 from Sandip University, Nasik. He served as Assistant Professor in Sandip Foundation, Nasik from 2009 to 2011. He is working as Assistant Professor in Government Polytechnic since 2011. He is now working with Tribal Minister as Officer on Special Duty (OSD), Government of Maharashtra. He has a vast experience in various domains like Soft Computing, Machine Learning, Deep Learning, Qunatum Computing, Big Data Analytics, and Data Science.

DR. PRITI A. KHODKE completed her B.E. (Computer Science & Engg) from Govt. College of Engineering, Amravati in the year 1995. She completed her Master's degree M.E. in Computer Science & Engg from College of Engineering Badnera in the year 2001 and Ph.D in 2017. She has a varied experience of 30 years in various domains ranging from Technical to administrative. She served various organizations including Tata Unisys Ltd. Education Centre Amravati ,C-DAC, ACTS Badnera, Khodke Computers Pvt. Ltd., Amravati, I²IT, Infosys Technologies Ltd Pune. She is with Prof Ram Meghe College of Engineering & Management, Badnera- Amravati since 2009. She has to her credit 2 patents granted, 4 patents filed, 31 research papers published in National and International Journal and 2 book chapters published.

DILIP R. UIKE completed B.E. degree in Computer Science & Engineering from Government College of Engineering, Aurangabad in the year 2005 and M.E. in Computer Science & Engineering from Sipna's College of Engineering and Technology, Amravati in the year 2016. He served as a lecturer in HVPM's College of Engineering and Technology, Amravati from the year 2006 to January 2011. Currently he is working as Assistant Professor in the Department of Information Technology, Government College of Engineering, Amravati, Maharashtra, India since January 2011. He has total 18 years of experience in teaching field. His areas of interest are Artificial Intelligence, Machine Learning, and Deep Learning.

Prologue

The lines between the physical and digital worlds are blurring. As technology advances, Virtual Reality (VR) and Augmented Reality (AR) have emerged as revolutionary tools that redefine how we interact with our surroundings, engage with content, and connect with one another. These technologies are not just shaping industries; they are transforming our perceptions of reality itself.

Exploring the Virtual Frontier: An Introductory Guide to Virtual and Augmented Realities is your gateway to understanding these cutting-edge domains. Designed for students, professionals, and enthusiasts, this book provides a structured exploration of the principles, technologies, and applications of VR and AR, catering to both beginners and those looking to deepen their knowledge.

The journey begins with **Chapter 1**, where the world of Virtual Reality is introduced. From its basic concepts to the philosophical and practical implications of "fooling" the brain, this chapter lays a strong foundation. Topics such as the evolution of VR, key elements of virtual environments, and the interplay of human physiology and perception are covered to help you grasp the depth of VR's potential.

Building on this foundation, **Chapter 2** delves into the hardware and interfaces that enable VR experiences. Whether it's positional tracking, gesture interfaces, or haptic systems, this chapter provides a technical overview of the tools that connect us to immersive virtual environments.

In **Chapter 3**, we examine the computing architectures that make VR possible. From rendering pipelines to distributed architectures, this chapter offers insights into the complex systems that power virtual worlds, ensuring seamless and realistic experiences.

The focus then shifts to Augmented Reality in **Chapter 4**, where AR is defined and its underlying technologies explored. This chapter highlights the unique capabilities of AR, its history, and how it complements other technological advancements.

Chapters 5 and 6 dive deeper into the hardware, software, and applications of AR. From mobile AR systems to its transformative impact on industries like healthcare, education, and entertainment, these chapters offer a forward-looking perspective on AR's role in shaping our future.

Throughout this book, our goal is to demystify VR and AR while showcasing their incredible potential. Each chapter is crafted to provide a balance between foundational knowledge and practical applications, empowering readers to envision, create, and innovate within these rapidly evolving fields.

Whether you are a curious beginner, a seasoned professional, or an industry visionary, this book invites you to explore the virtual frontier. Let's embark on this journey together, uncovering the possibilities that await in the realms of VR and AR.

1. Virtual Reality

1.1 Introduction

Virtual reality (VR) technology is advancing at such a rapid pace that defining it based on specific devices is impractical, as those devices may become obsolete within a short period. To better understand VR, let's explore two illustrative examples:

In the first example, imagine a person experiencing the sensation of flying over a virtual San Francisco by flapping their own wings, as demonstrated in Figure 1.1.

Figure 1.1: Birdly experience

This scenario, known as the Birdly experience developed by the Zurich University of the Arts, involves the user wearing a VR headset while engaging in wing-flapping motions. The setup includes a motion platform and a fan to provide additional sensory inputs, enhancing the realism of the experience. The figure also illustrates how visual stimuli are delivered separately to each eye for a fully immersive experience.

The second example involves a mouse navigating a virtual maze projected onto a surrounding screen while running on a freely rotating ball.

Figure 1.2 depicts this experimental arrangement, which is utilized by neurobiologists at LMU Munich. In this setup, visual stimuli are presented to the mouse as it moves on the spherical treadmill, allowing researchers to study its behaviour and perception.

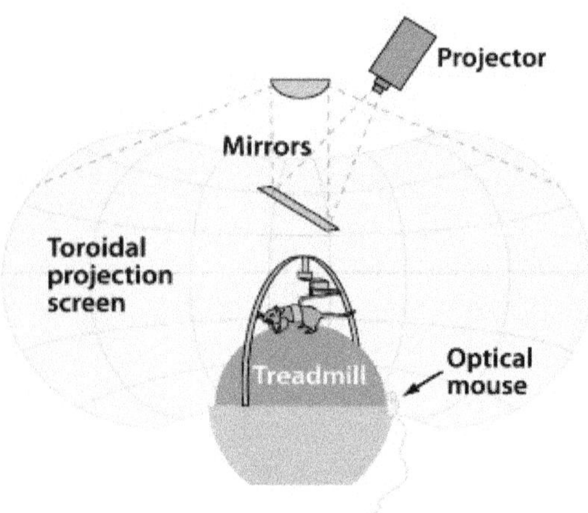

Figure 1.2: (Figure by Kay Thurley).

Based on these examples, VR can be defined as follows:

Definition: VR refers to the process of inducing specific behaviors in an organism through artificial sensory inputs, wherein the organism has minimal or no awareness of the external intervention.

This definition highlights four key components:

1. **Targeted Behavior:** The organism engages in a designed "experience" such as flying, walking, exploring, watching a film, or interacting socially.

2. **Organism:** This could include humans, other species, or even smaller life forms like fruit flies, cockroaches, fish, mice, or monkeys—all of which have been subjects of VR studies.

3. **Artificial Sensory Stimulation:** VR leverages engineering techniques to partially or entirely replace natural sensory inputs with artificial ones, creating a convincing alternate reality.

4. **Awareness:** During the experience, the organism is typically unaware of the sensory manipulation, resulting in a sense of presence within the virtual environment. This lack of awareness creates a convincing illusion of being in a different world.

In essence, VR systems rely on maintaining a perceptual illusion for the organism. This makes human physiology and sensory perception fundamental elements of VR technology.

1.2 Expanding the Boundaries of VR

When someone wears a modern VR headset, also known as a head-mounted display (HMD), and participates in an immersive session, they are unquestionably engaging with virtual reality. However, how far can the concept of VR stretch beyond such direct examples? Could listening to music through headphones count as VR? What about watching a movie in a theatre, where technologies like projectors and audio systems deliver artificial sensory experiences?

Taking it further, consider a painting or portrait hanging on a wall. In this case, the technology involves paints and a canvas, yet it still provides a form of sensory stimulation. Even reading a novel might be considered a type of VR. Here, the technologies involved are writing and printing, with visual stimulation being less direct compared to a movie or audio system.

Defining VR's precise boundaries may not be necessary. While debates can arise over these borderline cases, the primary focus should remain on understanding the foundational principles that define VR. These boundary examples, however, offer valuable insights into VR's evolution and historical context.

1.3 Does "Fooling" the Brain Really Make Sense?

The notion of "fooling" an organism, as mentioned in the VR definition, may initially seem abstract. However, research in neurobiology provides tangible evidence for this concept. When an animal navigates its surroundings, its brain creates neural structures called *place cells*, which store spatial information. These cells activate when the organism revisit's specific locations, as illustrated in Figure 1.3 (a). Additionally, *grid cells* encode spatial locations in a grid-like pattern, akin to Cartesian coordinates, as shown in Figure 1.3 (b).

Remarkably, studies reveal that such neural patterns can form even during VR experiences. In other words, the brain may create place cells for environments that do not physically exist. This strongly indicates that VR successfully "fools" the brain into perceiving a virtual world as real.

This phenomenon raises intriguing questions: Could reading a vividly descriptive novel trigger similar neural response? If so, might our brains form mental maps for fictional places?

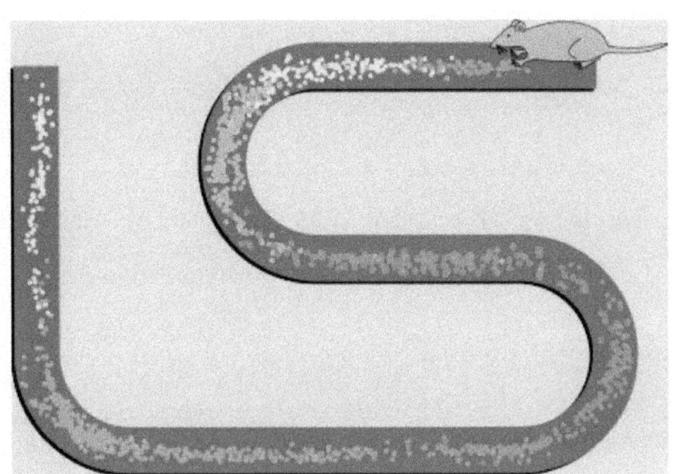
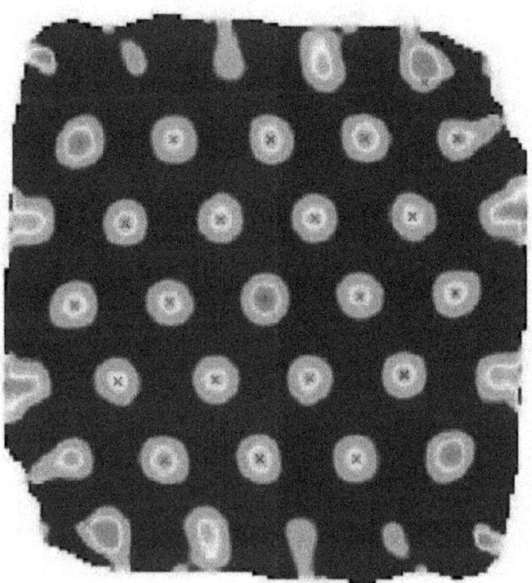

Philosophical Perspectives on Reality and Perception

The idea of being "fooled" by our perceptions is not new—it has fascinated philosophers for centuries. One of the earliest explorations of this concept is Plato's *Allegory of the Cave*, as described in *The Republic*. In this allegory, prisoners are chained inside a cave, able to see only shadows cast on the wall by objects passing in front of a fire. Socrates likens philosophers to individuals freed from the cave, able to perceive the true nature of reality rather than mere shadows.

In the 17th century, René Descartes proposed the thought experiment of an "evil demon" manipulating human perceptions to create the illusion of a physical world. This idea evolved further in 1973 when Gilbert Harman introduced the "brain in a vat" hypothesis, depicted in Figure 1.4. This scenario imagines a brain connected to a machine that simulates an entire reality, echoing themes explored in the 1999 film *The Matrix*. In this story, humans unknowingly live in a simulated world while their real bodies are harvested for energy by machines. The protagonist, Neo, faces a pivotal choice: embrace the harsh truth of reality or take a pill to return to the comforting illusion of the simulation.

These philosophical ideas challenge our understanding of perception and reality, compelling us to consider whether our current experiences are genuine or mere constructs of an even greater, undiscovered reality.

Figure 1.4: A VR thought experiment: The brain in a vat, by Gilbert Harman in 1973. (Figure by Alexander Wivel.)

1.4 Exploring Different Types of Realities

The concept of "virtual reality" (VR) has historical roots, dating back to German philosopher Immanuel Kant. However, Kant used the term in a philosophical context, describing the "reality" that exists within the mind, distinct from the external physical world. It wasn't until the 1980s that the modern technological interpretation of VR gained traction, largely popularized by Jaron Lanier. Despite its widespread use, the term *virtual reality* can appear contradictory—a philosophical dilemma that some have addressed by suggesting alternatives like *virtuality*. Nonetheless, for consistency, we will continue using the term *virtual reality*.

A distinction that becomes crucial here is the differentiation between the *real world*, which refers to the physical surroundings of the user during an experience, and the *virtual world*, which is the environment perceived as part of the VR simulation.

Related Terms and Evolving Definitions

While VR is a broad term, several related concepts are commonly used today:

1. **Virtual Environments (VE)**: This term predates VR's modern use and is preferred in academic settings. It is often considered synonymous with VR but can also refer to environments that may be based on real-world images or synthetic worlds. Hence, not all VEs seem strictly "virtual."

2. **Augmented Reality (AR)**: AR integrates digital elements, such as text or graphics, into the real world, often displayed through glasses or camera feeds. Unlike VR, AR keeps most of the user's real-world environment intact while adding digital overlays.

3. **Mixed Reality (MR)**: MR spans a spectrum that merges aspects of VR, AR, and the real world, blending these elements seamlessly.

Over time, as technology has advanced, distinctions between VR, AR, and MR have become less rigid. This has led to attempts to unify these concepts under terms like *Extended Reality (XR)*, *X Reality*, or combinations like VR/AR, AR/VR/MR, and so on.

4. **Telepresence and Teleoperation**: Telepresence refers to systems that allow users to feel as though they are in another real-world location. When users can interact or control objects, such as piloting a drone, the term *teleoperation* applies.

For simplicity, virtual environments, AR, MR, telepresence, and teleoperation can all be regarded as variations of VR, as they share the goal of altering the user's perception of reality.

The Essence of VR: Perceptual Illusions

At the core of VR lies the idea of engineering perceptual illusions. This is achieved not by debating whether the environment feels more "real" or "virtual" but by altering the user's perception through carefully designed systems. This concept could be aptly termed *perception engineering*, as it involves leveraging engineering methods to create, develop, and deliver immersive experiences that manipulate sensory input.

Figure 1.5 highlights the interplay of engineering and human physiology in perception engineering. While traditional VR systems focus on hardware and software components, understanding the nuances of human perception and physiology is equally critical. Since we cannot redesign human senses, these fields often involve reverse engineering to effectively manipulate perception. Together, these elements form the foundation of *perception engineering*, a field that blends technology with an understanding of how we experience the world

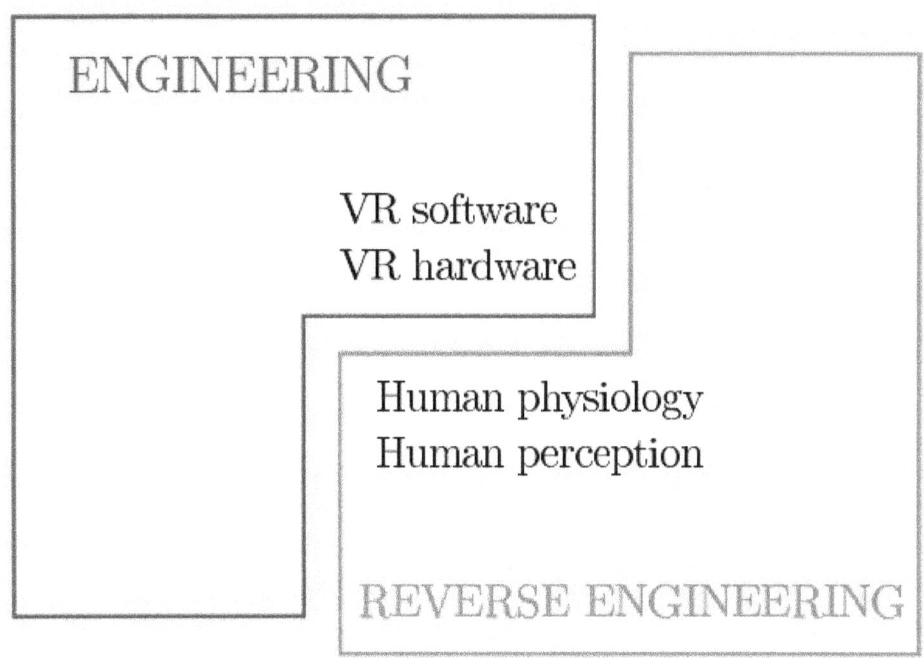

1.5 Key Elements of Virtual Reality

Interactivity

A fundamental aspect of most VR experiences is interactivity. This refers to whether the sensory stimulation in VR changes in response to the user's actions. If the system functions independently of the user's input, it is classified as *open-loop*. In contrast, a *closed-loop* system allows the user to influence sensory outputs through body movements such as turning the head, moving hands, or even via non-physical signals like voice commands, heart rate, or skin conductivity. This dynamic interaction helps create a more immersive and engaging VR environment.

First-Person vs. Third-Person Perspective

Developers of VR systems need to carefully consider the user's perspective. In scientific experiments, as illustrated in Figure 1.2, a clear distinction exists: the subject experiences the VR in the first person, while the scientist observes from a third-person perspective to test a hypothesis, such as the impact of altering neurons on a rat's navigation.

However, for developers creating VR experiences, this separation often blurs. They frequently switch between acting as the observer and the participant, which can introduce bias. Creators are naturally inclined to see their work positively, making it challenging to evaluate user experiences objectively. Furthermore, as developers adapt to flaws in their own creations, these issues become harder to notice. Much like proofreading your own writing, creators must actively counter these biases and critically assess the sensory and perceptual aspects of their designs.

Is VR More Real Than Reality?

An intriguing question in VR development is: How realistic should the experience be? One approach is the *universal simulation principle*, which aims to replicate real-world interactions as closely as possible. This principle has heavily influenced industries like gaming, where realistic graphics and physics dominate, particularly in first-person shooter (FPS) games.

However, realism isn't always necessary—or even ideal. Simplified or stylized environments can sometimes be more effective depending on the purpose of the experience. Developers should consider the intended goals: Are users meditating, playing a game, learning a skill, or exploring distant worlds? The realism required will vary significantly across these contexts. For instance, while programming in VR, one could recreate a traditional office setup or design a more imaginative workspace, such as a beachfront or forest setting, with floating screens and tools. The key is to define the criteria for a convincing and comfortable illusion tailored to each use case.

Synthetic vs. Captured Environments

Virtual worlds in VR can range from entirely synthetic environments to those based on real-world captures. Synthetic environments are built using geometric models and simulated physics, as seen in video games. Conversely, captured environments rely on imaging technologies like panoramic videos or 3D scans, enhanced with depth sensors and SLAM (Simultaneous Localization and Mapping) techniques to create a realistic and adaptive representation of the real world.

However, accurately capturing and rendering a dynamic, interactive environment remains a technical challenge, particularly without controlled settings like motion capture studios. Tracking human motions, facial expressions, or gestures becomes critical, especially when users interact with others in VR. Avatars, or digital representations of users, help bridge this gap by offering anonymity and customizable features. Yet, achieving highly realistic avatars can lead to discomfort, a phenomenon known as the *uncanny valley*, where minor imperfections in realism create unease.

Health and Safety in VR

Regardless of the level of realism, the health and safety of users must remain a priority. Unlike traditional media like TV or radio, VR can overwhelm the senses, leading to fatigue or discomfort. Known as *simulator sickness* or *VR sickness*, these adverse effects can arise from poorly designed hardware, software, or experiences.

Understanding human physiology and perception is critical to developing comfortable VR experiences. Fatigue often stems from the brain's struggle to integrate unfamiliar sensory inputs or reconcile inconsistencies between visual, auditory, and physical feedback, leading to nausea or dizziness.

Muscle strain can also occur with prolonged physical interactions. For instance, tasks requiring extended arm movements, like manipulating objects in VR, can result in "gorilla arms," where the user feels excessive fatigue. Designing more ergonomic interfaces, such as mimicking the small, efficient motions of a computer mouse, can reduce physical strain while maintaining effective interaction in the virtual environment.

In summary, successful VR experiences rely on careful engineering to balance interactivity, perspective, realism, and safety while tailoring the experience to the user's needs and expectations.

1.6 Contemporary Applications of VR

The modern era of virtual reality (VR) has been shaped by breakthroughs in display technology, sensors, and computing power—largely driven by advancements in the smartphone industry. Since Palmer Luckey introduced the Oculus Rift in 2012, VR has evolved from a concept to an accessible reality, with devices ranging from high-tech headsets to simple smartphone-based viewers. The rapid adoption of VR technology mirrors earlier revolutions, such as those of personal computers and web browsers, where broader access led to a dramatic expansion in applications and creativity.

This section provides a brief glimpse into how people are using VR systems today and offers a foundation for exploring similar experiences online. However, merely reading or viewing images about VR falls far short of the immersive impact of trying it firsthand. Much like newspapers in the 1890s struggled to describe the novelty of movie theatres, a written account can only convey so much. If possible, immerse yourself in a variety of VR experiences to develop a personal perspective and ignite your creativity to push the boundaries even further.

Video games

For decades, people have envisioned stepping directly into the worlds of their favorite video games—a dream popularized as early as 1982 by Disney's *Tron*. Virtual reality (VR) now makes that vision a tangible reality, as shown by the examples in Figure 1.6.

A major appeal for gamers is the ability to explore expansive, lifelike environments through an avatar. For instance, Figure 1.6 (a) features *Portal 2* on the HTC Vive headset, providing an immersive, first-person perspective. Complementing this is an innovative peripheral shown in Figure 1.6 (b): an omnidirectional treadmill that simulates walking by allowing players to slide their feet across a dish-like surface, enhancing the sense of movement within the virtual world.

Alternatively, some games offer a third-person perspective for a more relaxed experience. In Figure 1.6 (c), *Lucky's Tale* allows users to control a character while observing from above, creating a comfortable and detached viewpoint. Lastly, Figure 1.6 (d) illustrates a game designed specifically to harness VR's unique capabilities, showcasing how this technology can redefine gameplay in ways traditional formats cannot.

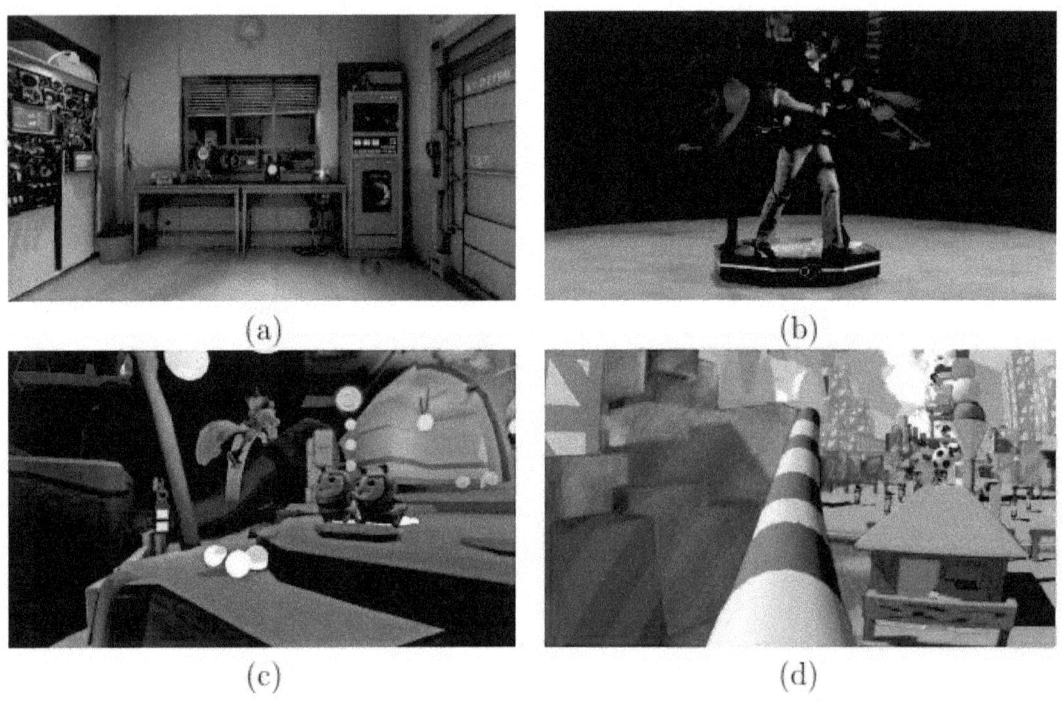

Figure 1.6 Descriptions:

(a) A demo of *Valve's Portal 2*, included in *The Lab* for the HTC Vive, offers players an engaging puzzle-solving adventure within a virtual environment.

(b) The Virtuix Omni treadmill enhances immersion in first-person shooter games by allowing players to simulate walking or running in the virtual world.

(c) *Lucky's Tale* for the Oculus Rift adopts a third-person perspective, letting players control their character while observing from a floating viewpoint above.

(d) *Dumpy*, a game developed by DePaul University, places players in the role of a character with a massive elephant trunk. The gameplay focuses on the fun of this unique embodiment, encouraging players to knock objects down by swinging the trunk.

Immersive cinema

Hollywood has always pursued greater levels of realism in filmmaking, so why not go one step further and let viewers feel like they're inside the story? Figure 1.7 illustrates a breakthrough in immersive storytelling. Virtual reality (VR) is ushering in a transformative era for cinema, challenging directors to rethink the techniques developed over the 20th century. Traditionally, the camera's perspective is tightly controlled by the cinematographer. In VR, however, viewers can freely explore the environment—looking in any direction or even moving through the scene.

This shift raises intriguing questions: What freedoms should viewers have? How do filmmakers ensure important story elements aren't missed? Should the narrative adapt to the viewer's actions or remain linear? Should the viewer take on the role of a character within the story or remain a passive, unseen observer? How can VR films become a shared experience for groups of friends? And when are real-world scenes preferable to animations, or vice versa?

Figure 1.7: A notable example is *Henry*, a short VR film produced by Oculus Story Studio in 2015. It tells the Emmy-winning story of a hedgehog longing for companionship, engaging the viewer as a potential friend.

While such experiments pave the way, it will likely take years to refine the storytelling techniques and answer these evolving questions.

In the meantime, VR can act as an immersive "wrapper" for traditional movies. The VR Cinema application, developed by Joo-Hyung Ahn in 2013 for the Oculus Rift, allows users to experience standard films in a virtual theatre (Figure 1.8). Users can select their seat, while the app simulates realistic theatre acoustics and flickering projector lights. Both 2D and 3D movies stored on the viewer's hard drive can be streamed on the virtual screen.

This approach also opens the door to creative enhancements without altering the original films. Imagine watching a zombie movie where virtual zombies infiltrate the theatre or a disaster film where the theatre itself collapses in the storm. VR even adds a social dimension, enabling movie nights with friends across the globe as you "sit" together in the virtual space. You might even enjoy the thrill of mischief—whispering or throwing popcorn— without worrying about real-world consequences

Figure 1.8: VR Cinema, developed in 2013 by Joo-Hyung Ahn for the Oculus Rift. Viewers could choose their seats in the theatre and watch any movie they like.

Telepresence

Achieving the sensation of being in a different place begins with capturing a panoramic view of a remote environment (Figure 1.9). Applications like Google Street View and Google Earth already use millions of panoramic images to map locations worldwide. VR technology leverages these images to create immersive experiences, allowing users to virtually stand in these locations and seamlessly transition between nearby areas (Figure 1.10).

Panoramic video captures provide an even more immersive experience. For example, Figure 1.11 shows a frame from an interactive VR recording of a Paul McCartney concert, where users felt as though they were on stage alongside the performer. Live panoramic video streaming takes this further by enabling people to virtually attend events like concerts and sports games in real time, offering the possibility of interaction.

Integrating panoramic cameras with robots adds an extra layer of engagement. Users can control robotic avatars to explore and interact with remote environments (Figure 1.12). Examples include the DORA robot from the University of Pennsylvania, which mimics head movements to offer a stereoscopic view of the surroundings, and the Plexidrone, a flying device designed to stream panoramic video.

Current VR technology bridges the gap between physical and virtual presence, enabling activities like virtual travel and remote interaction. This innovation has significant implications for telecommuting, allowing people to work remotely in a way that feels more connected and natural. Over time, such advancements might even drive societal shifts, such as de-urbanization. By making remote work and experiences more accessible, people could spread more evenly across the planet, reversing the urbanization trends that began with the Industrial Revolution.

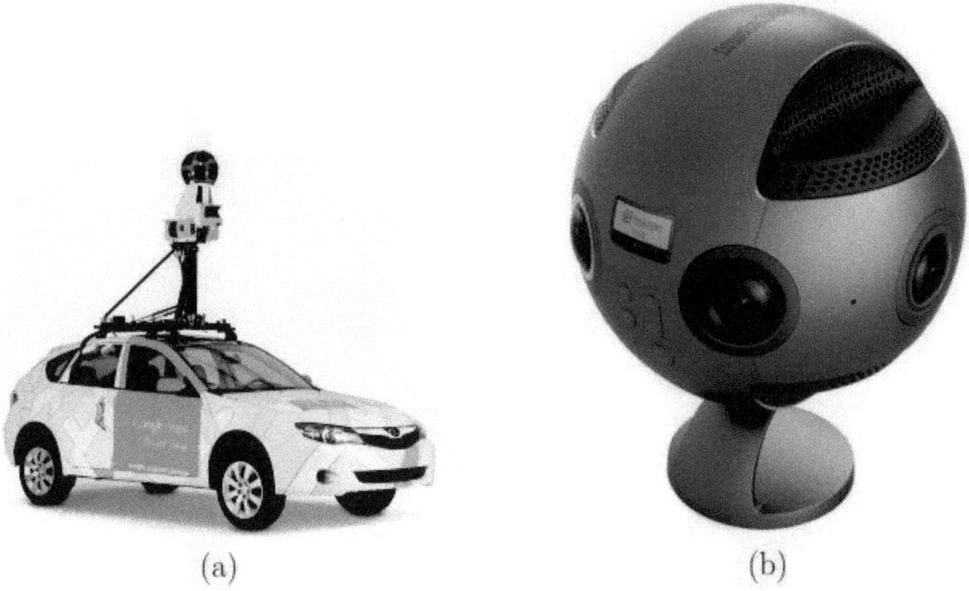

Figure 1.9: Capturing panoramic views is a crucial step in creating telepresence experiences. Examples include (a) a Google vehicle equipped with cameras and depth sensors for generating Street View imagery and (b) the Insta360 Pro, a device capable of recording and streaming full 360-degree videos.

Figure 1.10: A VR application that utilizes Google Street View imagery to create immersive experiences: (a) an iconic Parisian scene, and (b) VR headsets generating left- and right-eye perspectives while adjusting to the viewer's gaze direction for realistic interaction.

Figure 1.11: Jaunt's panoramic video of Paul McCartney performing *Live and Let Die* allows viewers to experience the concert as if they were on stage with the artist, offering an immersive musical experience.

Figure 1.12: Examples of robotic avatars that enhance telepresence capabilities: (a) the DORA robot from the University of Pennsylvania, which synchronizes with the user's head movements to enable exploration of remote environments with stereoscopic visuals, and (b) the Plexidrone, a flying robotic platform designed to transmit panoramic video footage for a more dynamic perspective.

Virtual societies

While telepresence places us in a remote physical environment, VR goes a step further by enabling the creation of entirely virtual societies. These synthetic worlds mirror aspects of the real world but are populated by avatars representing real individuals. Figure 1.13 illustrates a scene from *Second Life*, a virtual space where users interact with one another through customizable avatars. Originally designed for screen-based interaction, such environments are now accessible through immersive VR, making the experience more engaging and lifelike.

In these virtual spaces, people can gather for various purposes, such as sharing niche interests, pursuing educational objectives, or simply escaping the routine of daily life. These societies thrive on interaction, fostering connections in environments hosted on shared servers, offering endless possibilities for socialization and collaboration

.

Figure 1.13: Illustrates a scene from *Second Life*, a virtual space where users interact with one another through customizable avatars.

Empathy

Virtual reality's ability to place users in a first-person perspective makes it a transformative tool for fostering empathy. It provides a way for individuals to experience the world through the eyes of someone with a different identity—something the world continues to grapple with as it seeks greater acceptance and equality across lines of race, religion, age, gender, sexuality, and socioeconomic status. The challenge lies in understanding what it truly feels like to live as someone else, and VR bridges this gap in a profound way.

One example is *Clouds Over Sidra*, a VR project developed in 2015 under the sponsorship of the United Nations. Figure 1.14 shows this immersive experience, which allows viewers to step into the life of a Syrian refugee, evoking a visceral understanding of their hardships. While compassion often stems from sympathy, VR fosters a deeper emotional connection by simulating firsthand experiences

.

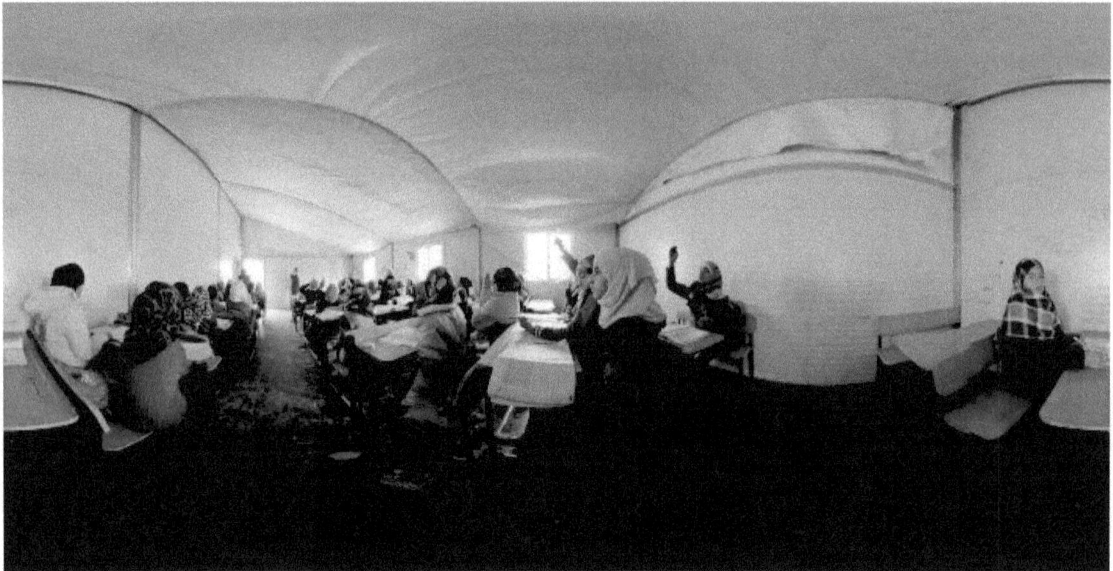

Figure 1.14: *Clouds Over Sidra*, a VR project developed in 2015 under the sponsorship of the United Nations (figure by Within, Clouds Over Sidra).

Similarly, Figure 1.15 depicts *The Machine to Be Another*, a 2014 project by BeAnotherLab. This system lets participants swap bodies with someone of a different gender. By wearing VR headsets equipped with forward-facing cameras, each person sees the world from their partner's perspective. Coordinated movements between the participants create the illusion of inhabiting the other's body, offering insights into the experiences of another gender

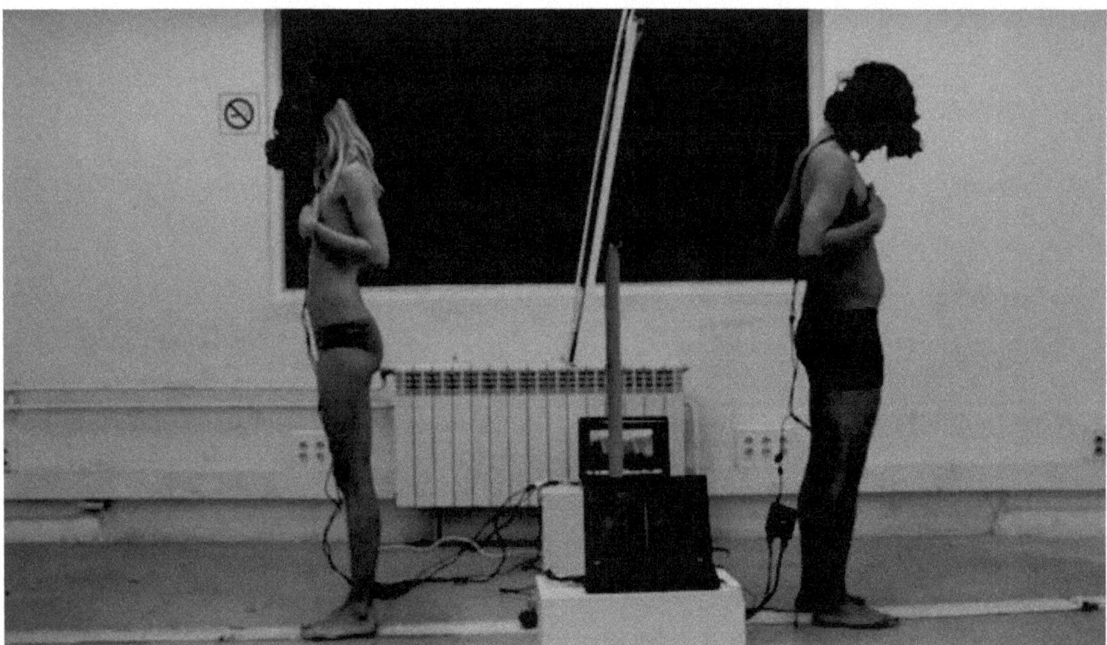

Figure 1.15: depicts *The Machine to Be Another*, a 2014 project by BeAnotherLab.

VR also opens the door to exploring broader social dynamics in virtual societies. Imagine scenarios where you are 10 cm shorter than everyone else, teaching a class as another gender, or facing racial discrimination. By simulating these experiences, VR creates interactive "life games" that reveal how societal biases and barriers affect different groups, fostering a deeper awareness of inequality and the challenges others face

Education

Beyond its ability to foster empathy, VR has the potential to revolutionize education by leveraging its immersive first-person perspective. In fields such as engineering, mathematics, and science, VR enables students to explore complex geometric relationships and visualize intricate data in ways traditional methods cannot achieve. This makes abstract or challenging concepts more accessible and engaging.

VR is particularly effective for hands-on training, as the skills practiced in realistic virtual environments often translate seamlessly to real-world applications. This is especially valuable in scenarios where the actual environment is costly to replicate or poses safety risks. One of the earliest and most notable uses of VR for training is in flight simulation. Figure 1.16 illustrates a flight simulator used by the U.S. Air Force, where trainees sit in a physical cockpit surrounded by displays simulating the external environment

Figure 1.16: A flight simulator in use by the US Air Force (photo by Javier Garcia, U.S. Air Force).

Other practical applications include training for firefighting, nuclear power plant safety, search-and-rescue operations, military exercises, and medical procedures. However, VR's potential in education extends far beyond technical disciplines. The humanities present exciting opportunities, such as history, anthropology, and language learning. Imagine the difference between reading about the Victorian era and virtually strolling through the streets of 19th-century London, recreated with historical accuracy. Similarly, VR can bring ancient ruins back to life, allowing users to explore reconstructed sites like the Nimrud palace of Assyrian King Ashurnasirpal II (Figure 1.17), a VR experience developed in 2016 by Learning Sites Inc. and the University of Illinois.

Figure 1.17: A tour of the Nimrud palace of Assyrian King Ashurnasirpal II, a VR experience developed by Learning Sites Inc. and the University of Illinois in 2016.

Virtual reality also paves the way for innovative approaches to digital heritage. Museums can create VR interfaces for virtual tours, or artifacts can be scanned and displayed in entirely virtual museum spaces. These possibilities expand access to cultural and historical education, making learning more dynamic, immersive, and inclusive.

Virtual prototyping

Prototyping in the physical world helps us evaluate how a design looks, feels, or performs. While technologies like 3D printing have made physical prototyping more accessible, virtual prototyping takes this process to another level. By stepping into a virtual environment that showcases their prototype (Figure 1.18), designers can interact with it in real time, experiment with changes, and refine their ideas efficiently.

This approach also facilitates communication. Designers can invite clients into the virtual space, allowing them to visualize and experience the design firsthand. For instance, if you're planning to renovate your kitchen, VR enables you to create a detailed virtual model and clearly convey your vision to a contractor, leaving little room for misinterpretation.

Virtual prototyping has vast applications across industries such as real estate, architecture, automotive and aerospace design, furniture creation, fashion, and medical instrument development. Figure 1.18 highlights a prime example: a virtual kitchen prototype called *Ty Hedfan*, developed by IVR-NATION. The upper portion of the image shows the real kitchen, while the lower section depicts its virtual counterpart, showcasing how VR can seamlessly bridge conceptualization and realization.

This technology empowers businesses to innovate with greater speed and precision, making it an invaluable tool for modern design and planning.

Figure 1.18: highlights a prime example: a virtual kitchen prototype called *Ty Hedfan*, developed by IVR-NATION.

Health care

While VR introduces unique challenges regarding health and safety, it also offers innovative solutions for improving well-being. A growing movement in distributed medicine uses VR to empower remote communities by training individuals to perform routine medical procedures. Through telepresence, doctors can provide real-time guidance while utilizing VR for immersive training experiences.

One transformative application involves visualizing 3D models of organs generated from medical scans (Figure 1.19). This allows surgeons to virtually explore a patient's anatomy in detail, aiding in preoperative planning and enhancing their understanding of complex procedures. It also serves as an effective tool for communicating medical options to patients and their families, enabling them to make more informed decisions.

VR extends beyond planning and education into direct therapeutic uses. Patients can address phobias and stress disorders through controlled exposure therapy, maintain cognitive function as they age, or improve motor skills to recover from balance, muscular, or neurological issues. Additionally, VR could enhance quality of life for aging populations by providing virtual travel experiences, engaging physical therapy exercises, and meaningful social interactions. Such systems can help mitigate loneliness by fostering connections with family and friends in a way that feels genuine and immersive.

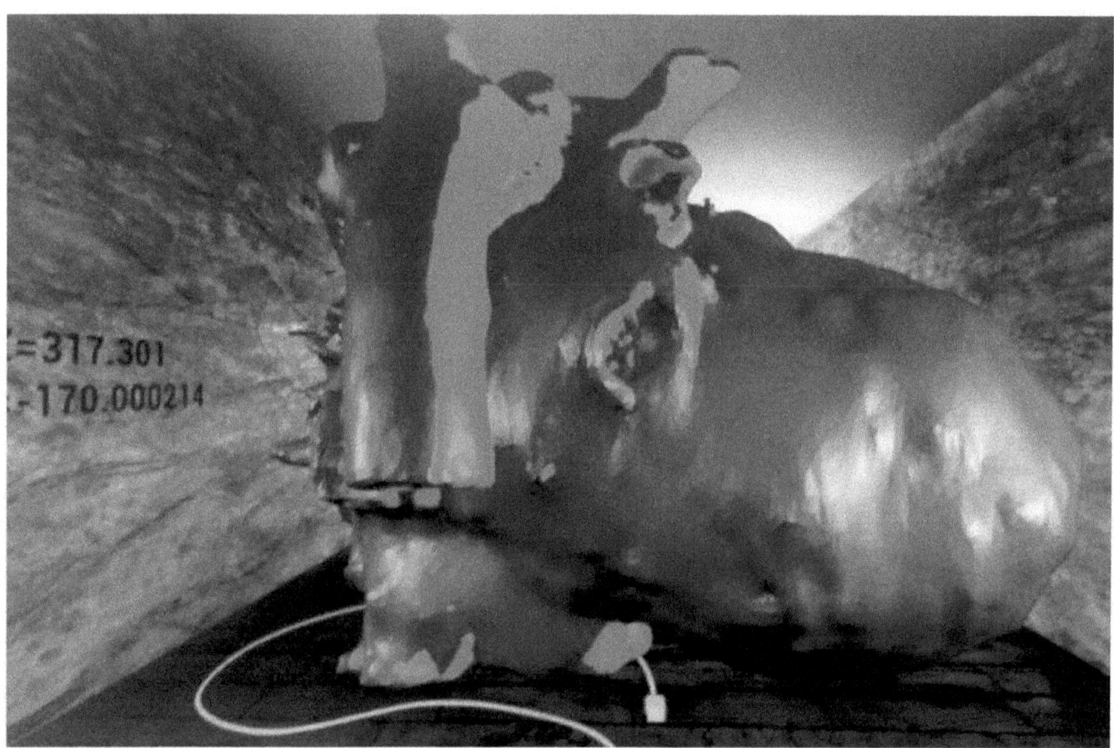

Figure 1.19 depicts a heart visualization system created by the Jump Trading Simulation and Education Center in collaboration with the University of Illinois. This example showcases how VR is revolutionizing health care by merging cutting-edge technology with human-centered medical practices

Augmented and mixed reality

In many scenarios, enhancing the real world with superimposed digital graphics can offer significant advantages (Figure 1.20). This approach, known as augmented reality (AR) or mixed reality (MR), seamlessly blends virtual elements into our physical environment. By integrating features like text, icons, and other graphics into the user's view, AR/MR can harness the power of the Internet to assist with tasks such as navigation, social interactions, or mechanical repairs.

Businesses have embraced this technology to optimize operations. For instance, in a factory setting, workers might see virtual labels floating above parts that need assembly or visualize internal components of machinery to identify replacements. This capability improves efficiency and accuracy in complex workflows.

Figure 1.20: shows the Microsoft HoloLens, a device that overlays digital graphics onto the physical world using advanced see-through display technology.

AR/MR applications rely heavily on cutting-edge computer vision techniques to recognize objects, reconstruct shapes, and analyse lighting conditions. These processes are essential for ensuring virtual objects appear naturally integrated into the real world, including casting realistic shadows or aligning perfectly with physical counterparts. However, achieving consistent reliability is challenging due to the unpredictable nature of real-world environments. Precise tracking and alignment, especially in dynamic settings, remain significant hurdles.

Figure 1.21: illustrates the popular geolocation-based game *Pokémon Go* by Nintendo. This 2016 phenomenon allowed players to see virtual Pokémon characters superimposed on their surroundings by viewing them through their smartphone screens.

AR/MR systems can utilize various display methods. Fixed screens paired with 3D glasses can provide enhanced visuals, while digital projectors can alter real-world surfaces with colors, textures, or informative overlays. Handheld devices like smartphones and tablets can act as windows into augmented environments, as demonstrated in *Pokémon Go*.

Head-mounted displays (HMDs), however, offer the most immersive experience. Two main types of HMDs exist: **see-through displays** and **pass-through displays**. See-through displays allow users to view their surroundings through transparent lenses while overlaying virtual graphics. Devices like Google Glass, Microsoft HoloLens, and Magic Leap are pioneering this technology, though challenges like resolution, field of view, and light-blocking persist in consumer-grade devices.

Pass-through displays, on the other hand, use external cameras to capture the real world and project it onto internal screens. While they address some limitations of see-through displays, they introduce issues like latency, distortion, and restricted dynamic range. Despite these challenges, advancements in AR/MR technology promise a future where affordable, high-performance devices become commonplace.

Exploring New Human Experiences

Virtual reality opens doors to entirely novel human experiences, often transcending the limits of what is possible—or even safe—in the real world. While telepresence allows us to see through the eyes of robots or others, VR can push boundaries further by creating immersive scenarios that defy reality. Artists, in particular, have embraced this potential, crafting imaginative and transformative experiences.

Take, for instance, the Birdly project, which simulated the sensation of human flight (Figure 1.1). Figure 1.22 highlights additional groundbreaking examples. What if you could drastically alter your scale? Imagine shrinking to just 2 millimetres and confronting an ant at eye level. Now contrast that with towering 50 meters above a city, watching as people flee in panic. The creative potential of VR allows for these fantastical shifts in perspective.

VR can also simulate altered states of consciousness, such as the effects of drugs, or let users embody animals, their favourite fictional characters, or even inanimate objects like a piece of food. The only real constraint is the tolerance of the human body

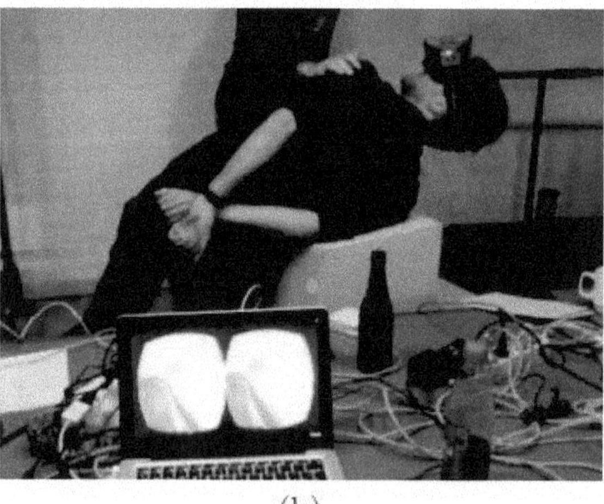

(a)   (b)

Figure 1.22: showcases two unique VR experiences:

- **(a)** Epic Games' 2014 virtual roller coaster ride, where users were taken on a wild adventure through a digital living room.

- **(b)** A 2013 guillotine simulator by André Berlemont, Morten Brunbjerg, and Erkki Trummal. Participants felt the chilling realism as friends lightly tapped their necks at the moment the virtual blade dropped, experiencing a surreal perspective as if their heads rolled away.

With VR, the horizon of artistic creativity seems limitless, paving the way for experiences we've only dreamed of. The adventures ahead promise excitement, wonder, and a profound reshaping of how we perceive reality.

1.7 Evolution of Virtual Reality

The Journey Beyond the Screen

How did we reach the immersive world of VR as we know it today? To truly understand, we must explore a history that predates modern technology, stretching back thousands of years. Long before the term "virtual reality" existed, humans engaged with visual representations that sparked imagination and transported them to different realities. Ancient societies developed the skill of interpreting flat surfaces as windows into three-dimensional worlds, forming the foundation of what would eventually become VR.

Figure 1.23: Journey Beyond the Screen

One example can be found in the cave paintings, like the one depicted in Figure 1.23(a), created approximately 30,000 years ago at the Bhimbetka rock shelters in India. These ancient murals told stories through static images, inviting viewers to imagine dynamic scenes. Centuries later, medieval European art, such as the depiction of John Ball rallying Wat Tyler's rebels in Figure 1.23(b), reflected similar storytelling instincts. Though the artwork displayed more detail, the perspective often appeared flawed, resulting in oddly proportioned figures and misaligned spatial elements.

As artistic techniques advanced, so did the understanding of perspective. In 1596, Hans Vredeman de Vries showcased an architectural painting (Figure 1.23(c)) with precise perspective lines, creating a vivid sense of depth that required no guesswork from the observer. By this point, art had become more realistic, almost photographic in its clarity.

However, realism wasn't the final frontier. By the late 19th century, the Impressionist movement emerged, challenging the notion that art should always mimic reality. Artists like Claude Monet, as shown in Figure 1.23(d), embraced the ambiguity of impressionism, blending forms and colors to evoke emotion and encourage imagination. Much like the cave paintings of old, these works left interpretation to the viewer, a characteristic that resonates with the immersive, subjective experience VR aims to deliver today.

From ancient cave walls to the avant-garde movements of the 19th century, the human desire to create and experience alternate realities has remained a constant thread, ultimately paving the way for the development of modern virtual reality.

The Birth of Motion Pictures

Once humans mastered the art of staring at static images, the next leap was bringing those images to life. The principle behind motion pictures lies in a fascinating optical illusion called stroboscopic apparent motion. When images are displayed in rapid succession, the human brain perceives movement. Remarkably, even as few as two images per second can create a sense of motion. When the frame rate exceeds ten images per second, the illusion becomes so smooth that the brain no longer distinguishes individual frames, creating the seamless flow we now associate with movies.

One of the earliest demonstrations of this concept came in 1878 when Eadward Muybridge produced the iconic "Horse in Motion" series at the request of Leland Stanford (yes, the founder of Stanford University). As shown in Figure 1.24, Muybridge arranged 24 cameras along a racetrack, each triggered by a trip wire as the horse galloped past. The resulting sequence of images, when played on a zoopraxiscope—a device similar in function to a record player but designed to project images—offered a groundbreaking glimpse into the moving image and served as a precursor to modern film projection.

This early exploration of motion paved the way for the film industry as we know it, transforming static visual art into dynamic storytelling.

Motion picture technology evolved rapidly, captivating audiences in ways that were once unimaginable. In 1896, during a screening of *Arrival of a Train at La Ciotat Station*, theatregoers panicked, believing the oncoming train might burst through the screen and into the room (Figure 1.25(a)). Remarkably, this moment occurred without any sound—just the flickering black-and-white images. Today, such a reaction might seem absurd, but at the time, it was a groundbreaking testament to the immersive power of early cinema.

Figure 1.24: This 1878 Horse in Motion, motion picture by Eadward Muybridge.

Evolution of Special Effects in Film

Figure 1.25: Advancements in Cinematic Effects: (a) *Arrival of a Train at La Ciotat Station* (1896)

(b) *A Trip to the Moon* (1902) (c) *2001: A Space Odyssey* (1968) (d) *Gravity* (2013).

As film audiences grew more sophisticated, so did their expectations for realism. By 1902, Georges Méliès' *A Trip to the Moon* (Figure 1.25(b)) dazzled viewers with imaginative, handcrafted effects, blending fantasy with early cinematic innovation. Fast-forward to 1968, when Stanley Kubrick's *2001: A Space Odyssey* (Figure 1.25(c)) delivered a visually stunning, meticulously crafted portrayal of space exploration, setting a new benchmark for realism. By 2013, Alfonso Cuarón's *Gravity* (Figure 1.25(d)) pushed the boundaries of visual effects even further, creating an experience so lifelike that it transported viewers into the vastness of space itself.

Interestingly, despite technological advances, audiences remain willing to embrace films that forgo hyper-realism. Just as with paintings, films that leave room for imagination can evoke powerful emotional responses, proving that the magic of cinema lies not only in what is shown but in what is left unseen

Evolution of Animation Styles

(a)

(b)

(c)

(d)

Figure 1.26: Milestones in Animated Film: (a) Fantasmagoria by Emile Cohl (1908) (b) Steamboat Willie featuring Mickey Mouse (1928) (c) Star Wars: The Clone Wars (2003) (d) South Park (1997)

The enduring appeal of animation—whether called cartoons, anime, or animated films—demonstrates how artistic style can evolve while maintaining mass appeal (Figure 1.26). Much like live-action movies, animation has undergone a fascinating transformation over the decades. In 1908, Emile Cohl's *Fantasmagoria* (Figure 1.26(a)) introduced audiences to whimsical, hand-drawn characters composed of simple, fluid lines. This early work laid the foundation for the animation industry.

By 1928, Walt Disney's *Steamboat Willie* (Figure 1.26(b)) brought Mickey Mouse to life, adding greater detail, synchronized sound, and a stronger narrative structure, capturing the hearts of viewers worldwide. Fast forward to 2003, when *Star Wars: The Clone Wars* (Figure 1.26(c)) pushed animation into new territory, delivering sophisticated visuals and dynamic action sequences that rivalled live-action filmmaking in terms of realism and complexity.

Interestingly, while technology has enabled stunningly realistic animation, simpler styles have also thrived. *South Park*, which premiered in 1997 (Figure 1.26(d)), embraced deliberately crude, minimalistic visuals, proving that strong storytelling and humour can captivate audiences just as effectively as intricate animation.

The evolution of animation reflects a broader trend in visual media: the balance between realism and imagination. Whether highly detailed or strikingly simple, animation continues to resonate with viewers by blending creativity, innovation, and narrative power

The Shift Toward Convenience and Portability

Advancements in technology often prioritize convenience over realism, driven by factors like cost and portability. As illustrated in Figure 1.27, families in the mid-20th century eagerly gathered around small, grainy black-and-white televisions for free broadcasts, despite the availability of theatres offering vibrant, high-resolution, panoramic, and even 3D films. By today's standards, those early TV screens would seem almost unwatchable, yet they offered an accessible way to enjoy entertainment without leaving home.

This shift highlights a clear progression in media consumption: 1) traveling to a theatre to experience it, 2) enjoying it from the comfort of home, and 3) eventually carrying it wherever you go. The trend applies not only to television but also to movies, phones, computers, video games, and more. Virtual reality is no exception.

What's remarkable is how much the gap between portability and quality has narrowed. Today, portable devices offer an experience that rivals—or even surpasses—the stationary, high-end systems of the past. As VR technology advances, we can anticipate that lightweight, mobile systems will continue to close the gap, delivering ever-more immersive experiences without sacrificing convenience.

Figure 1.27: A snapshot from 1958 showing a family gathered around a television, a reminder that even with theatres offering superior quality, people valued the convenience of home entertainment.

The Evolution of Video Games: From Simplicity to Realism—and Back

Unlike motion pictures, which provide a passive, third-person experience, video games offer a more immersive, interactive environment that feels closer to a first-person perspective. As discussed earlier in Section 1.1, this distinction mirrors the difference between open-loop and closed-loop VR systems. While movies follow an open-loop structure, where viewers passively receive content, video games represent a step toward closed-loop VR, where user actions influence the experience in real time.

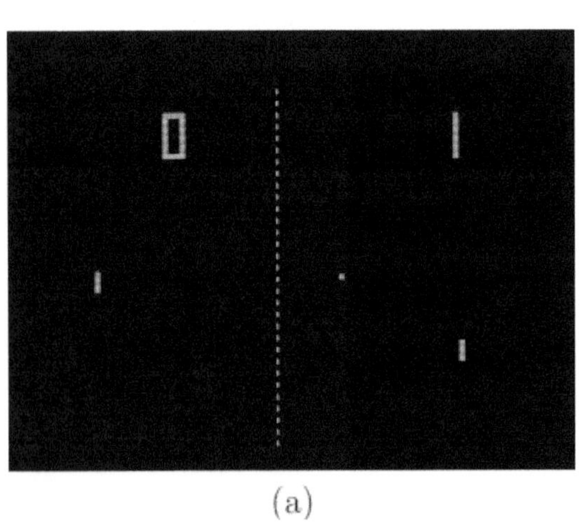

(a)

(b)

(c)

(d)

Figure 1.28: Milestones in Video Game Development: (a) Pong by Atari (1972) (b) Donkey Kong by Nintendo (1981) (c) Doom by id Software (1993) (d) Assassin's Creed by Ubisoft (modern)

As shown in Figure 1.28, video game design has followed a fascinating trajectory from simplicity to high realism—and, in many cases, back to simplicity. Early games like *Pong* and *Donkey Kong* relied on basic graphics, leaving much to the player's imagination. The 1993 release of *Doom* introduced the first-person shooter (FPS) genre, offering a player-centred perspective that sparked a race toward increasingly detailed, realistic visuals. By the time *Assassin's Creed* emerged, modern games had achieved breathtaking realism, with detailed environments and lifelike character animations.

Yet, simplicity has remained a powerful draw. Games like *Angry Birds* recall the straightforward design of 1980s classics, while *Minecraft* invites players to explore and build within blocky, pixelated worlds reminiscent of early gaming aesthetics. Interestingly, simpler games often have lower technical demands, running smoothly on basic smartphones, whereas cutting-edge FPS games may require powerful PCs with advanced graphics cards.

The lesson here is clear: greater realism doesn't always translate to better gameplay. Video games thrive on creativity, interaction, and engagement, showing that simplicity can be just as captivating as the most graphically sophisticated experiences.

Beyond the Rectangle: Expanding the Limits of Visual Immersion

Until now, much of the technology discussed revolves around the idea of viewing a flat, rectangular display fixed on a wall. However, two significant advancements have propelled visual experiences beyond this limitation: (1) delivering a distinct image to each eye to create a 3D effect and (2) broadening the field of view so users are not constrained by screen boundaries. One of the primary methods our brain uses to judge distance is stereopsis, where slight differences in the images seen by each eye provide depth perception.

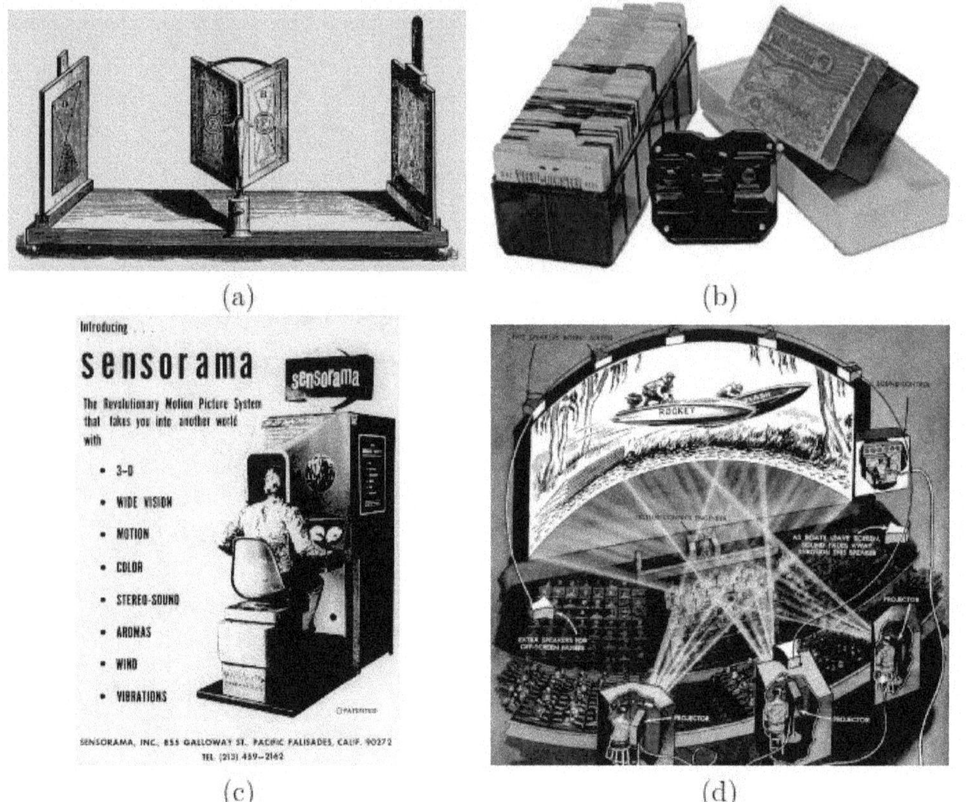

(a)   (b)   (c)   (d)

Figure 1.29: Pioneering Developments in Immersive Visuals: (a) Charles Wheatstone's stereoscope (1838) (b) The View-Master (1930s) (c) Morton Heilig's Sensorama (1957) (d) The Cinerama system (1950s).

The first demonstration of stereopsis was conducted by Charles Wheatstone in 1838 using a device called the stereoscope (Figure 1.29(a)). This invention used mirrors to project a unique image to each eye, later improved by replacing mirrors with lenses. By the 1930s, a portable, mass-market version known as the View-Master (Figure 1.29(b)) became a household favourite, offering an accessible way to experience 3D imagery.

In 1957, Morton Heilig expanded on this concept with the Sensorama (Figure 1.29(c)), a multi-sensory device that incorporated motion pictures, sound, vibration, and even scents to create a fully immersive experience. Despite its innovation, the Sensorama had a notable limitation: the user's head remained stationary relative to the screen, reducing mobility and flexibility. Around the same time, movie theatres introduced stereoscopic 3D films, where viewers wore polarized glasses that filtered distinct images for each eye. This technique, which gained popularity in the 1950s, remains the foundation of modern 3D cinema.

Another way to enhance immersion is by increasing the viewer's field of view. The Cinerama system of the 1950s (Figure 1.29(d)) utilized a wide, curved screen to envelop the audience's vision, much like today's curved LED displays. Taking this concept even further, the CAVE (Cave Automatic Virtual Environment) system was developed in 1992 at the University of Illinois (Figure 1.30(a)). In the CAVE, video is projected onto multiple walls surrounding the user, offering a fully immersive space. The system also incorporates stereoscopic viewing with polarized glasses and head-tracking technology to ensure that the images on the walls adjust dynamically based on the user's movements.

These innovations, from the stereoscope to VR systems like CAVE, illustrate how visual experiences have evolved from staring at a static rectangle to stepping into fully immersive environments, pushing the boundaries of how we perceive and interact with digital worlds.

The Evolution of VR Headsets: From Pioneering Concepts to Modern Innovation

The drive toward portability continues to shape the development of virtual reality. A pivotal moment occurred in 1968 when Ivan Sutherland introduced the *Sword of Damocles*, widely regarded as the first VR headset (Figure 1.30(b)). This early device utilized cutting-edge displays and computers of the time to present dynamic images that adjusted as the user moved their head. This adjustment created the illusion that virtual objects remained stationary in space, introducing a key concept: *perception of stationarity*. For this effect to work, the system had to track head movements and adjust the visual output accordingly, making sensors and tracking systems essential components of VR.

By the 1980s, commercial VR headsets began to emerge. Jaron Lanier's company, VPL, popularized the iconic image of VR goggles and gloves (Figure 1.30(c)), cementing the idea of immersive interaction. The 1990s saw the introduction of VR-based video games in arcades (Figure 1.30(d)) and home systems like the Nintendo *Virtual Boy* (Figure 1.30(e)). However, these early experiences were often uncomfortable and lacked the realism needed to capture widespread interest.

The current generation of VR headsets has revolutionized the field, thanks largely to advances driven by the smartphone industry. Devices like the Oculus Rift (Figure 1.30(f)), released in 2016, leverage high-resolution screens and sophisticated sensors to deliver lightweight, affordable, and immersive experiences. These innovations have significantly lowered the cost of entry for both developers and enthusiasts, sparking a renewed surge of interest in VR technology across industries.

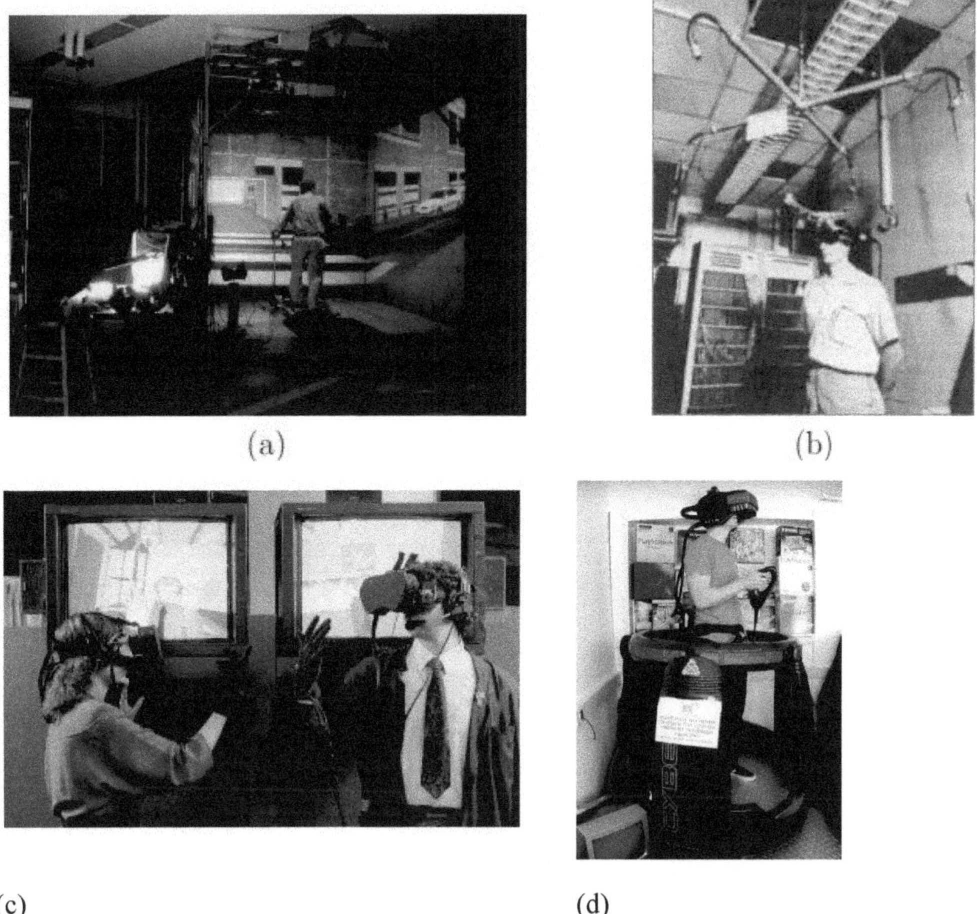

(a)

(b)

(c)

(d)

Figure 1.30: (a) CAVE system, 1992 (b) Sword of Damocles, 1968 (c) VPL Eyephones, 1980s (d) Virtuality gaming system, 1990s (e) Nintendo Virtual Boy, 1995 (f) Oculus Rift, 2016.

By blending technological advancements with accessibility, modern VR headsets have made virtual reality more compelling and mainstream than ever before, ushering in a new era of immersive digital experiences

Connecting People in Virtual Spaces

An essential element we've yet to fully explore is human connection—how we interact, collaborate, and share experiences with others. For centuries, social interaction has taken various forms, from live theatre performances and classrooms to the written word in letters and novels. Long before writing existed, oral storytelling passed experiences from generation to generation. In more recent times, technology has enabled instantaneous communication, evolving from the telephone's transmission of audio to the seamless video-conferencing we now enjoy online. Despite these advancements, text-based communication, such as messaging and online forums, remains a significant part of our interactions, illustrating how simplicity often rivals realism in value.

Since the 1970s, communities built around text-based exchanges have flourished on the internet. In gaming, the evolution from early Multi-User Dungeons (MUDs) to today's Massively Multiplayer Online Role-Playing Games (MMORPGs) showcases how virtual spaces can bring people together in expansive digital worlds. Similarly, in education, the PLATO system from the University of Illinois pioneered computer-assisted learning by introducing message boards, instant messaging, screen sharing, chat rooms, and even emoticons—laying the groundwork for modern platforms like Khan Academy and Coursera.

Today, social interaction online is dominated by platforms such as Facebook, where users communicate through text, share photos and videos, and exchange links. In virtual reality, this concept is taken further with platforms like *Second Life* and *Opensimulator*, where users create avatars to "live" and interact in immersive digital worlds (Figure 1.31). These platforms allow for dynamic social experiences, moving beyond the constraints of viewing life through a flat screen.

Figure 1.31: *Second Life*, launched in 2003, allows users to create avatars and engage in a shared virtual environment. The figure depicts a keynote address delivered at the 2014 Opensimulator Community Conference, highlighting the collaborative potential of such platforms.

As VR continues to develop, it raises profound questions: What kinds of virtual societies will emerge when we are no longer tethered to physical boundaries or two-dimensional screens? Science fiction often paints a vivid, though sometimes dystopian, picture of a future where humanity prefers virtual interactions over real-world connections. The outcome remains uncertain, but what is clear is that simplicity can be as powerful as hyper-realism in creating impactful VR experiences.

Regardless of technological advances, the fundamental design of human senses, minds, and bodies remains constant. To craft truly engaging VR systems, a deep understanding of human perception and cognition is essential. Whether VR's future leads to utopian collaboration or dystopian isolation, the balance between realism and imagination will continue to shape how we connect in these evolving virtual landscapes

1.8 Human Physiology and Perception

Our bodies did not evolve with virtual reality in mind. The delicate biological systems that have taken millions of years to develop in natural environments can be disrupted by artificial sensory input. VR introduces stimuli that may not align with the brain's accumulated experiences, potentially altering our perception. In some cases, our bodies adapt, making us less aware of system imperfections. In others, VR can enhance our ability to interpret complex 3D scenes. However, this comes at a cost—users may experience increased fatigue or headaches as the brain works harder to process the unfamiliar input. The most extreme reaction is VR sickness, manifesting as dizziness and nausea.

Perceptual Psychology explores how sensory input is transformed into perceived reality. It addresses crucial VR-related questions such as:

- How far does that object appear to be?

- What video resolution prevents pixel detection?

- How many frames per second are needed for smooth motion perception?

- Is the user's virtual head positioned correctly?

- Where is that sound coming from in the virtual environment?

- Why does VR sometimes induce nausea?

- Why is one VR experience more exhausting than another?

- What does "presence" in VR truly mean?

To answer these, three key areas need exploration:

1. The basic physiology of sense organs and neural pathways.

2. Core theories and findings from experimental perceptual psychology.

3. The impact of engineered VR systems on natural perception, including side effects and implications.

Many VR developers underestimate the importance of perception. In daily life, these processes operate so effortlessly that we barely notice them. Consider how easily you recognize a loved one's face—seemingly effortless but supported by complex neural processes. Experiments have demonstrated just how much the brain works during such tasks. For example, studies involving brain lesions show how damage to specific areas can impair facial recognition. Individuals with prosopagnosia cannot recognize familiar faces, including their own reflection, even though other cognitive functions remain intact.

Scientists also use single-unit recordings, primarily in animal studies, to observe individual neuron responses to stimuli. Imagine a neuron that fires only when you see a sphere—this highlights the incredible specificity of sensory perception. Understanding these intricate processes is essential for creating VR experiences that are not only immersive but also comfortable and engaging, ensuring users feel present without succumbing to the physical strain VR can sometimes cause

Optical Illusions: Windows into Perceptual Complexity

Optical illusions offer a fascinating glimpse into the intricacies of human perception, often revealing how our visual system can be tricked by cleverly designed stimuli. These illusions are harmless yet astonishing, crafted to expose subtle flaws in how we process visual information. They present scenarios that differ from the ordinary experiences our brains are accustomed to interpreting, thus creating surprising effects.

(a)   (b)

Figure 1.32: illustrates two such illusions that demonstrate the brain's remarkable yet sometimes fallible ability to interpret sensory data:

1. **Ponzo Illusion (Figure 1.32a)**: In this classic illusion, the upper line appears longer than the lower one, despite both being the same length. This effect is caused by the brain's interpretation of linear perspective, as if the lines are converging in the distance, akin to railroad tracks.

2. **Checker Shadow Illusion (Figure 1.32b)**: Here, tile B appears lighter than tile A, although they are the same shade of gray. The illusion is driven by the brain's assumptions about shadows and lighting, causing it to adjust the perceived brightness based on context.

These examples emphasize the brain's continuous effort to fill in gaps, infer context, and provide coherent interpretations of the world based on prior experiences and biological design. When designing virtual reality systems or other visual experiences, it is crucial to understand these mechanisms. Ignoring the complex interplay between sensory input and perception can lead to disorienting or uncomfortable user experiences. Optical illusions remind us that what we see is not always reality but rather the brain's best guess at interpreting the visual information it receives.

Classification of Human Senses

Perception extends beyond just what we see—our bodies are equipped with a diverse array of sensory systems, each tuned to detect specific types of stimuli. Table 1.1 categorizes these basic senses, highlighting how different forms of energy are transformed into neural signals. In essence, each sense acts as a biological sensor, converting external stimuli into signals the brain can interpret. This process is known as **sensory system selectivity**, where specialized receptors respond to distinct types of energy.

For instance, vision relies on over 100 million **photoreceptors** in each eye that detect electromagnetic energy in the visible spectrum. Some photoreceptors are sensitive to color, while others adjust to varying light intensities. In contrast, **mechanoreceptors** in the auditory, touch, and balance systems detect motion, vibration, and gravitational forces. **Thermoreceptors** embedded in the skin register changes in temperature, while **chemoreceptors** in the nose and mouth perceive the chemical makeup of substances, forming the basis for taste and smell.

Table 1.1: Human Sensory Systems Overview

Sense	Stimulus	Receptor Type	Sense Organ
Vision	Electromagnetic energy	Photoreceptors	Eye
Auditory	Air pressure waves	Mechanoreceptors	Ear
Touch	Tissue distortion	Mechanoreceptors	Skin, muscles
Temperature	Thermal changes	Thermoreceptors	Skin
Balance	Gravity, acceleration	Mechanoreceptors	Vestibular organs
Taste/Smell	Chemical composition	Chemoreceptors	Mouth, nose

Engineering Equivalents in VR

Remarkably, these biological senses have technological counterparts, many of which are already integrated into modern virtual reality (VR) systems. Imagine designing a humanoid telepresence robot to interact through a VR headset. Cameras could function as its "eyes," capturing visual data, while microphones would serve as its "ears," picking up sound. Pressure sensors and thermometers could replicate the sensations of touch and temperature. For balance, an **Inertial Measurement Unit (IMU)** would provide the robot with orientation and motion data, much like the human vestibular system. The similarity between the signals produced by IMUs and those from the vestibular organs is striking.

Even chemical sensing can be mimicked using devices like pH meters, which could measure chemical properties to simulate taste and smell. These parallels highlight how advances in sensory technology enable VR to create more immersive and lifelike experiences, bridging the gap between human perception and machine-based sensing.

Big Brains

Perception begins only after sensory organs convert external stimuli into neural signals. The human body is estimated to contain approximately 86 billion neurons, with around 20 billion residing in the **cerebral cortex**—the brain region responsible for processing perception, attention, memory, language, and consciousness. This thin layer of neurons, about three millimetres thick, is intricately folded to fit within the confines of the skull.

For comparison, consider the neuron counts in other species: a roundworm has 302 neurons, a fruit fly about 100,000, and a rat approximately 200 million. Interestingly, elephants surpass humans with over 250 billion neurons. However, neuron quantity alone does not determine cognitive superiority. Only mammals possess a cerebral cortex. In rats, it contains roughly 20 million neurons, while cats and dogs have around 300 million and 160 million, respectively. A gorilla's cortex contains about 4 billion neurons. Notably, the long-finned pilot whale's cerebral cortex holds an estimated 37 billion neurons—almost twice the number found in humans—but this does not necessarily translate to greater intelligence.

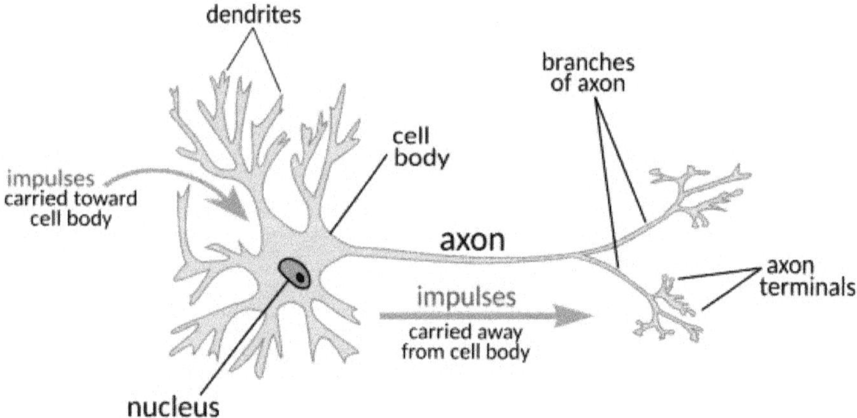

Figure 1.33: Neuronal Structure

A typical neuron receives signals through dendrites (input pathways) and sends output signals through axons to other neurons.

The Neural Network of the Brain

Neurons function as interconnected nodes in an immense directed graph, where each neuron processes information it receives. The **cell body** or nucleus acts as the central node, **dendrites** serve as the input edges, and **axons** represent output edges. Each neuron gathers input from thousands of others through its dendrites, processes it, and transmits the signal to additional neurons via its axon.

Communication between neurons occurs at the **synapse**, a tiny gap where chemical or electrical signals are exchanged. On average, each neuron in the human brain forms roughly 7,000 synaptic connections, resulting in an estimated **quadrillion (10^{15})** synaptic connections across the brain's neural network. This vast web of connections underscores the complexity and power of human cognition.

Hierarchical Processing in Perception

Once sensory signals leave the receptors of sense organs, they traverse a complex network of neurons before reaching the cerebral cortex. This journey involves **hierarchical processing**, as illustrated in Figure 1.34. Each receptor is highly selective, responding only to specific types of stimuli, such as variations in time, space, or frequency. As these signals pass through successive layers of neurons, they integrate input from numerous receptors, allowing the detection of increasingly intricate patterns within the stimulus.

In vision, for example, early stages of this process involve **feature detectors**, which help identify basic elements like edges, corners, and motion. By the time the signals reach the cerebral cortex, they are combined with previous life experiences, enabling the interpretation of complex stimuli such as recognizing familiar faces or identifying a melody. The cerebral cortex thus creates a cohesive representation of the surrounding world.

Interestingly, **topographic mapping** techniques have revealed that the spatial relationships among receptors can be preserved in the arrangement of neurons within the cortex. Moreover, specialized cells like **place cells** and **grid cells** play crucial roles in forming spatial maps of familiar environments, further aiding in navigation and spatial awareness.

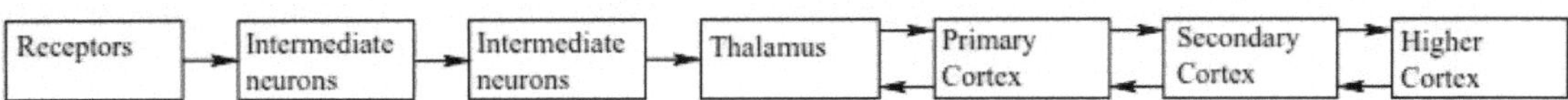

Figure 1.34:

The sensory information captured by receptors moves through a hierarchical neural network. In early stages, signals are integrated from multiple receptors and transmitted upward, while in later stages, information flows bidirectionally, enhancing perception through feedback loops.

Proprioception: The Body's Hidden Sense

Beyond relying on our senses and memories, we also engage proprioception—our innate ability to perceive the positions and movements of our body parts and the effort involved in those movements. Imagine closing your eyes and waving your arms in a spacious area. You can still sense the location of your arms, even if accurately touching your fingertips together without sight proves difficult. This sense is so vital that the motor cortex, responsible for controlling movement, sends signals known as efference copies to other brain regions, informing them of the actions being performed.

Proprioception functions much like an additional sense. In the context of robotics, it is akin to the role of encoders on joints or wheels that track movement distances. A fascinating aspect of this sense is its role in tickling: you cannot tickle yourself because you are aware of your own movements. However, when someone else tickles you, their efference copies are inaccessible to your brain, making the tickling sensation possible.

Fusion of Senses: The Brain's Balancing Act

Throughout our lives, the brain continuously integrates input from multiple senses, along with proprioception, and combines these signals with past experiences. In everyday situations, without the influence of virtual reality (VR) or substances, this complex process usually results in a seamless perception of the world. However, disrupting these sensory integrations can lead to conflicting signals. Sometimes, these conflicts go unnoticed, but they may still cause subtle effects like fatigue or headaches. In more pronounced cases, the brain's response might trigger dizziness or nausea. Occasionally, the conflict becomes so apparent that we immediately recognize the experience as artificial, undermining VR's immersive effect. To ensure VR is both convincing and comfortable, rigorous testing with human participants is essential, as predicting brain responses to novel scenarios is nearly impossible without prior research on similar experiences.

One of the most striking examples of sensory conflict in VR is *vection*, the illusion of self-movement. This occurs when the eyes report acceleration to the brain, but the inner ear's balance system indicates stillness. In real life, such conflicts rarely happen because vision and balance usually work in harmony, like when walking down a street. You might have experienced vection when sitting in a stationary car or train and feeling as if you are moving backward while watching another vehicle move forward nearby. A historical example dates back to the 1890s, when Amariah Lake designed an amusement park attraction called the "haunted swing." The swing remained stationary, but the surrounding room rotated, creating the illusion of movement. Although thrilling, it often caused nausea due to extreme vection.

In VR, vection frequently arises during locomotion, such as when a player uses a controller to simulate forward motion. The visual system perceives acceleration, but the vestibular system remains at rest, leading to sensory conflict and discomfort. Ensuring a smoother, more immersive VR experience requires understanding these sensory dynamics and their effects on the human brain.

Figure 1.35: The Haunted Swing Illusion

This illusion created the sensation of swinging by rotating the surrounding room while the swing remained still. Though entertaining, it often caused nausea due to strong vection effects. (Adapted from Albert A. Hopkins, *Magic Stage Illusions*, 1898.)

Adaptation: The Brain's Ever-Changing Perception

A key feature of all sensory systems is *adaptation*—the way our perception of stimuli shifts over time. This can happen across any sense and over varying durations. For instance, the loud hum of an engine in a car or airplane seems less noticeable after a few minutes. Similarly, our eyes adjust to changes in brightness as the optical system and photoreceptors recalibrate. Over longer periods, *perceptual training* can enhance adaptation. In military simulations, for example, soldiers report less motion sickness, possibly due to frequent exposure. Likewise, seasoned gamers, particularly those playing first-person shooters, often experience less vection in VR due to their prolonged interaction with immersive screens.

In VR development, adaptation plays a double-edged role. Developers, through repeated exposure, may grow accustomed to experiences that could feel uncomfortable or disorienting to new users, creating an inherent bias. This is akin to the classic mistake of confusing the scientist for the test subject. On the positive side, frequent exposure can sharpen developers' ability to detect subtle issues that newcomers might overlook, such as:

- Increased latency, disrupting the sense of stability.

- Swapped visuals between the left and right eyes.

- Objects appearing in one eye but not the other.

- Unequal latency between eye views.

- Slight warping of straight lines due to optical distortion.

This disconnects between stimulus and perception leads directly into the next important concept.

Psychophysics: Exploring the Link Between Stimuli and Perception

Psychophysics is the scientific study of how physical stimuli give rise to perceptual experiences. For instance, what conditions must be met for someone to perceive an object as "red"? In this case, the stimulus is light entering the eye, while the perception occurs when the brain identifies the colour "red." Other perceptual experiences include concepts like "straight," "louder," "sour," or "ticklish".

Figure 1.36 illustrates a typical psychophysical experiment. As a variable, such as light frequency, is adjusted, there is often a range where participants cannot confidently categorize the stimulus. For example, within a certain range, a person might be uncertain whether the light appears red. At one end of the spectrum, they consistently perceive it as "red," while at the other, they consistently see it as "not red." In the ambiguous middle region, researchers track the probability of detection, which measures how often participants identify the light as "red".

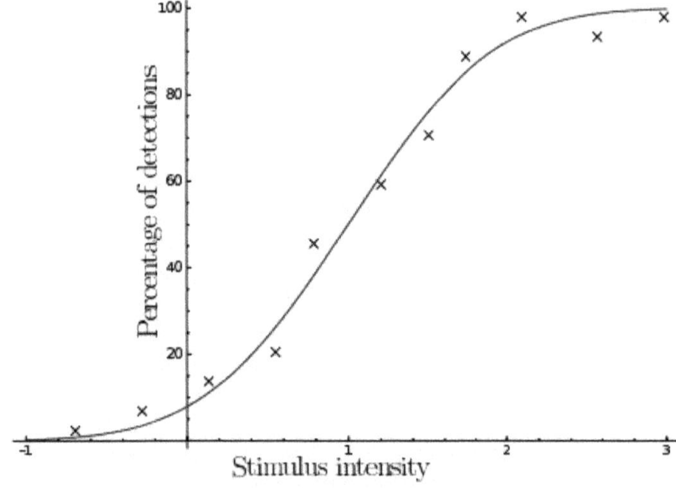

Figure 1.36: Psychometric Function Overview

This graph shows how the detection rate increases as the intensity of a stimulus rises. The point where 50% of participants detect the stimulus marks a critical threshold, often modelled using a cumulative distribution curve, typically assumed to follow a Gaussian (normal) distribution.

Stevens' Power Law: The Link Between Stimulus and Perception

Stevens' power law is a key concept in psychophysics that describes how the perceived intensity of a stimulus relates to its actual physical magnitude. The law suggests that this relationship follows an exponential form across many sensory systems and types of stimuli:

$$p = cm^x$$

Where:

- **m** is the stimulus magnitude or intensity,

- **p** is the perceived magnitude,

- **x** is an exponent that defines how the actual magnitude translates into perception,

- **c** is a constant determined by the units used (less important in interpretation)

When **x = 1**, the equation becomes linear: p=c·mp = c \cdot mp=c·m. A good example is the perception of line length—if you look at a line segment, the perceived length is directly proportional to its actual length.

More intriguing cases occur when **x ≠ 1**. For instance, when observing the brightness of an object in the dark, **x = 0.33**, meaning that even a substantial increase in brightness only results in a modest perceived difference. In contrast, with electrical shocks through the fingers, **x = 3.5**, meaning that even a small increase in current feels significantly more intense, highlighting how perception can amplify certain stimuli.

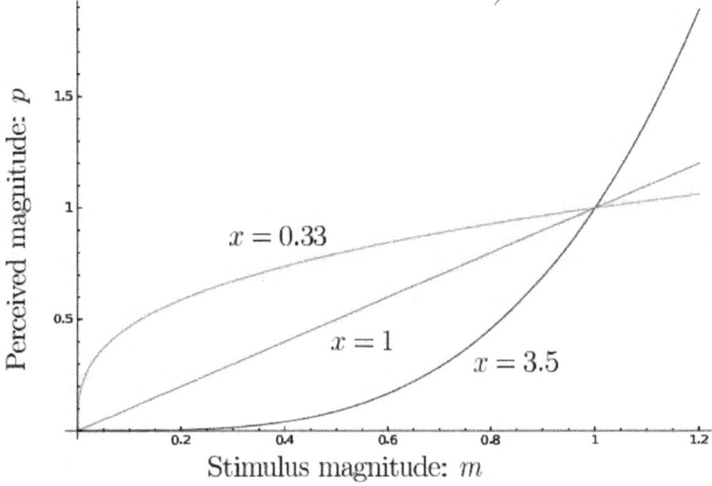

Figure 1.37: Stevens' Power Law Visualization

This figure illustrates the exponential relationship between a stimulus's physical magnitude and its perceived intensity, where the curve's shape is determined by the value of **x** and varies depending on the type of stimulus

Just Noticeable Difference (JND): Detecting Subtle Changes

A fundamental concept in psychophysics is the ***just noticeable difference*** (JND), which refers to the smallest change in a stimulus that can be detected at least 50% of the time. If the change is large, nearly all participants will perceive it, while a very small change may go unnoticed by most. The challenge in experiments is to adjust the stimulus until the likelihood of detection reaches that 50% threshold.

Take brightness as an example: as the intensity of light increases, how much more must it change for people to notice the difference? This relationship is explained by *Weber's Law*:

$$\frac{\Delta m}{m} = c$$

Here:

- Δm represents the JND (the smallest detectable change),

- **m** is the current magnitude of the stimulus,

- **c** is a constant specific to the type of stimulus.

Weber's Law shows that the JND is proportional to the stimulus's initial magnitude, meaning that as the stimulus grows stronger, a larger change is needed for it to be perceived.

Designing Experiments for VR: Challenges and Considerations

Virtual reality (VR) disrupts users' typical sensory processes, making it essential to test new VR systems and experiences to ensure they achieve the desired outcomes without causing unintended side effects. This involves applying the scientific method: observing, hypothesizing, and conducting experiments to validate those hypotheses. However, working with human participants presents unique challenges.

Key questions arise: How many participants are needed? What if they adapt to the VR environment during the study? How do their past experiences or even their current state—like feeling slightly unwell or what they had for breakfast—impact the results? These seemingly small variables can significantly influence outcomes.

Complications increase if participants are aware of the hypothesis, which could bias their responses. Researchers must also decide how to collect data. Will they rely on subjective questionnaires, or will they use objective measures like head movements, heart rate, or skin conductance? These decisions can greatly affect the validity of the findings.

Moreover, VR technology evolves rapidly. A simple online search will reveal the latest headsets and development tools. Yet, the fundamental principles of human perception and physiology remain consistent. For further exploration, refer to resources focusing on "Sensation and Perception."

Exercise Questions

1. Define virtual reality. Explain the key components in the VR definition.

2. What is the importance of physiology and perception in virtual reality explain with examples?

3. Explain 5 key components in virtual reality systems.

4. Are we making organisms really fool in virtual reality? Elaborate.

5. List and explain applications of virtual reality.

6. What are differences between real world and synthetic world?

7. Give differences between virtual reality and augmented reality with examples.

8. Explain open loop and close loop virtual reality systems with examples.

9. What is Virtual Reality? What are applications of VR?

10. What are the historical perceptive of virtual reality? What were the initial commercial VR products?

11. What was Helig's role in development of VR?

12. What are commonalities and difference between virtual reality and 3 D computer graphics?

13. What are the five classic components of a VR system?

14. What was NASA'S role in early VR developments and why was it interested?

15. What happened with the VR industry in 1990s?

16. How virtual reality is differ from augmented reality and telepresence?

17. Explain history of virtual reality.

18. Explain human physiology and perception

2. Input and Output Devices for Virtual Reality

Virtual Reality (VR) systems rely on various input and output devices to create immersive experiences for users. Input devices play a crucial role in virtual reality (VR) experiences, enabling users to interact with and navigate virtual environments. Following are some common input devices used in VR.

1. VR Controllers

VR controllers are handheld devices specifically designed for VR interactions. They typically feature buttons, triggers, thumbsticks, and touchpads, allowing users to manipulate objects, navigate menus, and perform actions within VR environments. Examples include Oculus Touch controllers, HTC Vive controllers, and PlayStation Move controllers as shown in figure 2.1.

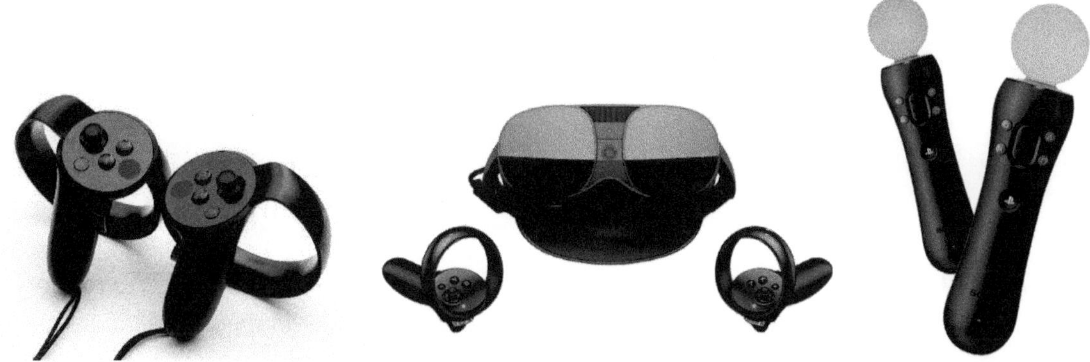

Figure 2.1: Oculus Touch, HTC Vive, and PlayStation Move controllers

2. Motion Tracking Systems

Motion tracking systems capture the movement and orientation of the user's body and translate it into the virtual environment. These systems often use external sensors, cameras, or inside-out tracking technology embedded in VR headsets to track the user's position and gestures. Examples include Oculus Constellation tracking, HTC Vive Base Stations, and Windows Mixed Reality inside-out tracking.

3. Gesture Recognition Devices

Gesture recognition devices enable users to interact with VR environments using hand gestures and motions. They typically use cameras and sensors to detect and interpret the user's gestures, allowing for intuitive and natural interactions. Examples include Leap Motion hand tracking devices and Intel RealSense cameras (Figure 2.2).

Figure 2.2: Leap Motion hand tracking devices and Intel RealSense cameras

4. Voice Recognition Systems

Voice recognition systems allow users to control and navigate VR experiences using voice commands. These systems utilize built-in microphones or external devices to capture and interpret user voice inputs, enabling hands-free interaction in VR. Examples include built-in voice assistants in VR headsets and third-party voice recognition software integrations.

5. Eye Tracking Devices

Eye tracking devices monitor the movement and gaze direction of the user's eyes within the VR environment. They enable features such as foveated rendering, which optimizes graphics rendering based on the user's gaze, improving performance and visual quality. Eye tracking also enhances interaction by enabling gaze-based selection and navigation. Examples include Tobii eye tracking technology integrated into some VR headsets (Figure 2.3).

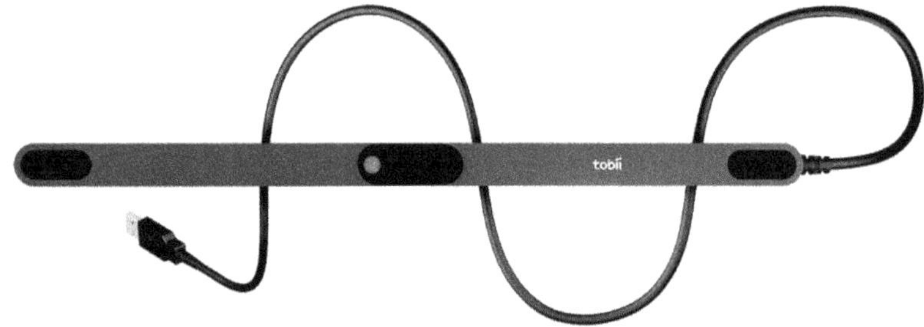

Figure 2.3: Tobii eye tracking

6. Biometric Sensors

Biometric sensors measure physiological responses such as heart rate, skin conductance, and facial expressions. They provide valuable data for enhancing immersion, adapting experiences based on user feedback, and monitoring user engagement and emotional responses. Examples include wearable biometric sensors and VR peripherals equipped with biometric tracking capabilities.

These input devices work in tandem to provide users with immersive and interactive VR experiences, enabling them to engage with virtual environments in intuitive and natural ways. As VR technology continues to evolve, new input devices and interaction paradigms may emerge, further enhancing the user experience in virtual reality.

Output devices in virtual reality (VR) are essential for delivering immersive experiences to users, allowing them to perceive and interact with virtual environments.

1. VR Headsets

VR headsets are the primary output devices in VR systems, providing users with visual and auditory immersion. They feature built-in displays, lenses, and head-tracking sensors to create stereoscopic 3D visuals and simulate depth perception. VR headsets also incorporate integrated headphones or audio jacks to deliver spatial audio, enhancing immersion. Examples include Oculus Rift, HTC Vive, PlayStation VR, and Valve Index.

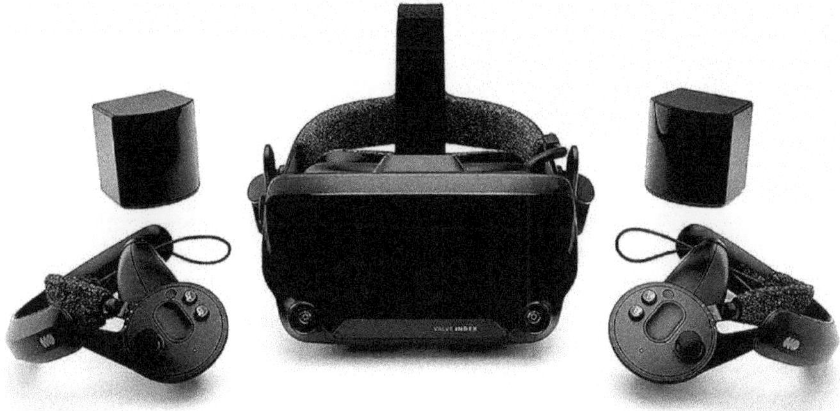

Figure 2.4: Valve Index

2. Haptic Feedback Devices

Haptic feedback devices enhance immersion by providing tactile sensations to users, simulating touch and force feedback. These devices may include handheld controllers, vests, gloves, or accessories equipped with vibration motors, force sensors, or pneumatic actuators. Haptic feedback can simulate interactions with virtual objects, environmental effects, and physical feedback from virtual environments. Examples include the Oculus Touch controllers with vibration feedback, haptic gloves like the Dexmo, and full-body haptic suits such as the Teslasuit.

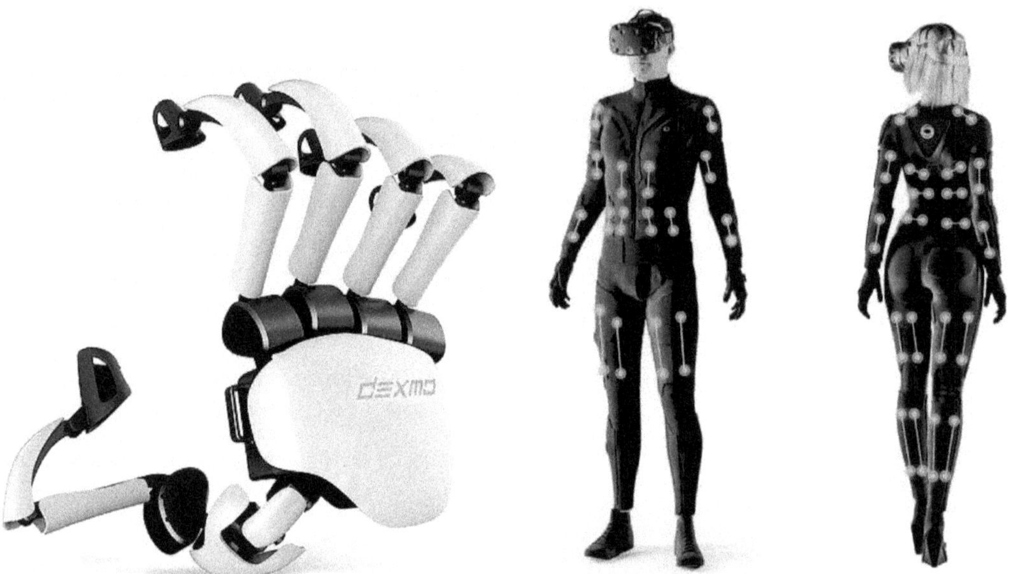

Figure 2.5: Dexmo and Teslasuit

3. Spatial Audio Systems

Spatial audio systems create realistic soundscapes in VR environments by simulating the direction, distance, and intensity of virtual sounds. These systems use head-related transfer functions (HRTFs) to accurately position audio sources in 3D space relative to the user's head position and orientation. VR headsets typically feature integrated headphones or audio systems to deliver spatial audio cues, enhancing immersion and situational awareness. Examples include Oculus Spatial Audio, Steam Audio, and Dolby Atmos for VR.

4. Visual Output Enhancements

VR systems may incorporate visual output enhancements to improve image quality, reduce motion sickness, and enhance comfort. Features like dynamic depth of field, foveated rendering, and variable refresh rates optimize graphics rendering and performance based on user behavior and system capabilities. High-resolution displays, adjustable interpupillary distance (IPD), and lens technologies contribute to sharper visuals and reduced eye strain in VR headsets. Examples include adaptive resolution scaling in VR games, lens adjustments in VR headsets, and anti-aliasing techniques for smoother graphics.

These output devices work together to create compelling and immersive VR experiences, engaging user's senses and enabling interaction with virtual environments. As VR technology continues to evolve, advancements in display technology, audio rendering, and haptic feedback systems will further enhance the realism and immersion of virtual reality experiences.

2.1 Three dimensional position tracker

A three-dimensional position tracker is a device or system that is capable of determining the location and alignment of an object or user in three-dimensional space. These trackers are crucial components in various applications such as virtual reality, augmented reality, motion capture, robotics, and navigation systems.

Optical Tracking Systems

Optical tracking systems use cameras and markers to track the position and orientation of objects in three-dimensional space. Infrared cameras detect the position of reflective markers placed on objects, enabling real-time tracking with high accuracy. These systems are commonly used in motion capture studios for animation, virtual reality setups, and augmented reality applications. Examples include Vicon, OptiTrack, and PhaseSpace optical tracking systems.

Figure 2.6: Vicon, OptiTrack, and PhaseSpace

Inertial Measurement Units (IMUs)

IMUs utilize a combination of gyroscopes, accelerometers, and sometimes magnetometers to measure the acceleration, angular velocity, and magnetic field of an object. By integrating the sensor data over time, IMUs can estimate the object's position and orientation in three-dimensional space. IMUs are often used in wearable devices, motion tracking systems, and navigation applications where GPS signals may be unavailable or unreliable.

Electromagnetic Tracking Systems

Electromagnetic tracking systems utilize electromagnetic fields to determine the location and orientation of objects equipped with specialized sensors. A transmitter emits electromagnetic signals, and receivers in the tracked object measure the signal strength and direction, allowing for precise localization. These systems are used in surgical navigation, virtual reality, and motion tracking applications where high accuracy is required. Examples include the Ascension Flock of Birds system and Polhemus electromagnetic trackers.

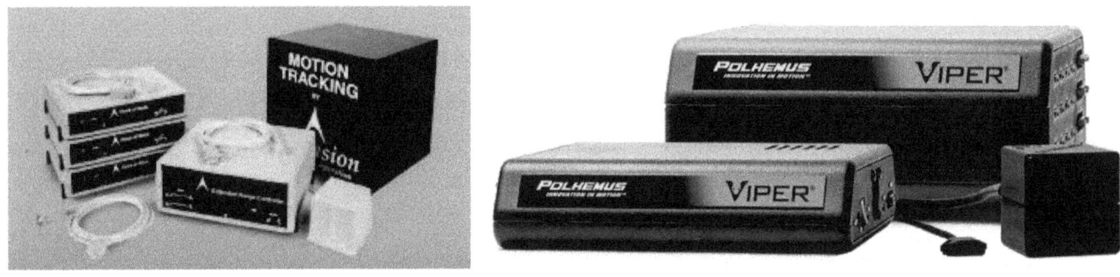

Figure 2.7: Ascension Flock of Birds and

Laser-based Tracking Systems

Laser-based tracking systems use laser emitters and receivers to measure the distance between the tracking device and reflective targets placed on objects. By triangulating the reflections from multiple targets, the system can determine the object's position and orientation in three-dimensional space. Laser trackers are commonly used in industrial metrology, 3D scanning, and large-scale motion tracking applications.

Table 2.1: Comparison table outlining the advantages, limitations, and applications of various types of three-dimensional position trackers

Tracker Type	Advantages	Limitations	Applications
Optical Tracking Systems	High accuracy	Line-of-sight limitations	Motion capture
	Real-time tracking	Susceptible to marker occlusion	Virtual reality
	Scalable systems for large environments	Calibration requirements	Augmented reality
Inertial Measurement Units (IMUs)	Compact and portable	Drift and cumulative error	Wearable devices
	No external infrastructure required	Integration errors	Motion tracking systems
	Low-latency tracking	Limited accuracy over time	Navigation systems
	Works in GPS-denied environments	Sensitivity to vibration	
Electromagnetic Tracking Systems	High accuracy and precision	Costly infrastructure	Surgical navigation
	Low-latency tracking	Electromagnetic interference	Virtual reality
	No line-of-sight requirement	Limited tracking volume	Motion tracking systems
Laser-based Tracking Systems	High accuracy	Limited tracking volume	Industrial metrology
	Long-range tracking capabilities	Line-of-sight requirements	3D scanning
	Suitable for outdoor environments	Susceptible to environmental factors	Robotics
Ultrasonic Tracking Systems	Non-line-of-sight tracking	Limited accuracy over long distances	Indoor positioning
	Low-cost hardware	Susceptible to interference	Virtual reality
	Scalable systems for large spaces	Limited range	Robotics

Ultrasonic Tracking Systems

Ultrasonic tracking systems rely on the transmission and reception of ultrasonic signals to calculate the time taken for these signals to travel between devices. By analysing the time-of-flight from multiple transmitters, the system triangulates the position and orientation of an object. These systems are widely used in applications such as indoor navigation, virtual reality, and robotics.

The examples provided illustrate various three-dimensional position tracking technologies, each offering distinct benefits and limitations depending on accuracy, environment, and cost considerations. The selection of a suitable system is influenced by specific requirements and constraints.

Understanding Positional Tracking

Positional tracking refers to the ability of a device to determine its precise location relative to its surroundings. Combining hardware and software, this technology enables absolute position detection, which is critical for creating immersive virtual reality (VR) experiences. It supports six degrees of freedom (6DOF), allowing for full movement tracking in three-dimensional space.

Degrees of Freedom (DOF)

Degrees of freedom describe the ways an object can move within a three-dimensional space. There are six in total, categorized into rotational and translational movements, with three degrees in each category:

- **Rotational Movements:** Pitch, yaw, and roll. These are typically tracked by inertial measurement units (IMUs), which combine accelerometers, gyroscopes, and magnetometers to detect an object's orientation and movement. While marketed as "9 DOF" systems, IMUs essentially measure the same three rotational movements.

- **Translational Movements:** Forward/backward, up/down, and left/right. These are usually captured using external cameras or other sensors, as internal sensors rarely track translational movement. Accurate positional tracking is essential for determining an object's absolute position in a 3D space.

Head Tracking vs. Positional Tracking

While head tracking captures only rotational movements (pitch, yaw, roll), positional tracking encompasses both rotational and translational data, registering precise movements such as leaning, jumping, or shifting position within a space.

Advantages of Positional Tracking in VR

Positional tracking significantly enhances the VR experience by:

- Adjusting the user's perspective based on their movements.

- Accurately representing hand and object positions in virtual environments.

- Strengthening the connection between physical and virtual worlds, such as enabling object manipulation through gestures.

- Improving 3D depth perception using parallax, which helps the brain interpret distance.

- Minimizing motion sickness by aligning visual inputs with the body's vestibular system.

Various techniques are available for positional tracking, with the choice depending on factors like accuracy, refresh rate, environment (indoor/outdoor), cost, power efficiency, and whether the tracked object is rigid or flexible.

In VR, positional tracking is indispensable for creating a seamless, immersive experience. By precisely mapping movements such as head or hand positioning, this technology fosters a heightened sense of presence and engagement within virtual spaces.

2.2 Methods of Positional Tracking

There are several techniques utilized for positional tracking, each with its own unique principles and applications:

Acoustic Tracking

Acoustic tracking determines the position of an object by measuring the time it takes for an acoustic signal to travel from an emitter to a receiver. Typically, multiple transmitters are positioned within the tracking area, while receivers are placed on the object to be tracked. By calculating the time taken for the signal to reach the receiver, the distance between them is determined. For accurate measurements, the system must know the exact time the signal was sent. When an object has multiple receivers in fixed positions, the system can also deduce the object's orientation by comparing the signal arrival times at each receiver. While effective, acoustic tracking requires precise calibration and can be affected by environmental noise. Additionally, it lacks high update rates, making it less suitable for certain applications. To enhance accuracy, it is often combined with other tracking technologies, such as inertial sensors. Companies like Intersense have successfully developed systems based on acoustic tracking.

Wireless tracking

Wireless tracking employs anchors placed around the tracking space and tags attached to the objects being monitored. Functioning similarly to GPS, this system operates in both indoor and outdoor environments, often referred to as "indoor GPS." Tags determine their 3D position by triangulating signals received from the anchors. Advanced wireless technologies, such as Ultra-Wideband (UWB), have achieved remarkable precision, sometimes below 100 mm. When paired with high-speed algorithms and sensor fusion, accuracy improves further, reaching precision levels of about 5 mm with update speeds as high as 200 Hz, or a latency of just 5 milliseconds.

Inertial Tracking

Inertial tracking relies on accelerometers and gyroscopes to determine an object's position and orientation. Accelerometers measure linear acceleration, which is used to compute velocity and position relative to an initial point. Gyroscopes measure angular velocity, allowing the calculation of angular position. These measurements, combined with the mathematical relationships between acceleration, velocity, and position, provide the object's movement data. While this method is cost-effective and offers high update rates with low latency, it is prone to positional drift due to the cumulative errors in calculations. This drift limits the long-term accuracy of inertial tracking.

Magnetic Tracking

Magnetic tracking determines position and orientation by measuring variations in magnetic field strength. A base station generates a magnetic field, and as the distance between the tracked object and the base increases, the field's strength diminishes. Changes in the magnetic field's distribution allow for orientation detection. Magnetic tracking systems are generally accurate in controlled environments but can be disrupted by nearby conductive materials, other magnetic fields, or ferromagnetic interference. Devices like the Razer Hydra motion controllers demonstrate practical applications of this technology. Many modern devices, such as head-mounted displays (HMDs) and smartphones, use magnetometers to detect Earth's magnetic field for orientation.

2.3 Optical Tracking

Optical tracking methods utilize cameras to capture positional data. Various approaches within this category include.

Tracking with markers

This method uses specific marker patterns on objects, which are detected by cameras. Algorithms analyze the marker arrangement to determine the object's position and orientation. Marker patterns are designed strategically to maximize information and minimize data loss. Markers can be either passive or active. Passive markers reflect infrared (IR) light back to the camera's source, while active markers emit IR signals themselves. The choice of marker type depends on factors such as distance, surface properties, and required detection angle.

Tracking with visible markers

Visible markers, arranged in predefined patterns, can also facilitate optical tracking. Cameras detect these markers to compute the object's position and orientation. These markers vary in shape and size but must be easily recognizable by the camera system.

Markerless tracking

In markerless tracking, the system relies on known geometric features of objects rather than external markers. By comparing camera images with a 3D model of the object, features such as edges or color transitions are used to track the object's position and orientation.

Depth map tracking

Depth cameras create real-time maps of object distances within the tracking area. The object to be tracked, such as a hand, is extracted from this depth map and analysed. Microsoft's Kinect is a prominent example of a device using depth map tracking technology.

Sensor Fusion

Sensor fusion combines multiple tracking techniques to enhance accuracy and compensate for individual limitations. For instance, inertial tracking can mitigate optical tracking's susceptibility to occlusion, while optical tracking can address inertial tracking's drift issues. The integration of these methods results in more reliable positional data.

Oculus Rift and HTC Vive's positional tracking

The Oculus Rift and HTC Vive employ distinct tracking technologies. The Rift uses an IR-LED array, tracked by a camera in a system known as Constellation. This system is limited to the camera's field of view and relies on IMU sensors in the headset when LEDs are not visible. In contrast, the HTC Vive utilizes Valve's Lighthouse technology, which employs lasers to flood the tracking area with invisible light, detected by photosensors on the device.

Positional tracking and smartphones

Mobile VR systems face challenges in achieving accurate positional tracking due to power limitations and the design constraints of mobile devices. Current solutions, such as using QR codes and cameras, compromise the simplicity and portability of mobile VR. As a result, smartphones primarily track head movements. Despite these limitations, companies are investing in advanced tracking systems for mobile devices to broaden VR accessibility and adoption.

Types of positional tracking

- **Inside-Out Tracking**: Cameras are placed on the device (HMD) being tracked.
- **Outside-In Tracking**: Cameras are positioned externally in the environment to monitor the device.
- **Markerless Tracking**: A tracking method that does not use fiducial markers.
- **Markerless Inside-Out Tracking**: Combines markerless tracking with inside-out tracking.

- **Markerless Outside-In Tracking**: Integrates markerless tracking with outside-in tracking

Modern consumer tracking systems, originally designed for traditional video games, are now widely applied in VR environments, showcasing their versatility and evolution.

Table 2.2: Comparison of tracking systems

Brand and Model	Tracking system	Inside -out	Outside -in	Marker -based	Marker light frequency	IM U	Spacial resolutio n (mm)	Latenc y (ms)
Facebook/Oculus Rift	Constellatio n	No	Yes	Yes	Infrared	Yes	--	--
IndoTraq	HSVT	Yes	No	No	Infrared	Yes	0.3	10
HTC Vive/SteamVR	Lighthouse	Yes	No	Yes	Infrared	Yes	0.3	15
Microsoft HoloLens	--	Yes	No	No	Infrared	Yes	--	--
Nintendo Wii Remote	--	Yes	No	Yes	Infrared	Yes	--	--
Sony PSVR	--	No	Yes	Yes	Red/Green/Blu e	Yes	--	18
Google	WorldSense	Yes	No	No	--	Yes	--	--

2.4 Mechanical trackers

A mechanical tracker, on the other hand, typically refers to a device or system that mechanically tracks the movement of an object or system. Using a mechanical tracker in virtual reality (VR) setups is less common compared to electronic and sensor-based tracking systems due to several limitations. However, mechanical trackers can still play a role in certain VR applications, particularly in specialized or experimental setups. Unlike electronic or sensor-based trackers, mechanical trackers often rely on physical linkages, gears, or mechanisms to follow the motion of an object. They may use principles such as gears, linkages, or cams to translate motion from one element to another. These systems have been used historically in various applications including:

- **Antenna Tracking Systems:** Mechanical trackers used to orient antennas towards specific satellites or radio sources.

- **Solar Tracking Systems:** Mechanisms that adjust solar panels to face the sun for maximum energy capture.

- **Machine Tool Tracking:** Systems that maintain precise alignment and positioning of cutting tools or machining heads during manufacturing processes.

In summary, while both three-dimensional position trackers and mechanical trackers serve the purpose of tracking movement or position, the former relies on electronic sensors and computational methods, while the latter operates through mechanical linkages and mechanisms.

2.5 Position tracking and orientation

This section explores methods for tracking all six degrees of freedom (6 DOF) for a moving rigid body, with a primary focus on head tracking. The combined position and orientation of a body is often referred to as its pose. By accurately estimating position, the parallax effect—a crucial depth cue—becomes more pronounced, enabling users to observe objects from various angles, such as from above, below, or the sides. These techniques are also applicable for tracking hand movements or manipulating objects during VR experiences.

Accelerometer

Using an inertial measurement unit (IMU) alone for 6-DOF tracking might seem appealing. An accelerometer measures the sum of true linear acceleration and gravity. If the gravity component is filtered out, the remaining data represents body acceleration. In theory, integrating this acceleration twice should yield position estimates. However, the practical challenges include significant drift errors, which grow quadratically due to calibration inaccuracies and the double integration process. These errors make standalone IMU-based tracking unreliable for positional accuracy. Furthermore, true body acceleration is difficult to extract during rapid rotations. Despite these limitations, IMUs remain critical components in 6-DOF systems, thanks to their high sampling rates and precise rotational tracking capabilities.

Active Wave-Based Tracking

While IMU-based tracking systems operate passively, leveraging pre-existing environmental data, an alternative is to use active tracking methods by emitting waves into the surroundings. Since humans share the same environment, perceptible waves like sound and visible light are less desirable. Instead, tracking systems often rely on energy sources such as infrared, ultrasound, or electromagnetic fields.

A practical example involves emitting ultrasonic pulses (frequencies above 20 kHz) from a speaker and detecting their arrival using a microphone. In this setup, the speaker acts as the emitter, while the microphone functions as the detector. If the timing is synchronized between the two, the time taken for the pulse to travel between them— known as the ***time of fligh***t (TOF or time or arrival)—can be measured. Using the medium's known speed of sound (approximately 330 m/s for ultrasound), the distance $d^\hat{d}d^$ between the emitter and detector can be calculated. However, one challenge with ultrasound systems is the occurrence of reverberation, where the pulse reflects off surfaces, leading to multiple signals received at the detector.

When correctly calibrated, the detector's position can be constrained to the surface of a sphere with radius $d^\hat{d}d^$, centred on the emitter. Adding more transmitters improves accuracy:

- **Two transmitters** refine the position to a circular path (where the spheres intersect).

- **Three transmitters** narrow it to two possible points.

- **Four or more transmitters** uniquely determine the position

In some cases, roles can be reversed—the tracked object can carry the emitter, with several detectors placed around it. The process of combining these measurements is known as **trilateration**. This method also works with electromagnetic waves like radio, infrared, or light, even if direct time measurement is challenging. When using electromagnetic waves, distances can alternatively be estimated based on signal strength reduction or phase shifts in reflected signals.

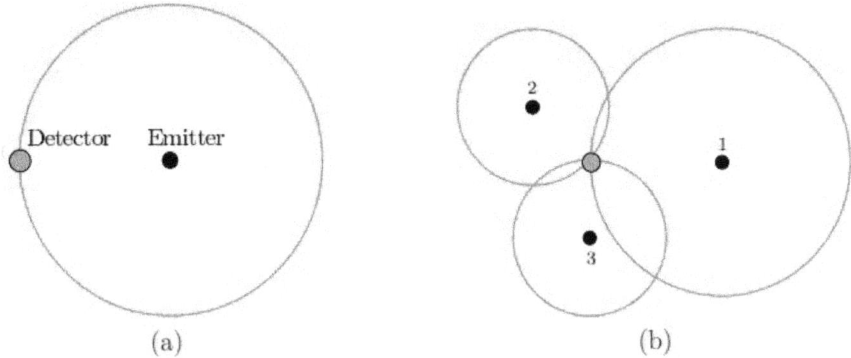

Trilateration in Action Figure 2.8 illustrates trilateration principles, which use distances to known emitters to pinpoint a detector's position:

a) A single emitter restricts the detector's possible locations to the circumference of a circle.

b) With three emitters, the detector's location is precisely determined.

Magnetic Fields for Tracking

Another approach involves creating a magnetic dipole, generating a field that changes in both strength and direction as the position varies. The magnetic field can be encoded to differentiate it from natural background interference. Systems like the Razer Hydra game controller utilize this principle, generating weak magnetic fields to track controller movements (Figure 2.9). A notable limitation of magnetic field tracking is environmental distortion, where the field becomes irregular, causing linear movements to appear curved. Unlike magnetometers, which require consistent fields across an area for yaw correction, positional tracking benefits from fields that vary significantly between locations

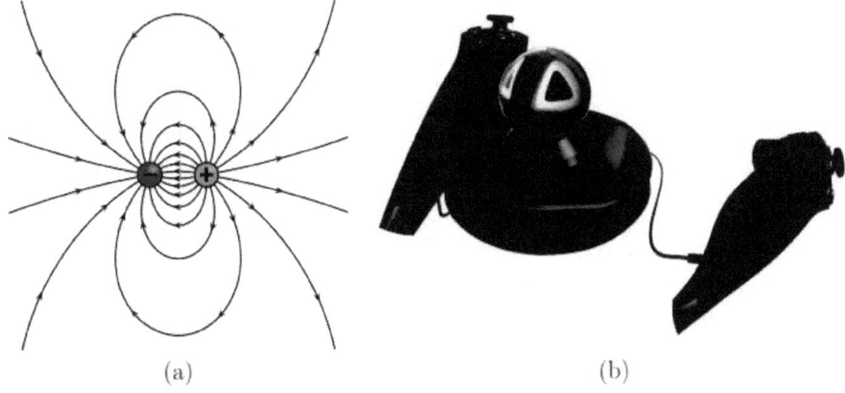

Figure 2.9: (a) A magnetic dipole produces a field whose intensity and orientation shift as the position changes (image credited to Wikipedia user Geek3). (b) The Razer Hydra, a gaming controller system, utilizes a base

station to emit a low-strength magnetic field, allowing precise tracking of controller movements (image courtesy of GamingShogun.com)

Multilateration and TDOA

If detectors lack precise timing for when a pulse begins, they can instead measure differences in arrival times at multiple points, a method known as **time difference of arrival (TDOA)**. Instead of a sphere, the possible positions form a hyperboloid. Multiple emitter-detector pairs are needed to refine the position further, using a process called **multilateration**. This technique, historically applied in the Decca Navigation System during World War II, was used to locate ships and aircraft. The human auditory system also uses a similar principle to locate sound sources.

Complex Fields for Tracking

Another method involves creating fields that vary spatially over the tracking area. Magnetic dipoles are one example: coded signals distinguish them from environmental fields, enabling the estimation of an object's position and orientation within the field. This principle has been successfully employed in devices like the Razer Hydra (Figure 2.9). However, magnetic fields are prone to distortions in real-world settings, leading to inaccuracies in tracking straight-line motion.

Visibility

An effective approach for achieving 6-DOF tracking is through visibility. This method involves identifying distinct elements within the physical environment, referred to as features, and determining their positions based on a line-of-sight ray extending to a known reference point. Figure 2.10 illustrates a concept influenced by a camera system, although other types of hardware can be utilized. A critical aspect of this tracking technique is featuring distinguishability. If all features appear identical, it becomes challenging to differentiate and consistently track them throughout the process. To address this, each feature must have a unique, persistent identifier that remains consistent as objects move. Failing to distinguish features accurately could lead to significant errors in estimating the pose of the tracked objec.

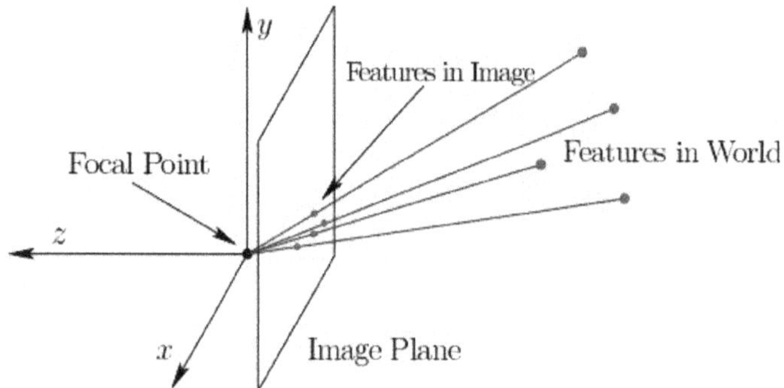

Figure 2.10: Distinct features in the real world can be identified along a line segment that connects them to the focal point through perspective projection.

Digital cameras are the most commonly used sensors for feature detection. Tasks such as recognizing, labelling, and tracking features fall under the domain of image processing and computer vision. Features can be classified into two categories:

- **Natural Features:** These are automatically identified and labelled during the tracking process without the need for external modifications.

- **Artificial Features:** These are purposefully designed and incorporated into the environment to facilitate easy detection, preassigned labelling, and tracking.

Natural features offer the advantage of requiring no setup, as the environment remains unaltered. However, they are generally less reliable. When using cameras, natural feature detection can be as complex as human vision, making it an inherently difficult task. Depending on factors such as texture, lighting, and the object itself, the method may work well in specific conditions but struggles to perform consistently across all scenarios. For instance, detecting and tracking features on a plain white wall is a significant challenge. As a result, artificial features are more commonly employed in practical applications.

Figure 2.11: Example of a QR code, which can be printed and utilized as an artificial feature. (Image sourced from Wikipedia.)

A straightforward approach to creating artificial features for tracking involves printing specialized markers directly onto the object. For instance, bright red dots can be applied to the surface and then identified in the image as red blobs. To address the need for unique identification, multiple colors—such as red, green, blue, and yellow—can be used. However, challenges may arise if these colors naturally appear elsewhere in the scene. A more robust solution is to design tags that stand out distinctly from the surrounding environment. Such tags can be encoded to carry extensive information, including a unique identifier. QR codes, as shown in Figure 2.11, are among the most widely used examples of coded markers.

The aforementioned features are considered *passive* because they rely on ambient light to reflect off the marker and onto the camera sensor. For more reliable results, *active* features that generate their own light can be employed. For example, colored LEDs can be attached to a headset or controller. However, this method has its drawbacks: it requires a power source, which increases the cost and weight of the device, and it may detract from the overall design aesthetic, potentially making the object resemble a lit-up decoration.

Infrared Tracking

The concepts described earlier can seamlessly transition to the infrared (IR) spectrum, allowing features to be visible to cameras without being noticeable to the human eye. For instance, patterns can be applied to objects using materials that strongly reflect IR light. Alternatively, IR LEDs can be integrated into devices. A notable example is the Oculus Rift headset, where IR LEDs are cleverly concealed behind plastic that is transparent to IR radiation but appears black to humans, as illustrated in Figure 2.14.

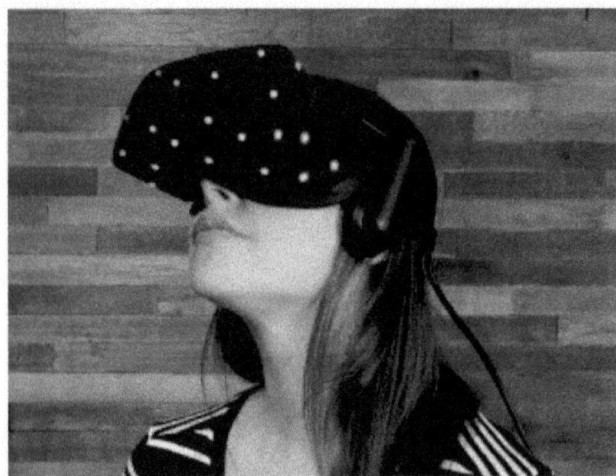

Figure 2.14: The Oculus Rift headset features IR LEDs hidden behind plastic transparent to IR light. (Image courtesy of www.ifixit.com.)

In certain scenarios, such as tracking fine movements across an entire human body, attaching LEDs directly to the subject may not be feasible. This method, known as motion capture (MOCAP), involves using high-powered IR LEDs placed around cameras to illuminate retroreflective markers positioned within the environment. These markers function like spherical mirrors, reflecting IR light back to the camera. However, one significant limitation is the reduced range due to the energy's need to travel to the target and back. As energy disperses quadratically with distance, doubling the distance results in only a quarter of the energy returning to the camera.

Considering the simplicity of the resulting image processing in such systems, one might question the need to capture an entire image. The widespread availability of affordable digital cameras and efficient image-processing software largely justifies this choice. However, a simpler design might involve an emitter-detector pair providing binary feedback to indicate whether a beam is obstructed. This principle is similar to how garage door safety systems work, where an IR LED directs energy to a photodiode detector. The system activates when sufficient energy is detected at the target wavelength.

To minimize energy loss, mirrors or lenses can focus IR energy more effectively. An even more precise option is to use an IR laser aimed directly at a detector. By incorporating lenses and movable mirrors, the beam can systematically illuminate every detector within view from a fixed location. For instance, the beam can be expanded from a dot to a line using a lens, and then the line can be swept across the space using a rotating mirror. This technology forms the foundation of the lighthouse tracking system employed in the HTC Vive headset.

The Perspective-n-Point (PnP) problem

To accurately determine the position and orientation of a moving rigid body, a set of n observed features is used. This challenge is known as the Perspective-n-Point (PnP) problem. In this scenario, rather than generating an image based on a known body position in a virtual world, we solve the inverse problem: deducing the body's placement in the real world from the observed points in an image

The features in question can either be located on the body itself or in its surrounding environment, depending on the sensing technique being utilized. Let's assume the features are on the body. Each feature represents a point, denoted as $p = (x, y, z)$ with its coordinates defined relative to the body's frame. To translate this point into real-world coordinates, a homogeneous transformation matrix, T_{rb}, which contains the pose parameters, is applied. However, in this case, T_{rb} is unknown.

By applying T_{rb}, each point on the body can be mapped to its corresponding position in the real world. Further transformations, such as T_{eye}, T_{vp}, and T_{can}, account for the camera pose, perspective projection, and image coordinate adjustments, respectively. These transformations ultimately determine the point's position in the image

Degrees of Freedom (DOF) and Feature Constraints

When features are visible, they impose constraints on the body's degrees of freedom (DOFs). Observing a single feature in the image reduces the body's DOFs by two, corresponding to the image coordinates (i, j). This scenario, known as the P1P problem, leaves the rigid body with four remaining DOFs, as depicted in Figure 2.15

.

Figure 2.15: Each visible feature reduces the rigid body's DOFs.

- *Left:* One visible feature reduces the DOFs to four.

- *Right:* Two visible features leave only two DOFs

If two features are observed (P2P problem), four DOFs are constrained, leaving two. As more features are identified, such as in the P3P problem, the remaining DOFs are reduced to zero, but this introduces multiple potential solutions unless the features are collinear. For example, in the P3P case, solving the problem involves fitting a triangle into a pyramid formed by rays from the image plane, typically yielding four distinct solutions.

As the number of features increases (P4P, P5P, etc.), ambiguities persist until at least six features (P6P) are observed. When six or more features are visible and no four points are coplanar, the problem yields a unique solution.

Practical Considerations

The PnP problem, as described above, assumes perfect observations and feature point assignments. However, in real-world scenarios, imperfections such as sensor noise, image quantization, and manufacturing variances introduce errors. These inaccuracies can lead to ambiguous or incorrect pose estimations.

To enhance precision, additional features are often employed, and calibration methods such as bundle adjustment can be used before the tracking system is deployed. Bundle adjustment helps refine the feature point locations for more accurate pose estimation. Additionally, techniques like RANSAC improve robustness by filtering out erroneous data and enhancing the reliability of the solution.

By combining these approaches, practical implementations of the PnP problem achieve greater accuracy and stability, ensuring reliable tracking in dynamic and complex environments.

Camera-based implementation

The challenge of visibility can be addressed using camera systems in two primary configurations, as illustrated in Figure 2.16. The camera frame, functioning similarly to the eye frame, can either be stationary relative to the world or move along with an object

In the case of a **world-fixed camera**, the camera remains stationary, and object movements relative to it are analyzed. A single transformation suffices to convert an object's pose, estimated in the camera's coordinate frame, into a corresponding world frame. For example, with the Oculus Rift headset, the user's head position can be mapped to a world frame where the negative z-axis points toward the camera, the y-axis points upward, and the origin is centred within the camera's tracking area or some default position based on the user's starting pose.

Alternatively, an **object-fixed camera** moves along with the object, with its pose estimated based on fixed features in the environment. For instance, QR codes mounted on walls serve as reference points for such systems. Here, the transformation provides the relationship between the camera frame and the world frame.

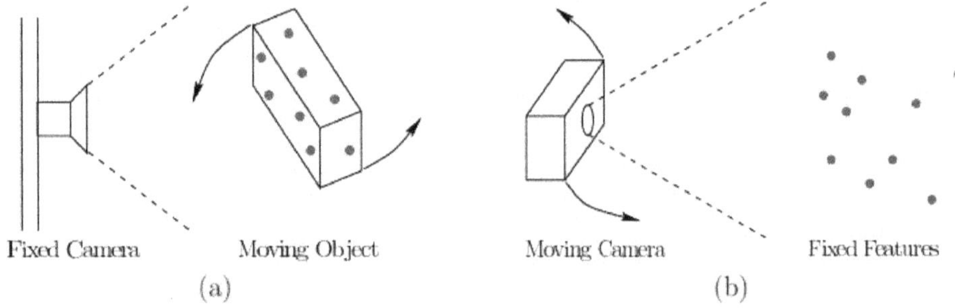

Figure 2.16: Two configurations for camera placement:

a)   A stationary world-fixed camera estimates object movements using features on the object.

b)   A moving object-fixed camera tracks features anchored to the world's coordinate frame

Calibration for Accuracy

Just as with inertial measurement units (IMUs), calibration plays a crucial role in enhancing the accuracy of camera-based sensing. A homogeneous transformation matrix can describe how an image is generated:

$$\begin{bmatrix} \alpha_x & \gamma & u_0 \\ 0 & \alpha_y & v_0 \\ 0 & 0 & 1 \end{bmatrix}$$

This matrix includes five intrinsic camera parameters:

- α_x and α_y control scaling,

- γ accounts for shearing, and

- u_0 and v_0 adjust for the optical axis offset.

These parameters are typically determined by capturing images of a precisely measured calibration object and applying a least-squares optimization to minimize errors. For cameras with wide-angle lenses, additional calibration is often required to compensate for optical distortions.

Detecting Features in Images

Once features are captured in an image, techniques such as blob detection are employed to isolate the corresponding pixels. This task is most straightforward with global shutter cameras, where all pixels represent the same moment in time. For rolling shutter cameras, motion correction may be necessary to mitigate distortions.

The feature's location is calculated statistically from the blob's pixel positions, often by averaging the pixels to yield non-integer coordinates. However, several factors can affect accuracy:

1. **Quantization errors** occur due to pixel locations being integers.

2. **Insufficient pixel coverage** for a feature exacerbates quantization errors.

3. **Lighting variations** complicate feature extraction, particularly for natural features.

4. **Feature overlap** in the image can hinder distinguishing individual blobs.

5. **Features entering or exiting the camera's view** may cause abrupt pose estimation changes.

Additionally, errors are typically more pronounced along the optical axis, where depth estimation is most challenging.

This systematic approach to camera-based tracking, coupled with effective calibration and feature detection, helps to overcome many of these challenges and ensures more reliable pose estimation in various real-world applications.

Laser-Based Implementation

The visibility challenge can be resolved with high precision and extended range using a specialized emitter-detector setup. This approach underpins the lighthouse tracking system found in the 2016 HTC Vive headset, as well as the Minnesota scanner developed in 1989. Figure 2.17 illustrates the hardware used in the HTC Vive's laser-based tracking system, which mimics the functionality of a virtual camera, as depicted in Figure 2.18(a).

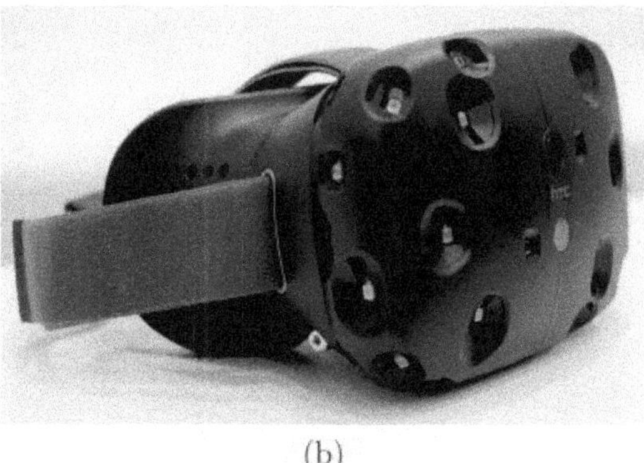

(a)   (b)

Figure 2.17: The HTC Vive's laser-based tracking system features:

a) A base station equipped with spinning drums emitting horizontal and vertical IR light sheets, along with an IR LED array that triggers a synchronization flash (photo by Ben Lang, Road to VR).

b) Photodiodes embedded in the headset detect incoming IR light (photo by Maurizio Pesce, CC BY 2.0).

The system operates by simulating a camera's function. A vertical sweeping stripe is analogous to determining the row in which a feature appears in an image, while a horizontal stripe corresponds to identifying the pixel column. The rotation rate of the spinning drum is precisely controlled, analogous to a camera's frame rate. As the IR beam strikes each photodiode, its timing is recorded, allowing for angular calculations.

Angular Positioning Using Polar Coordinates

Tracking relies on polar coordinates—distance and angle—from the base station. By knowing the beam's angular velocity and recording timing differences as the beam hits each photodiode, the angle between features can be computed. However, to reference these angles against a fixed direction, the system uses synchronized IR LED flashes. These LEDs, visible in Figure 2.17(a), emit simultaneous flashes detected by all photodiodes.

The synchronization flash marks the beam's orientation at a known reference point (e.g., zero degrees). The time interval between the flash and the IR beam striking a photodiode, combined with the beam's angular velocity, determines the precise angle of the detected feature. To minimize temporal drift, periodic synchronization flashes are employed during operation.

2D Angular Sweeping

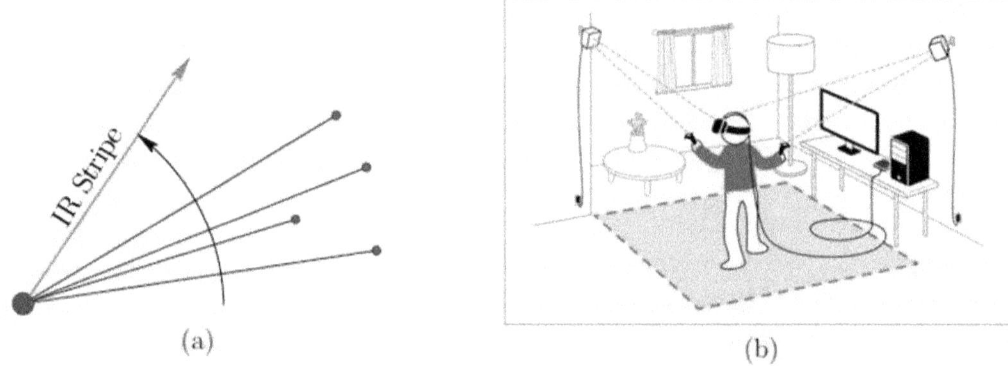

Figure 2.18(a) depicts a 2D visualization of the IR stripe's angular sweep in the laser-based system. In a top-down perspective, a vertically oriented stripe rotates with yaw motion, tracking horizontal angular positions akin to pixel columns in a camera. From a side view, the stripe spins with pitch rotation, capturing vertical angular locations. The timing data collected from the synchronization flash and beam strikes ensures accurate angular measurements for each feature.

Multi-Base Station Tracking

As with camera-based systems, the distance between the base station and tracked features is not directly known but can be deduced through solving the Perspective-n-Point (PnP) problem. Incorporating multiple base stations—similar to using multiple cameras or binocular vision—enables depth estimation and enhances tracking precision.

Figure 2.18(b) showcases a configuration with two base stations mounted on poles at opposite corners of the tracking area. This setup significantly expands the tracking region, enabling precise monitoring of headsets and controllers over a large space.

This laser-based approach achieves robust, accurate tracking, leveraging angular sweeps, synchronization flashes, and multi-station setups to maintain reliability and precision across substantial areas.

Filtering

Sensor outputs are integrated over time using filtering techniques to refine estimates. In the context of pose tracking, visibility data and IMU outputs are combined to maintain a reliable estimate. Orientation tracking within the pose can leverage a complementary filter, where a camera helps correct orientation drift errors. The optical axis of the camera serves as a direct reference for detecting yaw errors, effectively replacing the magnetometer. If the camera's tilt is known, it can also provide accurate corrections for tilt errors.

The IMU plays a pivotal role in precise orientation tracking, primarily due to the gyroscope's ability to deliver accurate, high-frequency angular velocity data. While a high frame rate from a camera or lighthouse system might suffice for accurate position tracking, directly measuring derivatives remains ideal. However, IMUs do not measure linear velocity directly. Instead, accelerometer outputs can be used to approximate linear velocity and position through numerical integration.

Estimating Velocity and Position

Assume the accelerometer provides the body's acceleration in the world frame, represented as

$$\hat{a}[k] = (\hat{a}_x[k], \hat{a}_y[k], \hat{a}_z[k])$$

where the gravity component has already been subtracted. Using numerical integration, velocity $\hat{v}[k]$ is calculated from acceleration, and position $\hat{p}[k]$ is derived from velocity. These estimates are updated using simple Euler integration

$$\hat{v}[k] = \hat{a}[k]\Delta t + \hat{v}[k-1]$$

$$\hat{p}[k] = \hat{v}[k]\Delta t + \hat{p}[k-1]$$

Each equation simultaneously handles the x, y, and z components. Accuracy can be further improved by adding $\frac{1}{2}\hat{a}[k]\Delta t^2$ to the position equation.

Addressing Position Drift

Double integration of acceleration tends to cause significant position drift error, denoted as $\widehat{d_p}[k]$. Errors detected from PnP solutions can estimate $\widehat{d_p}[k]$, though these updates may occur less frequently than IMU observations. For instance, a camera may operate at 60 FPS, while an IMU might produce data at 1000 FPS.

The complementary filter is extended to address drift correction

$$p_c[k] = \hat{p}[k] - \propto_p \widehat{d_p}[k]$$

$$v_c[k] = \hat{v}[k] - \propto_v \widehat{d_p}[k]$$

Here, $p_c[k]$ and $v_c[k]$ are corrected position and velocity estimates, respectively, derived through the complementary filter. The parameters α_p and α_v regulate the weight given to drift error estimates relative to IMU updates

Relation to Kalman Filtering

The complementary filter aligns with the Kalman filter under specific conditions. For a linear dynamical system with Gaussian noise and sensors also subject to Gaussian noise, the complementary filter becomes equivalent to a Kalman filter when:

$$\alpha_p = \sqrt{2\omega_d/\omega_s} \text{ and } \alpha_v = \omega_d/\omega_s$$

Here, ω_d^2 and ω_s^2 represent the variances of system and sensor noise, respectively. While alternative filtering methods exist, their impact is typically secondary to factors like calibration, sensor error models, and system dynamics specific to the application. Performance requirements are often *perceptually* driven and may differ from classical filtering design criteria.

Incremental PnP Problem Solving

Once the filter is operational, its pose estimates can enhance PnP problem-solving. Incremental adjustments to the filter's pose estimate, guided by the latest accelerometer outputs, can align observed features with the predicted model. This approach minimizes the sum-of-squares error, improving reliability in scenarios where few features are visible and the PnP problem has ambiguous solutions. Incremental refinement prevents abrupt shifts to incorrect PnP solutions, ensuring stability in pose estimation

2.6 Navigation Interfaces

Navigation interfaces in virtual reality (VR) play a vital part in enhancing user experience and enabling interaction within VR environments.

- **Teleportation:** Teleportation is one of the most popular navigation methods in VR. Users point to a location within the virtual environment and instantly teleport there. This method minimizes motion sickness and provides an efficient way to navigate large virtual spaces without physically walking.

- **Walking/Free Movement:** In VR setups with sufficient physical space, users can physically walk around to explore the virtual environment. This method provides a high level of immersion but requires ample physical space and may not be suitable for all VR applications.

- **Controller-based Movement:** Many VR systems utilize handheld controllers for navigation. Users can use thumbsticks or touchpads on the controllers to move forward, backward, strafe, and turn within the virtual environment. This method offers precise control but can contribute to motion sickness, especially in sensitive users.

- **Room-scale Tracking:** Room-scale VR setups use external sensors or cameras to track the user's movements within a defined physical space. Users can walk around freely within this space, and the virtual environment adjusts accordingly. Room-scale tracking enhances immersion and allows for natural movement within VR experiences.

- **Gesture-based Navigation:** Gesture recognition technologies enable users to navigate through VR environments using hand gestures or body movements. Users can interact with virtual objects and manipulate the environment by gesturing or pointing. Gesture-based navigation can be intuitive and immersive but may require calibration and may not always be precise.

- **UI Menus and Interfaces:** VR applications often feature user interfaces (UIs) that allow users to access menus, settings, and navigation options within the virtual environment. These interfaces can be presented as floating panels, holographic displays, or interactive objects within the VR space. Users can interact with these UI elements using controllers or gestures to select options and navigate within the application.

- **Hotspots and Waypoints:** Some VR experiences incorporate hotspots or waypoints within the virtual environment to guide users and facilitate navigation. Users can interact with these predefined points of interest to move between different locations or trigger specific events within the VR experience.

- **Map Overlays and Mini-maps:** VR applications may include map overlays or mini-maps to help users navigate large or complex virtual environments. These visual aids provide users with a bird's-eye view of the surroundings and can display points of interest, objectives, and navigation routes.

The choice of navigation interface in virtual reality (VR) hinges on factors such as the platform, the type of VR experience, user preferences, and the desired balance between immersion and comfort. Developers frequently experiment with various navigation techniques to identify the most suitable approach for their specific applications.

When the exact start time of a pulse is unknown, detectors can analyze differences in arrival times among themselves. This technique, known as time difference of arrival (TDOA), narrows down potential locations to a hyperboloid instead of a sphere. Multiple emitter-detector pairs can intersect hyperboloid sheets to achieve multilateration. This principle was applied in the Decca Navigation System during World War II for locating ships and aircraft and is also fundamental to how human ears pinpoint sound sources.

A movable model typically represents an object a user manipulates, such as a sword, hammer, or cup. These models are often created using a 3D scanner, which captures the object from multiple angles under controlled conditions. The object might be positioned on a turntable that rotates it for comprehensive imaging or placed in a stationary setup with sensors and cameras moving around it.

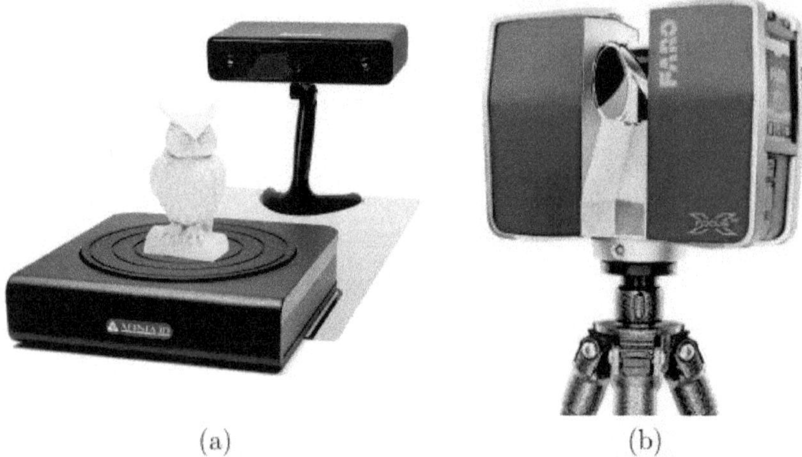

(a) (b)

For example, **Figure 2.19**: (a) illustrates the Afinia ES360 scanner, which generates 3D models of objects on a rotating platform, while **Figure 2.19**: (b) shows the FARO Focus3D X 330 Laser Scanner, designed to build detailed 3D maps of large environments with the aid of GPS for scan alignment.

Small objects are scanned using inward-facing sensors, while outward-facing sensors are used for larger or stationary models, such as building interiors. This technique is crucial for tasks like surveying and forensic analysis. It also relates to robotics, where a robot builds a 2D or 3D representation of its surroundings to navigate and avoid collisions. Estimating the robot's position using sensors, known as localization, often overlaps with VR tracking problems. Both involve simultaneous localization and mapping (SLAM), highlighting the deep connections between VR and robotics through shared models, algorithms, and technologies.

In VR, real-world navigation tools can be adapted to enhance virtual navigation. Virtual environments designed with familiar layouts, like streets and buildings, can include landmarks and signs to aid users. For instance, tall structures or boundary markers provide cues for navigation over long distances.

Special effects influencing the viewpoint can increase vection, or the sensation of movement. For instance, simulating an avatar jumping might induce vertical vection, while compensating for head sway during walking can create mismatches. Extreme cases, like observing the world from a flipping gymnast's perspective, could make the experience disorienting.

Various hardware solutions exist to facilitate movement in VR. Early examples include flight simulator cockpits.

(a) (b)

Figure 2.20: (a) shows an omnidirectional treadmill for multi-directional walking, while **Figure 2.20**: (b) depicts a stationary bicycle integrated with VR to allow pedalling through virtual environments.

These methods replicate real-world experiences in line with the universal simulation principle, although VR also permits non-physical movements like teleportation.

Locomotion techniques in VR often aim to mimic real-world experiences, aligning with the universal simulation principle. However, VR also offers opportunities for movement that defy physical limitations. One of the most popular methods is teleportation, reminiscent of the transporter technology from the TV show *Star Trek*, which allows users to instantly move to a chosen location.

But how does the system determine where the user wants to go? A straightforward solution is the use of a virtual laser pointer or a 3D mouse. This involves a controller, often shaped like a real-world laser pointer, which the user manipulates to direct a laser beam in the virtual environment. Even a smartphone could serve this purpose. By tilting or rotating the controller, the user can position a laser dot, and ray casting is used to calculate the nearest visible surface along the laser's path.

Figure 2.21: Demonstrates a virtual "laser pointer" with a parabolic trajectory, making it easier to select points on the floor. (Image from the Budget Cuts game on the HTC Vive platform.)

In some systems, the laser pointer follows a parabolic trajectory, as depicted in Figure 2.21, resembling the arc of a water stream influenced by gravity. This design makes it easier to target points on the ground. Once the user selects a destination, they can press a button to teleport instantly. For locations that are out of sight, additional tools such as pop-up maps, voice commands, or text-based searches can be employed.

Another innovative approach is the "world in miniature" technique, where users interact with a scaled-down virtual version of the environment. This miniaturized 3D map allows them to pinpoint and select destinations effortlessly, adding versatility to navigation in VR spaces.

2.7 Manipulation Interfaces

In everyday life, we interact with objects for countless purposes. For instance, you might use a spoon to eat soup, toss a rock into the distance, or put on a pair of pants. These actions, and many others like them, fall under the category of manipulation. Real-world manipulation is a complex process involving intricate sensorimotor coordination, honed through evolution and experience, allowing us to handle objects in diverse conditions. Objects vary in size, weight, texture, flexibility, temperature, and fragility, yet our bodies manage these challenges with remarkable adaptability.

Replicating human-like manipulation in robotics has proven to be a difficult and often frustrating task, with progress being incremental at best. This complexity in the physical world makes manipulation an excellent candidate for simplification through remapping techniques in virtual reality (VR). In VR, the physical rules governing manipulation can be altered or bypassed entirely. Instead of adhering to real-world physics, the goal is to make tasks such as selecting, grabbing, moving, carrying, and placing objects quick and effortless.

Minimizing physical effort, such as extensive reaching or other muscle strain, is also essential unless the VR experience is specifically designed for physical activity or exercise. By streamlining these interactions, VR can provide an intuitive and comfortable way for users to engage with virtual objects while avoiding unnecessary difficulty.

Figure 2.22: In the 2002 film *Minority Report*, Tom Cruise is seen rearranging windows on a holographic interface. While this interaction style looks impressive and futuristic on screen, it is highly impractical in real life. Prolonged use would lead to significant arm fatigue, a phenomenon humorously referred to as "gorilla arms."

Avoiding "Gorilla Arms"

One of the most widespread misconceptions is that the futuristic interface Tom Cruise uses in the 2002 movie *Minority Report* would be practical or desirable (Figure 2.22). In reality, prolonged use of such an interface would quickly lead to arm fatigue, often referred to as "gorilla arms." Imagine holding your arms outstretched in front of you for an extended period—how long could you last before feeling the strain?

Selection Techniques in VR

One of the simplest ways to interact with virtual objects is through a virtual laser pointer. Enhancements to this basic concept can improve the experience. For instance, instead of a laser, users might hold a virtual flashlight that illuminates potential targets, with an adjustable beam to refine the field of view. In scenarios where an object is obscured, a virtual mirror could be employed to allow selections around corners.

With a laser pointer, the user highlights the desired object and presses a button to select it. If the intent is to retrieve the item, it can instantly appear in the user's virtual hand or inventory. For repetitive tasks, pressing the button could trigger a preprogrammed action, such as turning a virtual doorknob to open a door. To ensure interactions remain immersive, developers might limit the laser pointer's range so users must be near the object— after all, opening a door from across the room could feel unnatural.

Challenges arise when objects are difficult to locate or select. For example, an item positioned behind the user might require an uncomfortable amount of turning. Similarly, objects that are very small or far away, occupying only a few pixels on the screen, can be hard to target. The situation becomes even more complicated if the object is surrounded by clutter or partially hidden from view.

Manipulation Techniques

When carrying objects over long distances in VR, the user should not need to continuously grip the controller, as this would lead to unnecessary fatigue. In certain scenarios, such as inspecting an object closely, the user may wish to move it around to understand its 3D structure. The object's orientation can be synchronized with the 3D position of the controller the user holds. Alternatively, the user could interact with a real-world object that is tracked by cameras but represented differently in the virtual environment, allowing for realistic force feedback.

Objects can also be manipulated in their original positions within the virtual world. Instead of moving the object toward the user's body, the virtual hand reaches the object while the user's physical hand remains stationary. Virtual tools like extended arms can even be simulated, enabling users to interact with distant objects without physically moving close.

Object Placement in VR

Placing an object back into the virtual environment should be as intuitive as possible. One simple method is pressing a button, causing the object to automatically snap into its target location. This is achieved using an attractive potential function, known as a "basin of attraction," which guides the object to its desired position and orientation (Figure 2.23). The function's minimum corresponds to the target pose, ensuring the object smoothly transitions into place once released.

This concept is similar to features in 2D drawing programs, where endpoints of line segments snap together for convenience. A notable example of easy object placement is seen in the game *Minecraft* (2011) by Markus Persson (Notch). In this sandbox game, building blocks seamlessly fall into position, enabling players to construct countless virtual worlds effortlessly—a feature embraced by millions, especially children.

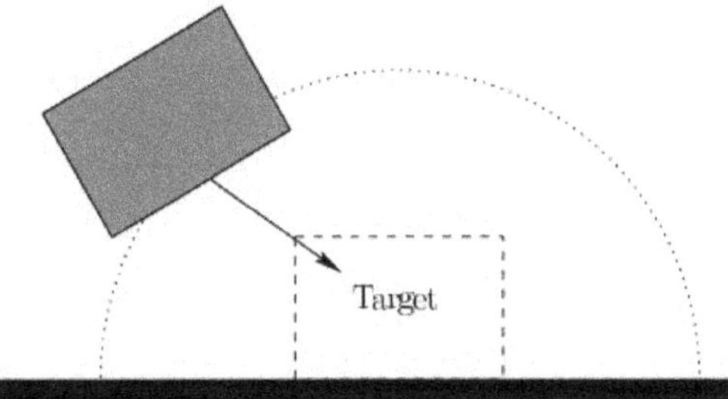

Figure 2.23: To simplify interactions for the user, a "basin of attraction" can be implemented around the target area. When an object enters this defined zone, it is automatically guided to the desired position and orientation, making placement seamless and intuitive.

Alternatively, certain applications may demand meticulous object placement. For example, tasks involving the careful stacking or balancing of objects to achieve maximum height require exceptional precision. In such scenarios, both the user and the controller's tracking system face increased challenges, as the margin for error is significantly reduced.

Remapping in VR Interaction

The concept of remapping offers immense potential in virtual reality. The simplest implementation involves using a button to select, grasp, or place objects. However, more dynamic interactions can also be achieved by tracking user-generated motions. Examples include turning a virtual knob, sliding a bar, swiping a finger across a touchscreen, or navigating a free-floating object through virtual space.

A crucial element of effective remapping is ensuring ease of learning. Simplifying the degrees of freedom involved typically makes the process more intuitive for users. To mitigate issues like "gorilla arms," scaling can be applied to the tracked input. For instance, a small physical movement of the controller could correspond to a larger motion in the virtual environment. While this improves comfort, it may come at the cost of reduced precision. Scaling can also extend to orientation, where the angular velocity in the real world is amplified in the virtual setting to achieve greater rotational movement. Such adjustments could be evaluated using principles like Fitts's law, as is done with computer mice.

Current Systems and Challenges

Developing effective manipulation mechanisms remains one of the biggest hurdles in virtual reality. Consumer VR headsets have taken varied approaches to addressing this challenge. Early systems often relied on existing gaming hardware, such as the XBox 360 controller bundled with the Oculus Rift in 2016. Others, like the HTC Vive controllers (Figure 2.24), embraced larger hand motions, moving closer to the futuristic but impractical interaction style depicted in *Minority Report* (Figure 2.22).

Some systems aim to eliminate the need for handheld hardware entirely. An example is the Leap Motion system, which tracks hand gestures without requiring physical controllers.

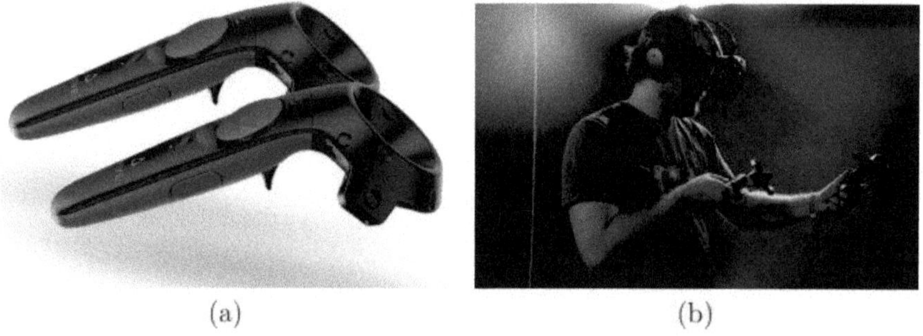

(a)   (b)

Figure 2.24 illustrates the evolution of VR interaction mechanisms. The HTC Vive controllers, introduced in 2016, featured side buttons, a trigger, and a thumb-operated touchpad. These devices reflect a progression from the "goggles and gloves" concept popular in the 1990s.

As VR technologies continue to advance, we can expect significant innovations in manipulation interfaces. Future developments are likely to prioritize user comfort, simplicity, and adaptability, paving the way for more seamless and intuitive interactions in virtual environments.

2.8 Gesture Interfaces

Gesture interfaces in virtual reality (VR) refer to the use of hand and body movements to interact with virtual environments instead of traditional input devices like controllers or keyboards. These interfaces aim to enhance immersion and make interactions in VR more intuitive and natural by allowing users to use gestures similar to how they would interact in the physical world, Figure 2.25.

Figure 2.25: Gesture Interfaces

- **Hand Tracking**: Advanced VR systems incorporate hand tracking technology, which allows the VR headset to recognize and track the movements of the user's hands without the need for handheld controllers. This technology enables users to interact with virtual objects directly using their hands, such as grabbing, pointing, or pushing objects.

- **Body Tracking**: In addition to hand tracking, some VR setups support full-body tracking, which captures the movements of the user's entire body. This enables more immersive experiences, as users can walk, jump, and perform other physical movements within the virtual environment.

- **Natural Interaction**: Gesture interfaces aim to provide a more natural way of interacting with virtual environments compared to traditional input devices. Users can perform gestures and movements that closely mimic real-world actions, enhancing immersion and reducing the learning curve for new users.

- **Immersive Experiences**: By enabling users to interact with virtual environments using their hands and body, gesture interfaces enhance the sense of presence and immersion in VR experiences. Users feel more connected to the virtual world and can engage with it in a more intuitive manner.

While gesture interfaces offer many benefits, they also present challenges. Accurately tracking hand and body movements in real-time requires sophisticated hardware and software algorithms. Issues such as occlusion (where the system loses track of a hand or body part due to obstruction) and latency (delay between the user's movement and its representation in the virtual environment) can affect the user experience.

Gesture interfaces find use in a wide range of industries, including gaming, education, training, healthcare, and design. In gaming, for instance, players can engage more immersively by physically interacting with objects within the virtual environment. Similarly, in healthcare, these interfaces enable surgeons to practice and refine their skills through realistic training and simulation scenarios.

As technology advances, gesture interfaces in VR are expected to become more accurate, responsive, and affordable. Improvements in sensors, algorithms, and machine learning techniques will likely drive further innovation in this area, leading to even more immersive and intuitive VR experiences. Overall, gesture interfaces play a crucial role in enhancing immersion and interaction in virtual reality, offering users a more natural and intuitive way to engage with virtual environments.

2.9 Graphic Displays

Graphic displays in virtual reality (VR) refer to the visual representation of virtual environments rendered to the user through VR headsets or other immersive display systems. These displays aim to provide realistic and immersive visual experiences that transport users to virtual worlds.

- **Head-Mounted Displays (HMDs)**: The primary method of experiencing VR environments is through head-mounted displays, which consist of a headset that the user wears over their eyes. These displays typically use high-resolution screens, lenses, and motion sensors to render and track the user's viewpoint in the virtual environment.

- **Immersive Visuals**: VR graphic displays aim to create highly immersive visual experiences by providing a wide field of view, high resolution, and low latency. This helps minimize motion sickness and enhances the sense of presence, making users feel like they are truly inside the virtual world.

- **3D Graphics Rendering**: VR graphic displays utilize 3D graphics rendering techniques to create realistic virtual environments. This includes rendering techniques such as real-time shading, lighting, and texture mapping to create visually rich and detailed scenes.

- **Stereo Vision**: VR graphic displays often employ stereo vision techniques to create depth perception in virtual environments. By rendering slightly different images to each eye, VR systems simulate the way human vision perceives depth, allowing users to perceive objects in the virtual world with depth and dimensionality.

- **Frame Rate and Latency**: Achieving smooth and responsive visuals is crucial for a comfortable VR experience. VR graphic displays must maintain a high frame rate (typically 90 frames per second or higher) and low latency to ensure that the user's movements are accurately reflected in the virtual environment without lag or stuttering.

- **Optimization and Performance**: Creating visually stunning VR experiences requires careful optimization of graphics performance. VR developers often employ techniques such as level of detail (LOD) rendering, occlusion culling, and texture compression to maximize performance while maintaining visual fidelity.

VR graphic displays have diverse applications across various industries, including gaming, entertainment, education, training, healthcare, architecture, and design. For example, in gaming, VR graphic displays enable players to explore immersive virtual worlds and interact with virtual objects, while in healthcare, VR simulations can be used for surgical training and medical education.

As VR technology continues to evolve, graphic displays are expected to become even more realistic and immersive. Advancements in display technology, graphics rendering algorithms, and hardware performance will likely enable higher resolutions, wider fields of view, and more realistic visual effects in VR environments. Graphic displays play a crucial role in delivering immersive and realistic experiences in virtual reality, enabling users to explore and interact with virtual environments in ways that were previously impossible.

2.10 Sound Displays

In VR, sound displays, often referred to as spatial audio or 3D audio, play a crucial role in enhancing immersion and creating realistic virtual environments.

- **Spatial Audio:** Spatial audio technology enables VR systems to simulate the perception of sound coming from different directions and distances in a virtual environment, just like in the real world. This means that users can perceive sounds as if they are emanating from specific locations within the virtual space.

- **Head-Related Transfer Function (HRTF):** HRTF is a key component of spatial audio in VR. It's a mathematical model that simulates how sound waves interact with the shape of the human head and ears to create directional cues. By applying HRTF to audio sources, VR systems can accurately replicate how sounds would be perceived by the user based on their head orientation and position.

- **Binaural Rendering:** Binaural rendering techniques are used to create realistic 3D audio experiences in VR. By processing audio signals with HRTF algorithms, VR systems can generate binaural audio that simulates the way sound waves interact with the user's ears, resulting in a sense of directionality and immersion.

- **Environmental Audio Effects:** In addition to spatial positioning, VR sound displays often incorporate environmental audio effects to further enhance immersion. This includes effects such as reverberation, occlusion, and attenuation, which simulate how sound behaves in different virtual environments (e.g., large halls, outdoor spaces, or confined rooms).

- **Dynamic Soundscapes:** VR sound displays can dynamically adjust audio based on the user's movements and interactions within the virtual environment. For example, sounds may change in volume or direction as the user moves their head or approaches virtual objects, adding to the sense of realism and presence.

- **Integration with Visuals:** Sound displays in VR are often tightly integrated with visual elements to create cohesive and immersive experiences. For example, audio cues may accompany visual events or objects in the virtual environment, helping users locate and interact with them more intuitively.

Spatial audio has diverse applications in VR, including gaming, entertainment, education, training, and simulations. For example, in gaming, spatial audio enhances immersion by providing directional cues for approaching enemies or environmental hazards. In educational VR experiences, spatial audio can help users locate important information or navigate complex environments.

As VR technology continues to advance, sound displays are expected to become even more realistic and interactive. Future developments may include improved HRTF algorithms for more accurate spatial positioning, enhanced environmental audio effects, and better integration with other sensory feedback modalities, such as haptic feedback. In summary, sound displays are an essential component of virtual reality, contributing to immersion, realism, and presence by providing users with spatially accurate and dynamic audio experiences within virtual environments.

2.11 Human Haptic System

Haptics, one of the five primary human senses, plays a crucial role in perceiving external environments. It provides valuable insights into object properties such as shape, size, temperature, and surface texture. Through tactile interaction, humans can explore and understand objects even without visual cues. For example, when handling an unfamiliar item while blindfolded, a person can deduce its geometric shape through various forms of touch-based exploration.

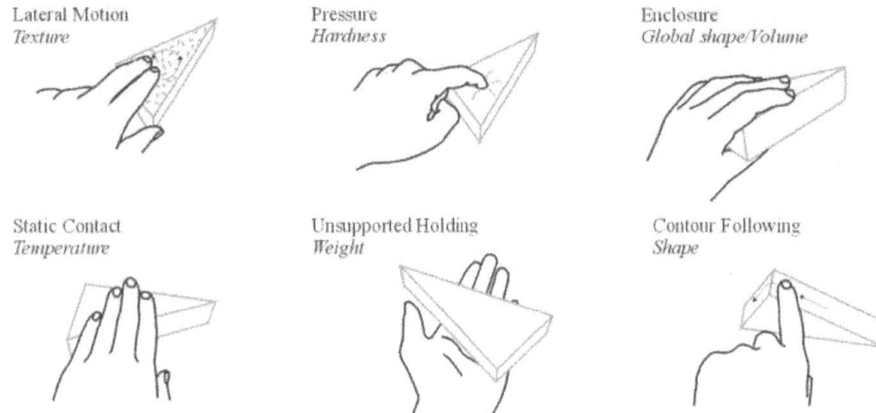

Figure 2.26 illustrates six distinct methods of haptic exploration, each engaging different types of sensory receptors and integrating spatial and temporal information. By interpreting these somatosensory signals during object manipulation, a mental model of the object's geometry is formed. (Figure by Allison Okamura, adapted from Lederman and Klatzky.)

Engineered systems have been designed to deliver touch sensations using diverse approaches. For instance, **Figure 1.1** demonstrated a setup where users push mechanical wings to simulate flight, accompanied by a fan mimicking wind intensity relative to speed. Additionally, body tilting stimulates the vestibular system, enhancing the experience.

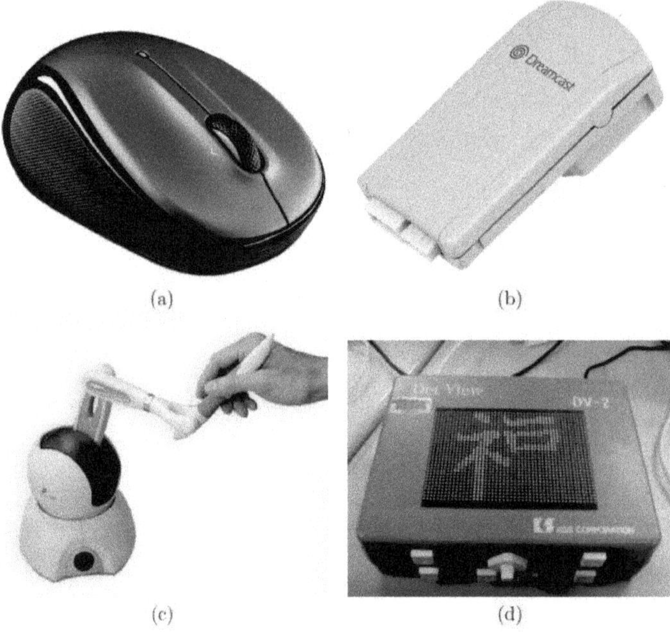

(a)

(b)

(c)

(d)

Figure 2.27 highlights several examples of haptic feedback systems:

- **(a)** The Logitech M325 wireless mouse provides tactile feedback via 72 discrete bumps on its scroll wheel, enabling precise control during use.

- **(b)** The Sega Dreamcast Jump Pack (1999) generates vibrations at key moments in gaming, such as collisions or explosions.

- **(c)** The Haptic Omni device, a pen-based system linked to a robotic arm, delivers forces and vibrations to the user's fingers. When the pen interacts with virtual surfaces, the robot applies resistance to simulate texture and friction. This level of feedback is particularly important in medical devices that allow surgeons to perform delicate procedures remotely. Without precise haptic feedback, surgeons might unintentionally exert excessive force, leading to errors.

- **(d)** The KGS Dot View Model DV-2 features a haptic pin array. Each pin can rise to simulate textures, shapes, or vibrations, providing a tactile experience for fingertips scanning its surface.

When a pen interacts with a virtual surface, a robotic system can simulate force feedback by restricting the pen's motion. This allows the user to drag the pen across the surface, experiencing textures as if they were real. Such force feedback is crucial in designing medical devices that let doctors perform surgical procedures remotely through connected interfaces. Without precise and immediate haptic feedback, executing these tasks becomes challenging. For example, cutting through tissue layers without sensing the resistance of a scalpel could lead to unintended overextension.

Figure 2.27 (d) illustrates a haptic display that functions similarly to a visual display. It is composed of a rectangular grid of rows and columns, where small pins can be raised to create shapes above the surface. These pins also generate varying pressures and vibration frequencies, enabling users to feel intricate tactile details.

While most haptic feedback devices focus on hand-based interactions, the human body contains touch receptors across its entirety. To engage a larger portion of these receptors, haptic suits have been developed. These suits can deliver localized forces, vibrations, or even electrical stimulation at specific points on the body. However, a significant limitation of such systems is the inconvenience of putting on and taking off the suit for each session, which may detract from their practicality.

Touch Feedback in Augmented Reality (AR):

Given the challenges of designing haptic displays, some systems use tangible objects in the real world to provide feedback, aligning them with virtual elements. Known as tangible user interfaces, these systems integrate physical and virtual environments to enhance immersion. For instance, a see-through display like the Microsoft HoloLens allows users to interact with their surroundings while overlaying virtual elements. This approach is widely adopted in augmented and mixed reality applications, combining real-world interactions with virtual enhancements.

Exercise Questions

1. What is tracker? Enumerate some important tracker performance parameter(draw diagram to illustrate your concepts)

2. How mechanical tracker works? Explain its advantage & disadvantage

3. What is gesture interface? Explain in detail any one gesture input devices.

4. Explain with diagram the Human Visual System.

5. What is difference between stereo sound and 3D sound?

6. Explain with example how does touch feedback differ from force feedback?

7. What is differences between older head mounted display (HMDs)and newer face mounted display (FDMs) in terms of ergonomics and optics?

8. How is the depth perceived by human vision system? Make a drawing and explain.

9. What is difference between an absolute and a relative position input devices? What are advantage/ disadvantage of each?

10. Explain with diagram, how is depth perceived by the human vision system.

11. What is relationship between HMD field of view and resolution and why it is important?

12. What are the ideal characteristics of haptic feedback actuators?

13. List and describe input devices for virtual reality.

14. Explain mechanical tracker and three dimensional position tracker.

15. List and describe output devices for virtual reality.

16. How navigation and manipulation interfaces works? Explain with example.

17. Explain: Gesture Interfaces, Graphic Displays and Sound Displays.

18. Explain various components of human haptic system.

3. Virtual Reality Computing Architectures

3.1 Rendering in Virtual Reality

Rendering refers to the process of generating sensory visuals that represent a virtual environment. In virtual reality and other forms of interactive, computer-generated media, these sensory outputs must be created quickly enough to appear as a seamless flow, rather than a series of disconnected frames. This capability to generate and display visuals at a lifelike pace is known as real-time rendering.

The process of producing sensory images for a VR participant can be divided into two primary stages. The first stage focuses on decisions regarding how the virtual environment will look, sound, and feel to the user. This is referred to as the *representation* phase, where the virtual world's attributes are defined. The second stage involves executing these decisions through software and hardware systems, which is the *implementation* phase of rendering. These two stages are inherently interconnected, as the capabilities and limitations of the rendering hardware and software influence the complexity and scope of the virtual environment that can be displayed in real time.

A crucial aspect of designing a VR experience is determining how abstract concepts, ideas, and data will be translated into visual, auditory, and tactile elements that the user will experience. The method of representing the virtual world significantly affects the overall quality and impact of the VR experience. In essence, representation determines what elements of the virtual environment will be rendered.

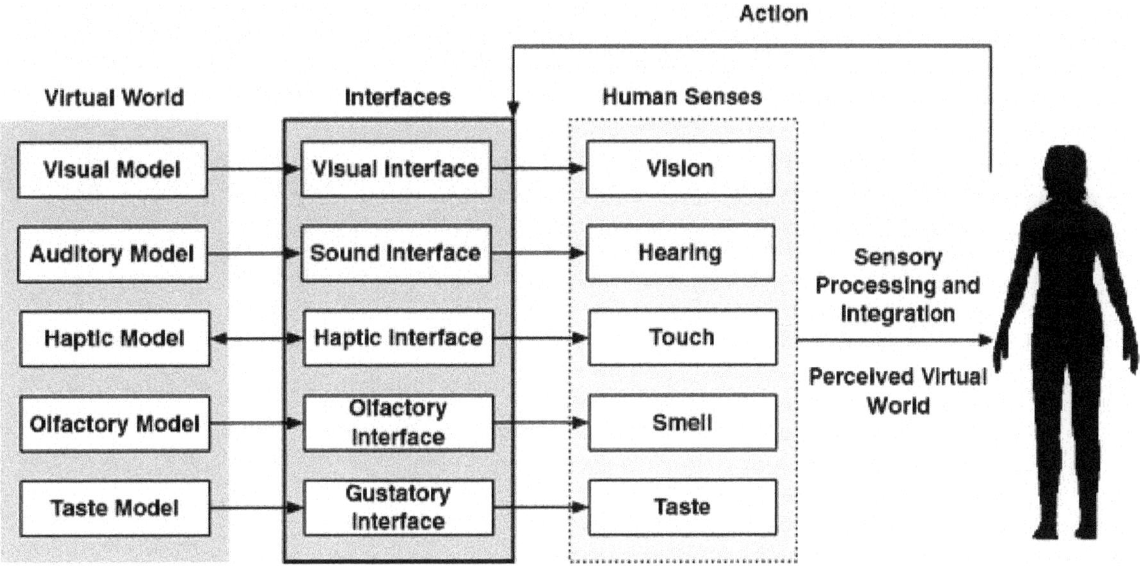

Figure 3.1: Representation of the Virtual World

3.2 Graphics Rendering Pipeline

Rendering, particularly in the context of computer graphics, refers to the process of transforming 3D geometric models within a virtual environment into 2D visuals that users can perceive. To enhance efficiency, pipeline architectures, which have been employed in CPU design for years, are also applied to rendering. This approach involves breaking the rendering process into distinct stages and allocating these tasks to specialized hardware components for simultaneous execution.

The computer graphics pipeline—often referred to as the rendering pipeline or graphics pipeline—serves as a structured framework within computer graphics. It outlines the steps required to convert a three-dimensional (3D) scene into a two-dimensional (2D) image on a display. Once a 3D model is created, the pipeline processes it into a format that is visually rendered on a screen. However, since rendering requirements vary based on hardware, software configurations, and display attributes, a universally standardized pipeline does not exist. To address this, graphics application programming interfaces (APIs) like OpenGL and Direct3D have been developed. These APIs provide a standardized abstraction over various graphics hardware accelerators such as those from AMD, Intel, and NVIDIA. They simplify development by eliminating the need for programmers to create hardware-specific code.

The graphics pipeline is most commonly utilized for real-time rendering. Many of its steps are hardware-accelerated, allowing for optimized performance. Like CPU pipelines, rendering pipelines run multiple stages concurrently, provided that each stage has the required inputs.

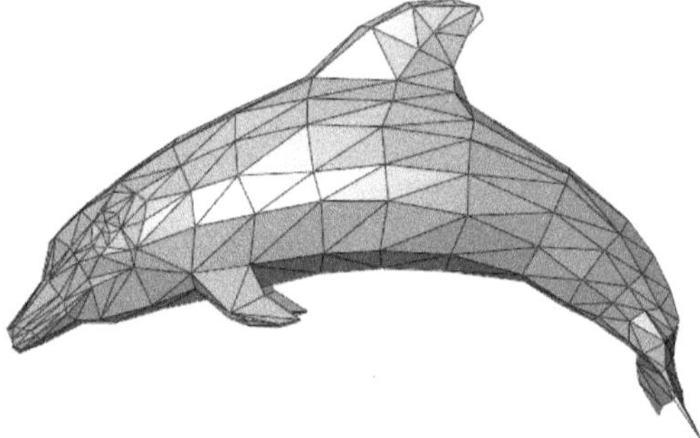

Figure 3.2: 3D Polygon Rendering

The most widespread method of 3D rendering is *3D polygon rendering*, which differs from methods like ray tracing and ray casting. In ray casting, rays originate from the camera's position, and their intersections with surfaces determine the color and lighting at those points. Conversely, in 3D polygon rendering, the process is reversed: the visible area within the camera's view is calculated first, and then rays are traced from each part of the visible surfaces back to the camera.

The graphics pipeline is typically divided into three main components: **Application**, **Geometry**, and **Rasterization**. Each of these stages contributes uniquely to the rendering process, ensuring the virtual environment is efficiently transformed into an immersive visual experience for the user.

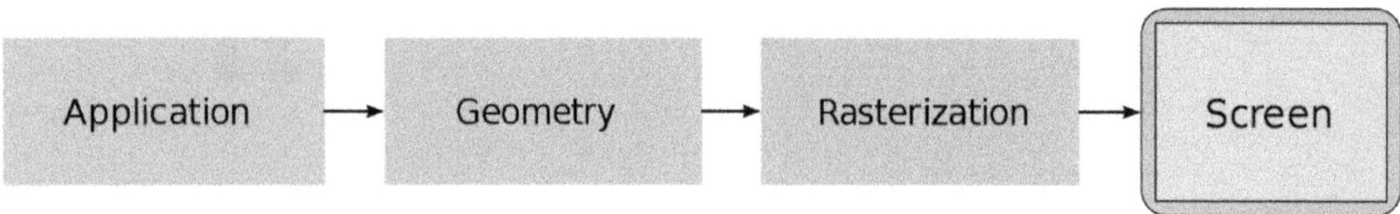

Figure 3.3: Graphics Pipeline

<u>**Application Stage**</u>

The application stage of the rendering pipeline operates within the software, running on the central processing unit (CPU). At this stage, updates to the virtual scene are performed as needed, often influenced by user interactions via input devices or ongoing animations. Once the scene is updated, including all its basic elements like triangles, lines, and points, it is forwarded to the subsequent stage of the pipeline for further processing.

Tasks typically handled during the application stage include collision detection, animation updates, and morphing. Additionally, techniques like spatial subdivision—using structures such as Quadtrees or Octrees—are employed to optimize performance and reduce memory usage. These techniques help manage the complexity of large-scale virtual environments by ensuring that only the necessary portions of the world are loaded into memory at a time. This is especially crucial for modern computer games, where the virtual worlds often exceed the capacity of the system's memory to accommodate them all at once.

Geometry Stage

The geometry stage, also referred to as the **geometry pipeline**, is pivotal for processing polygons and their associated vertices. Often divided into multiple tasks, the organization and parallelization of these tasks vary based on the specific implementation of the system.

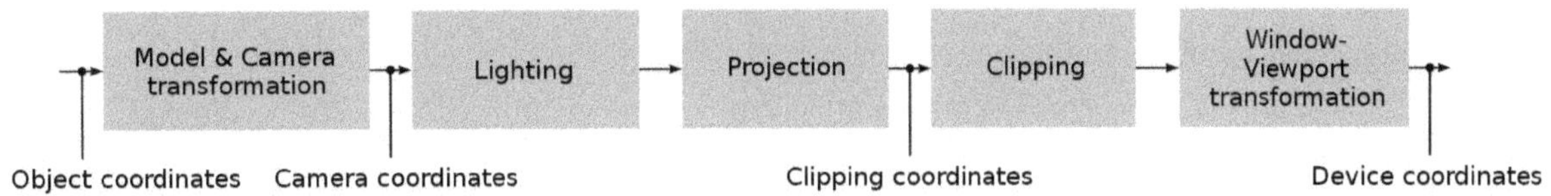

Figure 3.4: Geometry pipeline

Key Concepts of Geometry Processing

1. **Vertices**: A vertex (plural: vertices) represents a single point in 3D space. These points are used to define and join the surfaces of objects. While vertices can sometimes be displayed individually as point clouds, this approach remains rare.

2. **Triangles**: Among all geometric primitives, triangles are the most commonly used in computer graphics. Each triangle is defined by three vertices and a **normal vector**—a vector perpendicular to the triangle's surface that identifies its front-facing side. Triangles can either be assigned a color or have a texture applied, which appears as an image mapped onto their surface.

Triangles are preferred over rectangles or other polygons because their three vertices always lie on the same plane, ensuring stability and consistency during rendering processes.

Visual Representation

The geometry stage encompasses all the operations required to handle these fundamental shapes, as illustrated in Figure 3.4. It ensures that geometric data is efficiently prepared for subsequent steps in the rendering pipeline

The World Coordinate System

The **world coordinate system** serves as the foundation for creating the virtual environment. To ensure that mathematical operations can be applied seamlessly, the system must adhere to certain principles:

1. **Rectangular Cartesian System**: The coordinate system should be rectangular and Cartesian, with all axes equally scaled. This uniformity simplifies calculations.

2. **Unit Definition**: The unit of measurement within the system is flexible and depends on the specific application. Developers have the freedom to decide whether the unit corresponds to one meter, an Ångström, or any other scale suitable for the project.

3. **Handedness**: The choice between a right-handed or left-handed coordinate system is often dictated by the graphic library in use

Example: Flight Simulator

Consider the case of developing a flight simulator. The world coordinate system can be set up with the origin at the Earth's center, using a unit of one meter. For better alignment with real-world references, the following conventions can be adopted.

- The **X-axis** intersects the equator at the prime meridian (0° longitude).

- The **Z-axis** aligns with the Earth's poles.

- In a **right-handed system**, the **Y-axis** runs along the 90° East meridian, placing it somewhere in the Indian Ocean

This setup provides a Cartesian coordinate framework for accurately modeling Earth's features such as mountains, valleys, and oceans

Note on Geographic Coordinates

While Cartesian coordinates are ideal for computer geometry, Earth's surface is typically described using geographic coordinates (latitude, longitude) and altitude above sea level. The conversion between Cartesian and geographic coordinates is straightforward, though it simplifies the Earth's shape by assuming it is a perfect sphere:

$$\begin{pmatrix} x \\ y \\ z \end{pmatrix} = \begin{pmatrix} (R + hasl) * \cos(lat) * \cos(long) \\ (R + hasl) * \cos(lat) * \sin(long) \\ (R + hasl) * \sin(lat) \end{pmatrix}$$

with R = Radius of the Earth [6.378.137m], lat = Latitude, long = Longitude, hasl = height above sea level.

These calculations are typically applied in a right-handed coordinate system. If using a left-handed system, the signs may need adjustment to maintain consistency.

Object Coordinate Systems

Objects within a scene—such as houses, trees, or cars—are generally designed using their **local coordinate systems** (also known as object or model coordinate systems). This simplifies the modelling process. To position these objects within the **global coordinate system** of the virtual world, transformations such as translation, rotation, or scaling are applied. This is achieved by multiplying the relevant **transformation matrices**.

For instance, multiple variations of a single object, like a tree, can be transformed to create an entire forest. This technique is referred to as **instancing**.

Positioning a Model

To place an object, such as an aircraft, in the virtual world, several steps are required using **4x4 homogeneous transformation matrices**, as calculations in three-dimensional space demand four-dimensional representations.

$$T_{x,y,z} = \begin{pmatrix} 1 & 0 & 0 & 0 \\ 0 & 1 & 0 & 0 \\ 0 & 0 & 1 & 0 \\ x & y & z & 1 \end{pmatrix}$$

1. **Rotation Matrices:** Rotation transformations account for the aircraft's orientation along its three primary

$$R_x = \begin{pmatrix} 1 & 0 & 0 & 0 \\ 0 & \cos(\alpha) & \sin(\alpha) & 0 \\ 0 & -\sin(\alpha) & \cos(\alpha) & 0 \\ 0 & 0 & 0 & 1 \end{pmatrix}$$

axes:

First, we need three rotation matrices, namely one for each of the three aircraft axes (vertical axis, transverse axis, longitudinal axis).

☐ **X-axis (Longitudinal axis)**: Rotates around the aircraft's length.

☐ **Y-axis (Transverse axis)**: Rotates around the aircraft's width.

☐ **Z-axis (Vertical axis)**: Rotates around the aircraft's height.

2. **Translation Matrix A translation matrix** moves the aircraft to a specific location within the virtual

$$\begin{pmatrix} \cos(\alpha) & 0 & -\sin(\alpha) & 0 \\ 0 & 1 & 0 & 0 \end{pmatrix}$$

$$R_z = \begin{pmatrix} \cos(\alpha) & \sin(\alpha) & 0 & 0 \\ -\sin(\alpha) & \cos(\alpha) & 0 & 0 \\ 0 & 0 & 1 & 0 \\ 0 & 0 & 0 & 1 \end{pmatrix}$$

world.

The matrices described are arranged slightly differently than those in the standard rotation matrix article. This distinction arises from specific operational requirements, which will be clarified further below.

To calculate the positions of an aircraft's vertices in world coordinates, we multiply each vertex by four transformation matrices sequentially. However, performing these matrix-vector multiplications for every point can be computationally intensive. Instead, an optimized approach involves multiplying the four matrices together first. Although matrix-matrix multiplication is computationally expensive, it needs to be done only once for the entire object. The mathematical operations *((((v * R_x) * R_y) * R_z) * T)* and *(v *((((R_x * R_y) * R_z) * T))* are mathematically equivalent. Once the combined matrix is computed, it can be applied to all vertices. In practice, however, the vertex transformations are often deferred until the camera matrices are computed (discussed later

For the earlier example, the translation matrix must be adjusted differently because the commonly accepted "up" direction—except at the North Pole—does not align with the positive Z-axis. Therefore, the model must also be rotated around the Earth's center. The translation T_{Sphere} is calculated as follows:

$$T_{Sphere} = T_{x,y,z}(0,0, R + hasl) * R_y \left(\frac{\pi}{2} - lat\right) * R_z(long)$$

- **Step 1:** Move the model's origin to the correct height above the Earth's surface using the first translation matrix.

- **Step 2:** Rotate the model by its latitude and longitude to align it with the Earth's surface

Importance of Matrix Order

The sequence of applying these transformations is critical because **matrix multiplication is non-commutative**— the order of operations affects the result. This principle extends to rotational transformations as well.

For example, consider the point (1, 0, 0), located on the X-axis.

- If rotated first by 90° around the X-axis and then around the Y-axis, the point moves to the Z-axis, as the initial X-axis rotation does not affect points on the axis.

- Conversely, if the rotations occur in the reverse order (first around the Y-axis and then the X-axis), the point ends up on the Y-axis.

While the specific sequence of rotations is arbitrary, maintaining consistency is essential. A common, intuitive sequence is to apply rotations in the order of X (roll), Y (pitch), and Z (heading). This ensures the final orientation aligns with the "nose" direction, matching the intended compass heading

Matrix Conventions: Row vs. Column Vectors

Matrix definitions vary based on whether computations use **column vectors** or **row vectors**, with different graphics libraries favouring one convention over the other. For instance:

- **OpenGL** uses column vectors, requiring matrix multiplication from the right:

$$v_{out} = M * v_{in}$$

Here, v_{in} and v_{out} are 4×1 column vectors. Similarly, matrix concatenation proceeds from right to left, e.g., $M = T_x * R_x$ when rotation precedes translation.

- **DirectX**, on the other hand, employs row vectors, reversing the operations. Multiplication now happens from the left:

$$v_{out} = v_{in} * M$$

Row vectors are 1×4, and matrix concatenation follows the same order, $M = T_x * R_x$, for first rotating and then translating

The matrices shown earlier adhere to the row vector convention. To switch to column vectors, these matrices must be transposed. Transposing alters the multiplication order:

$$(v * M)^T = M^T * v^T$$

This enables flexibility in switching conventions without altering the transformation logic

Chaining Transformations and World Matrix

Matrix chaining enables the definition of new coordinate systems with each transformation. For example, if an aircraft model includes a separately modelled propeller, the propeller can be aligned to the aircraft's nose using a translation matrix. This aligns the propeller's local coordinate system with the aircrafts.

Rendering the complete model involves first calculating the aircraft's transformation matrix to position its points in the world coordinate system. Next, the propeller's transformation matrix is applied, combining it with the aircraft's matrix. This combined matrix defines the propeller's position and orientation relative to the world.

This computed matrix is called the **world matrix** and must be determined for every object in the scene before rendering. Applications dynamically update these matrices, for instance, adjusting an aircraft's position based on speed in each frame.

Camera and View Transformation

Scenes also include a **virtual camera**, defining the viewer's position and direction. To render the scene, objects are transformed so the camera is positioned at the origin, looking along the positive Z-axis. This transformation is called the *camera transformation or view transformation*, and the resulting coordinate system is referred to as the *camera coordinate system*

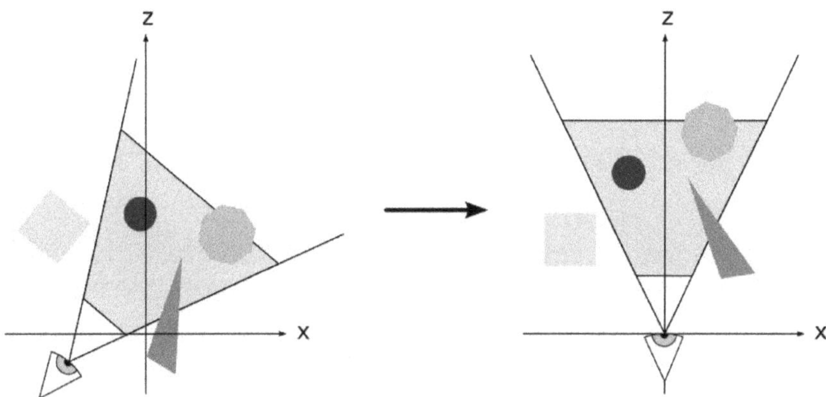

Figure 3.5: Left: The camera's position and orientation, as specified by the user. **Right:** The objects in the scene, reoriented after applying the camera transformation. The light gray area represents the visible volume (view frustum)

View Matrix & Normalized Vectors

The view matrix positions and orients the camera relative to the scene. It is calculated using:

- **Camera position**: The origin of the camera.

- **Target point**: The focal point where the camera is aimed.

- **Up vector**: Defines the "up" direction from the camera's perspective.

To compute the view matrix, three auxiliary vectors are derived:

1. **Z-axis**: Direction from the camera to the target:

$$Z_{axis} = normalize\ (cameraPosition - cameraTarget)$$

2. **X-axis: Perpendicular to the Z-axis and up vector:**

$$X_{axis} = normalize\ (cameraUpVector, Z_{axis})$$

3. **Y-axis: Cross product of the Z-axis and X-axis:**

$$Y_{axis} = cross\ (Z_{axis}, X_{axis})$$

Normalize Vector: Normalized vectors form the foundation of the **view matrix**, ensuring proper alignment of the scene with the camera's perspective. These vectors are calculated using.

- **Normal(v):** Normalization of vector v.

- **Cross (v_1, v_2):** Cross product of vectors $v_1, and\ v_2$

The view matrix is then represented as:

$$\begin{pmatrix} xaxis.x & yaxis.x & zaxis.x & 0 \\ xaxis.y & yaxis.y & zaxis.y & 0 \\ xaxis.z & yaxis.z & zaxis.z & 0 \\ -dot(xaxis, cameraPosition & -dot(yaxis, cameraPosition & -dot(zaxis, cameraPosition & 1 \end{pmatrix}$$

Here, dot (v_1, v_2) represents the dot product of vectors $v_1, and\ v_2$

Projection Transformation

The **3D projection step** converts the view volume into a cube bounded by coordinates (-1, -1, 0) and (1, 1, 1). Although this step transforms one volume into another, it is called **projection** because only the resulting X, Y, and Z coordinates are relevant for subsequent operations like Z-buffering during rasterization.

Perspective Projection

A central projection is used for perspective views, creating a truncated pyramid (frustum) as the visual volume. This shape helps restrict the objects displayed to those within the frustum. The perspective projection matrix is given by:

$$\begin{pmatrix} w & 0 & 0 & 0 \\ 0 & h & 0 & 0 \\ 0 & 0 & \dfrac{far}{near - far} & -1 \\ 0 & 0 & \dfrac{near * far}{near - far} & 0 \end{pmatrix}$$

Where:

- $h = \cot\left(\dfrac{fielfOfView}{2}\right)$ (aperture angle of the camera).

- $w = \dfrac{h}{aspectRation}$ (aspect ratio of the target image.

- near: Minimum visible distance

- far: Maximum visible distance.

The $near$ and far values are crucial for scaling Z-values to the 0..1 range for the Z-buffer, which often has a limited resolution (e.g., 16 bits). Improper selection of these values can lead to artifacts like **Z-fighting**, where surfaces incorrectly overlap due to insufficient Z-buffer precision

Parallel Projection

Used in technical and orthogonal visualizations, parallel projection preserves scale and parallel lines, making it ideal for maps and engineering designs. The matrix for parallel projection is:

$$\begin{pmatrix} \dfrac{2.0}{w} & 0 & 0 & 0 \\ 0 & \dfrac{2.0}{h} & 0 & 0 \\ 0 & 0 & \dfrac{1.0}{(near - far)} & -1 \\ 0 & 0 & \dfrac{near}{(near - far)} & 0 \end{pmatrix}$$

Where:

- w: Width of the target cube.

- $h = \dfrac{w}{aspectRation}$ Adjusts for aspect ratio.

Combined Transformation Matrix

For efficiency, the camera and projection matrices are combined into a single transformation matrix, bypassing the intermediate camera coordinate system. This combined matrix is pre-calculated for the frame, while only the world matrix is updated for individual objects. This approach simplifies rendering and allows for advanced effects, such as **vertex blending** or **geometry shaders**, to modify object geometry dynamically

For reasons of efficiency, the camera and projection matrix are usually combined into a transformation matrix so that the camera coordinate system is omitted. The resulting matrix is usually the same for a single image, while the world matrix looks different for each object. In practice, therefore, view and projection are pre-calculated so that only the world matrix has to be adapted during the display. However, more complex transformations such as vertex blending are possible. Freely programmable geometry shaders that modify the geometry can also be executed.

Rendering and Lighting

During rendering, the final transformation is computed as:

World Matrix * Camera Matrix *Projection Matrix

This composite matrix is applied to all vertices, converting them into screen coordinates.

To enhance realism, scenes often include light sources. Lighting calculations are based on the material properties of objects and the light source characteristics. Ambient light provides uniform brightness, while directional light sources, such as the sun, depend on the scalar product of the light's directional vector and the surface's normal vector. Surfaces facing away from the light source (negative scalar product) are not illuminated

Clipping and Culling: Enhancing Rendering Efficiency

Once the projection step is complete, only the primitives within the **visible volume**, known as the frustum, are processed for rendering. The frustum, which resembles a pyramid with its top cut off, defines the boundaries of what the virtual camera can see. This visual volume ensures that computational resources are focused solely on the objects relevant to the final scene

Frustum Culling and Clipping

Primitives entirely outside the frustum are eliminated through a process called **frustum culling**. For instance, if a triangle (such as the blue triangle in the figure) lies completely outside this volume, it is discarded without further processing, reducing unnecessary computational load.

Objects or primitives that are only partially within the frustum, such as the orange triangle in the figure, undergo a process called **clipping**. In this step, the geometry of the object is trimmed to fit within the frustum's boundaries. This operation may involve creating new vertices at the points where the object's edges intersect the frustum's planes, effectively modifying the shape of the primitive to conform to the visible region.

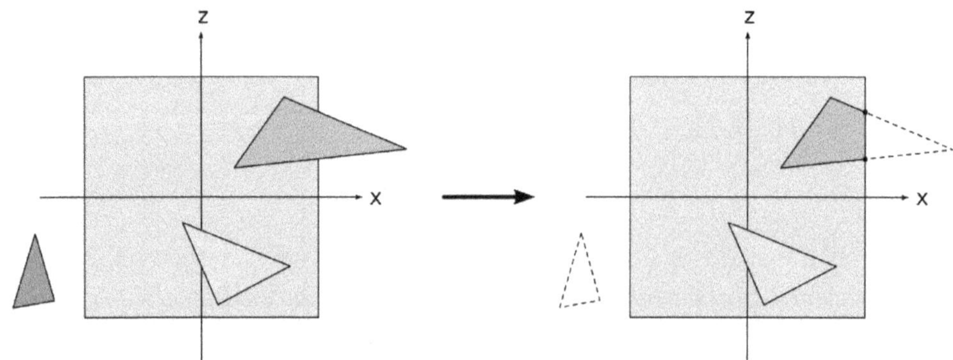

Figure 3.6: Clipping of primitives against the cube.

- The blue triangle outside the frustum is discarded.

- The orange triangle intersecting the frustum is clipped, creating new vertices.

Additional Culling Methods

To further enhance rendering efficiency, additional techniques like **back-face culling** are employed. Back-face culling eliminates surfaces that are oriented away from the camera's view. These surfaces, typically the back sides of objects, do not contribute to the visible scene and can thus be ignored during rendering.

Through the combined application of frustum culling, clipping, and back-face culling, only the necessary primitives—those fully or partially visible—are sent forward to the **rasterization stage**. This streamlined approach optimizes the rendering pipeline, ensuring that only relevant geometry is processed and displayed in the final image

The Window-Viewport Transformation: Mapping to the Screen

To render a 3D scene onto a 2D screen, an additional transformation called the **Window-Viewport Transformation** is applied. This process ensures the image is correctly scaled and positioned within a specific target area, or **viewport**, on the screen. The viewport defines the rectangular area where the final image is displayed, allowing for precise control over the output.

Transformation Steps

The Window-Viewport Transformation involves two key operations:

1. **Translation:** The coordinates of the projected 3D points are shifted to align with the viewport's origin on the screen.

2. **Scaling:** The points are then scaled to fit the dimensions of the viewport, ensuring the image is displayed at the correct size.

After applying these transformations, the resulting coordinates are referred to as **device coordinates**, which correspond to the physical output device, such as a monitor.

Viewport Parameters

The viewport is defined by the following six parameters:

- **Width:** The width of the viewport in pixels.

- **Height:** The height of the viewport in pixels.

- **Upper Left Corner Coordinates:** The starting position of the viewport in window coordinates, typically set to (0, 0).

- **Minimum Z Value:** The nearest depth value for objects, usually set to 0.

- **Maximum Z Value:** The farthest depth value for objects, typically set to 1.

The transformation formula for converting a point's coordinates vvv (after projection) into viewport coordinates is:

$$\begin{pmatrix} x \\ y \\ z \end{pmatrix} = \begin{pmatrix} vp.X + (1.0 + v.X) * vp.\dfrac{width}{2.0} \\ vp.Y + (1.0 - v.Y) * vp.\dfrac{height}{2.0} \\ vp.minz + v.Z * (vp.maxz - vp.minz) \end{pmatrix}$$

Here:

- vp: Represents the viewport parameters.

- v: Refers to the coordinates of the point after projection

Modern Implementation on Hardware

On contemporary graphics hardware, most of the computational work for geometry transformations is handled by the **vertex shader**, a programmable component of the GPU. While the vertex shader can be customized for various tasks, it typically handles two fundamental processes:

- **Point Transformation:** Converting 3D points into their corresponding device coordinates.

- **Lighting Calculations:** Determining the illumination of vertices based on light sources and material properties.

DirectX Specifics

With **DirectX**, the use of custom vertex shaders became mandatory starting from version 10, providing developers with greater flexibility in defining transformation and rendering processes. Earlier versions of DirectX offered a standard shader for these computations, reducing the need for manual programming but limiting customization

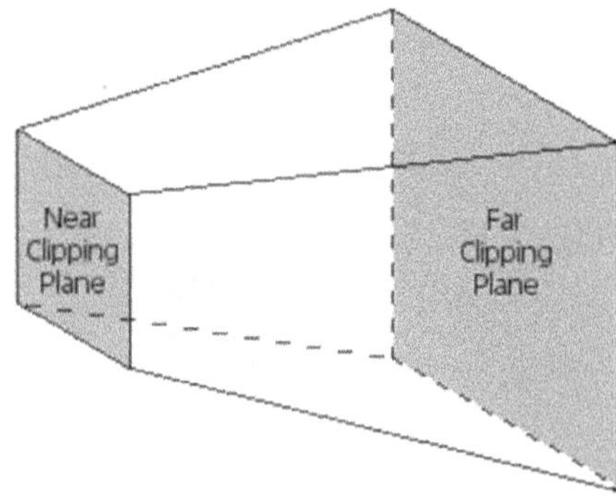

Figure 3.7: Frustum: Illustrates the 3D view volume (frustum) used during projection

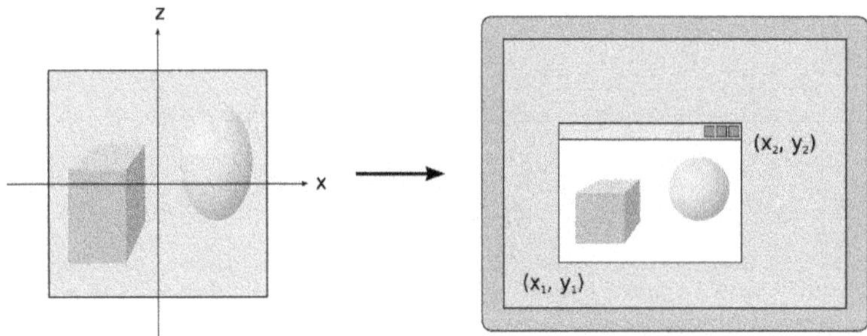

Figure 3.8: Window-Viewport Transformation: Depicts the process of mapping the 3D scene onto the screen's viewport, demonstrating how points are scaled and shifted to fit the target display area

By combining the Window-Viewport Transformation with earlier steps in the rendering pipeline, the scene's geometry is accurately projected and displayed within the designated area of the screen, ensuring a consistent and visually coherent final output

Rasterization: Finalizing the Rendering Process

The rasterization phase marks the last stage of the graphics pipeline before fragments enter the fragment shader pipeline. During this step, continuous geometric primitives—such as triangles or lines—are converted into discrete fragments that correspond to individual pixels on the screen.

Fragments and Their Role

In the rasterization process, the grid points generated are referred to as **fragments** to distinguish them from pixels in the frame buffer. Each fragment corresponds directly to one pixel on the screen. These fragments are then assigned colors, textures, and lighting effects based on the properties of the associated primitive.

However, when overlapping polygons are present, only the fragment closest to the viewer remains visible. The **Z-buffer**, a specialized memory buffer, is commonly employed to determine which fragments are visible and which are obscured. This process is referred to as **hidden surface determination**

Fragment Shading and Transparency

The color and visual properties of a fragment are calculated using various factors, including:

- **Illumination:** Light interactions with the primitive.

- **Textures:** Applied surface patterns or images.

- **Material Properties:** Characteristics such as reflectivity and shininess.

These values are typically interpolated from the vertices of the associated primitive. If available, a **fragment shader** (also known as a **pixel shader**) is executed for each fragment. The shader enhances the fragment by applying advanced visual effects, such as shadows, reflections, or dynamic lighting.

In cases involving transparency or multi-sampling (used for anti-aliasing), visible fragments are blended with existing color data in the frame buffer. This ensures smooth transitions and visually coherent overlapping elements. Ultimately, one or more fragments are combined into a single pixel.

Double Buffering for Smooth Rendering

To ensure smooth and seamless visuals, **double buffering** is employed. Rasterization occurs in an off-screen memory buffer. Once the entire image has been processed, it is swapped into the visible memory, preventing the viewer from seeing the gradual rendering process

Mathematical Properties of Transformation Matrices

All matrices used in the graphics pipeline are **nonsingular** (invertible). Since the product of nonsingular matrices is also nonsingular, the entire transformation matrix remains invertible. This property is critical for tasks such as converting screen coordinates back into world coordinates.

For instance, when determining which object the user clicked on, the system uses the mouse position to project a ray into the 3D scene. The intersection of this ray with scene polygons is then computed to identify the clicked object. Since the mouse position and screen coordinates are two-dimensional, the depth (Z-axis) is unknown and must be inferred using the inverse transformations.

Evolution of GPUs and Shader Pipelines

Classic graphics cards adhered closely to a rigid graphics pipeline. However, as demand for complex visuals grew, these rigid pipelines evolved into **shader-controlled pipelines**, offering greater flexibility and computational power. Modern GPUs now perform many additional processing tasks previously handled by the CPU.

Key Shader Units

1. **Vertex Shaders:** Process vertex data, including transformations and lighting.

2. **Geometry Shaders:** Manipulate entire primitives such as triangles or lines.

3. **Pixel Shaders:** Calculate fragment properties, such as color and transparency.

Unified Shader Architecture

Modern GPUs utilize a **Unified Shader Architecture**, where all shader units are pooled together. This architecture dynamically allocates resources, allowing greater flexibility and efficiency. Traditional distinctions between shader types (vertex, geometry, pixel) have become less rigid.

The most important shader units are vertex shaders, geometry shaders, and pixel shaders.

Advanced GPU Computation: GPGPU

Beyond graphics rendering, modern GPUs support **general-purpose computing on graphics processing units (GPGPU)**. Using compute shaders, GPUs can perform highly parallel computations unrelated to graphical output. While GPGPU excels at parallel tasks, it has certain limitations in terms of task complexity.

Mesh Shaders: The Next Evolution

A recent advancement in GPU technology is the introduction of **mesh shaders**, designed to overcome limitations in the fixed layout of traditional geometry pipelines. Mesh shaders offer greater control and efficiency, streamlining the rendering process for complex scenes

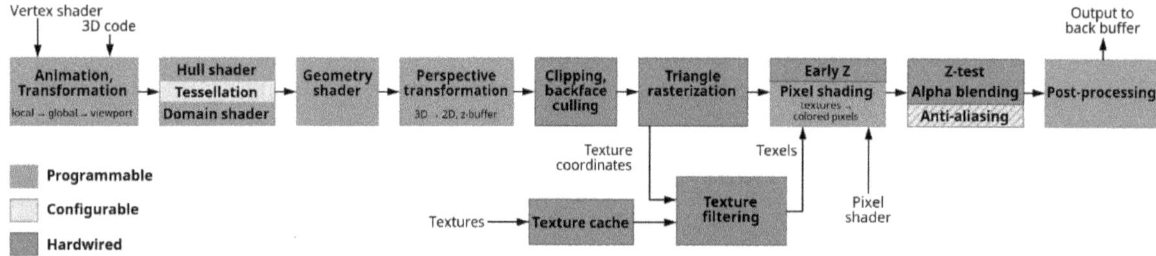

Figure 3.9: Flow chart of a 3D graphics rendering pipeline

This figure illustrates the complete rendering pipeline, highlighting key stages such as vertex processing, rasterization, fragment shading, and final image composition. It encapsulates how modern GPUs leverage programmable shaders to deliver high-performance, visually stunning graphics.

3.3 Haptic Rendering Pipeline

In virtual reality (VR), the haptic rendering pipeline is specifically tailored to provide users with immersive tactile feedback in addition to visual and auditory stimuli. Similar to non-VR haptic rendering, virtual objects in VR environments need to be digitally represented. This includes defining their geometry, material properties, and physical attributes such as mass, friction, and elasticity. A physics engine simulates the dynamic interactions between virtual objects in the VR environment. This involves calculating forces such as collisions, gravity, and object manipulation based on the laws of physics.

In VR, haptic feedback is generated to simulate the sensation of touching and interacting with virtual objects. This can involve various techniques such as:

- Vibrotactile Feedback: Vibrations are applied to haptic devices worn by the user, such as gloves or vests, to simulate tactile sensations.

- Force Feedback: Force-feedback devices apply physical forces to the user's hands or body, allowing them to feel resistance, pressure, or texture when interacting with virtual objects.

- Skin Stretching and Tension: Advanced haptic devices may simulate the sensation of skin stretching or tension, enhancing the realism of interactions.

Haptic devices are controlled to deliver feedback synchronized with the user's interactions and the virtual environment. This involves integrating haptic hardware with the VR system and coordinating feedback based on user actions and environmental cues. As in non-VR haptic rendering, optimization techniques are employed to maintain real-time performance and minimize latency. This includes optimizing physics simulations, haptic feedback generation, and synchronization with visual and auditory rendering.

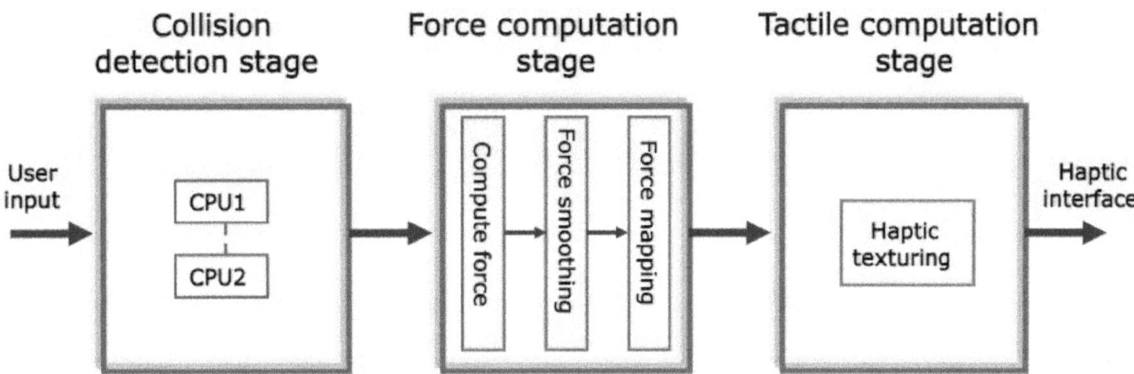

Figure 3.10: Haptic Rendering Pipeline

Users interact with virtual objects in the VR environment, receiving haptic feedback that enhances their sense of presence and immersion. Haptic feedback provides additional sensory cues that complement visual and auditory stimuli, improving the overall VR experience. The haptic rendering pipeline needs to be seamlessly integrated with VR platforms and development frameworks. This ensures compatibility with different VR hardware devices and software applications, allowing developers to create immersive haptic experiences across various VR platforms. The haptic rendering pipeline in virtual reality combines physics simulation, haptic feedback generation, device control, and user interaction to deliver immersive tactile experiences that complement the visual and auditory aspects of VR environments.

It is a process of applying forces to the user through a force-feed back device. The major difference between haptic devices and other input interface such as mouse and keyboard is that it will give force feedback based on the virtual environment.

Using haptic rendering, we can enable a user to touch, feel and manipulate virtual objects. Enhance a user's experience in virtual environment.

Imaging after twenty years, when we play computer games, we can wear some haptic device. Then we can do some exercise while playing games.

Goal of haptic rendering

- Enable a user to touch, feel and manipulate virtual objects

- Enhance a user's experience in a synthetic environment

- Provide a natural intuitive interface

Collision detection stage

- **Load Object Data:** Retrieve the physical characteristics of 3D virtual objects from a database.

- **Detect Collisions:** Identify when and where virtual objects interact or collide

Force computation stage

- **Calculate Collision Forces:** Determine the forces resulting from detected collisions.

- **Smooth Force Transitions:** Apply smoothing techniques to ensure realistic force feedback.

- **Map Forces:** Convert calculated forces into outputs suitable for haptic devices

Tactile computation stage

- **Simulate Touch Sensations:** Render tactile effects like texture, vibration, or surface resistance.

- **Combine Effects:** Add tactile effects to the computed force vector and send it to the haptic display output

The haptics rendering pipeline has a much less consistent construction compared to its graphics counterpart.

Future Vision: A Fully Immersive Experience

The potential of haptic technology is enormous. From gaming to virtual training simulations, haptic rendering opens the door to a more immersive, natural, and intuitive interaction with digital worlds. As the technology evolves, we may see the integration of haptic devices into everyday applications, transforming how we interact with virtual environments and making the line between physical and digital experiences increasingly blurred

3.4 PC Graphics Architecture

Graphics Processing Units (GPUs): An Overview

A **graphics processing unit (GPU)** is a specialized electronic circuit originally designed to enhance computer graphics and image processing. These components can be found in various devices, such as video cards, embedded systems, mobile phones, personal computers, workstations, and gaming consoles. While GPUs were initially tailored for graphical tasks, their parallel architecture has made them invaluable for a range of non-graphic computations, such as neural network training and cryptocurrency mining, particularly for embarrassingly parallel problems.

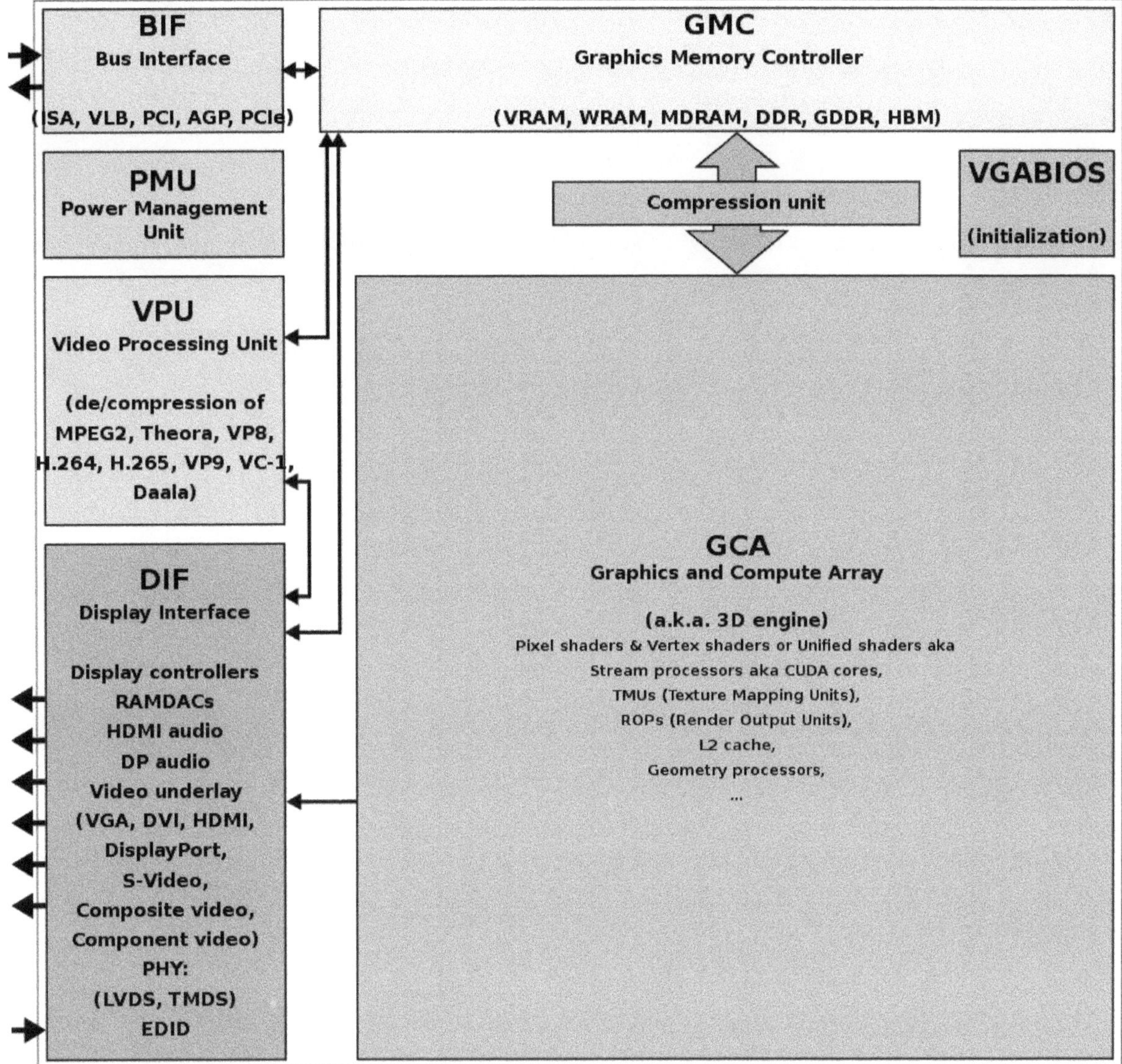

Figure 3.11: Key Components of a GPU

Over time, numerous companies have developed GPUs under various brand names. As of 2009, Intel, Nvidia, and AMD/ATI dominated the market with shares of 49.4%, 27.8%, and 20.6%, respectively. Other notable producers, such as Matrox, have also contributed to the GPU industry. In modern smartphones, GPUs like Qualcomm's Adreno, Imagination Technologies' PowerVR, and ARM's Mali are commonly used.

Evolution and Functionality of GPUs

Modern GPUs primarily allocate their transistors to computations for 3D computer graphics. Alongside these capabilities, they also offer basic 2D acceleration and framebuffer functions, often including VGA compatibility. However, some modern cards, like AMD/ATI's HD5000–HD7000 series, no longer include dedicated 2D acceleration, which is now emulated using 3D hardware.

Originally, GPUs were employed to manage the memory-heavy tasks of texture mapping and rendering polygons. Over time, their functionality expanded to include hardware for geometric calculations such as rotating and translating vertices between coordinate systems.

Recent advancements in GPU technology encompass:

- **Programmable Shaders**: Capable of manipulating vertices and textures with CPU-like operations.

- **Anti-Aliasing Techniques**: Employing oversampling and interpolation to reduce visual artifacts.

- **High-Precision Color Spaces**: Ensuring enhanced color accuracy and quality.

Factors Influencing GPU Performance

Several elements of GPU architecture directly impact their performance, particularly for real-time rendering tasks. Key considerations include:

1. **Semiconductor Pathways**: The size of these pathways influences data transfer efficiency.

2. **Clock Speed**: Determines how quickly the GPU processes instructions.

3. **On-Chip Memory Caches**: The size and number of caches contribute to the GPU's speed and data handling capabilities.

Performance is also shaped by the number of computational units:

- **Streaming Multiprocessors (SM)** in Nvidia GPUs.

- **Compute Units (CU)** in AMD GPUs.

- **Xe Cores** in Intel discrete GPUs.

These units work in parallel to execute core computations efficiently. GPU performance is typically gauged in **floating-point operations per second (FLOPS)**, with modern GPUs often achieving teraflop (TFLOPS) levels of performance. While this metric provides an estimate of computational power, factors like memory bandwidth and architecture design also influence actual rendering speeds.

GPUs have evolved from being solely graphics accelerators to multifunctional processors driving innovations in gaming, AI, and scientific computing. Their parallel processing capabilities continue to push the boundaries of performance, making them indispensable in modern computing systems

<u>GPU-Accelerated Video Decoding and Encoding</u>

Since the mid-1990s, graphics processing units (GPUs) have supported the YUV color space and hardware overlays, critical components for digital video playback. By the early 2000s, many GPUs also began incorporating support for MPEG primitives, such as motion compensation and inverse discrete cosine transform (iDCT). This innovation, where portions of video decoding and post-processing are delegated to GPU hardware, is known as GPU-accelerated video decoding. It may also be referred to as GPU-assisted, GPU hardware-accelerated, or GPU hardware-assisted video decoding.

Modern GPUs, especially recent graphics cards, have significantly advanced this capability, offloading high-definition video decoding tasks from the central processing unit (CPU) to the GPU. Commonly used APIs for enabling GPU-accelerated video decoding include **DxVA** for Microsoft Windows and **VDPAU, VAAPI, XvMC,** and **XvBA** for Linux-based and UNIX-like systems. While most of these APIs can handle video codecs such as MPEG-1, MPEG-2, MPEG-4 ASP (e.g., DivX 6), MPEG-4 AVC (H.264), VC-1, WMV9, and others, **XvMC** is limited to decoding MPEG-1 and MPEG-2.

Key Processes Accelerated by GPU Hardware

Modern GPUs enhance video processing by accelerating the following operations:

- **Motion Compensation (mocomp):** Improves video smoothness.

- **Inverse Discrete Cosine Transform (iDCT):** Handles key mathematical computations for video decoding.

- **Inverse Telecine:** Corrects 3:2 and 2:2 pull-down errors.

- **Inverse Modified Discrete Cosine Transform (iMDCT):** Processes advanced transformations in certain codecs.

- **In-Loop Deblocking Filter:** Smooths blocky video artifacts.

- **Intra-Frame Prediction:** Optimizes individual frame processing.

- **Inverse Quantization (IQ):** Converts compressed data back to its original form.

- **Variable-Length Decoding (VLD):** Also known as slice-level acceleration.

- **Spatial-Temporal Deinterlacing:** Enhances video clarity and detects interlaced or progressive sources.

- **Bitstream Processing:** Handles advanced encoding techniques, such as context-adaptive variable-length coding and perfect pixel positioning.

These functionalities are not limited to video playback but are also utilized in video editing, encoding, and transcoding workflows.

Evolution of GPU Technology

In earlier generations, GPUs primarily supported 2D graphics APIs like GDI and DirectDraw or 3D graphics APIs such as DirectX, OpenGL, OpenGL ES, Vulkan, and Metal. The term **GPU** was first used in the 1970s to describe a programmable processing unit designed for independent graphics manipulation. Sony later redefined the term in 1994 when referring to the PlayStation's graphics chip, designed by Toshiba. Nvidia popularized the concept in 1999 by introducing the GeForce 256, the first GPU with integrated features like transform, lighting, and rendering engines. Meanwhile, ATI Technologies (now part of AMD) coined the term **visual processing unit (VPU)** in 2002 with the release of the Radeon 9700.

In 2023, AMD introduced the **Alveo MA35D**, which features dual VPUs manufactured using a 5nm process, marking another leap in GPU innovation.

Types of GPUs

GPUs come in two main categories:

1. **Dedicated Graphics:** Also known as discrete GPUs, these are standalone components designed for high-performance tasks.

2. **Integrated Graphics:** Often referred to as shared graphics, these GPUs are embedded within the CPU or system architecture, using shared system memory

Applications of GPUs

GPUs are tailored for specific applications, ranging from gaming to AI training. Below is a breakdown of their diverse use cases:

1. **Gaming GPUs:**

   - Nvidia GeForce (GTX, RTX)

   - Nvidia Titan

   - AMD Radeon (HD, R5, R7, RX, Vega, Navi series)

   - Radeon VII

   - Intel Arc

2. **Cloud Gaming GPUs:**

   - Nvidia GRID

   - AMD Radeon Sky

3. **Workstation GPUs:**

   - Nvidia Quadro

   - Nvidia RTX

   - AMD FirePro

   - AMD Radeon Pro

   - Intel Arc Pro

4. **Cloud Workstation GPUs:**

   - Nvidia Tesla

   - AMD FireStream

5. **AI Training and Cloud Processing:**

   - Nvidia Tesla

   - AMD Radeon Instinct

6. **Autonomous Vehicle Systems:**

   - Nvidia Drive PX

Modern GPUs are more than just graphics accelerators; they are versatile computing powerhouses driving innovation in gaming, AI, cloud computing, and even autonomous vehicles. By offloading demanding computations to specialized hardware, GPUs not only boost performance but also open new horizons for technological advancements

Dedicated Graphics Processing Units

A **dedicated graphics processing unit (GPU)** refers to a GPU that has its own memory (RAM) exclusively reserved for its operations. Unlike integrated GPUs, which share system memory, dedicated GPUs utilize specialized RAM, often optimized for the sequential data processing required in graphics workloads, such as **GDDR** memory. It is worth noting that the term "dedicated" does not necessarily imply that the GPU is removable or interfaces with the motherboard in a standard fashion.

Dedicated GPUs are frequently found in discrete graphics cards, which connect to the motherboard via expansion slots like **PCI Express (PCIe)** or the now-outdated **Accelerated Graphics Port (AGP)**. While most discrete GPUs are designed to be replaceable or upgradable, the upgrade feasibility depends on the motherboard's compatibility. In rare cases, graphics cards may still use the older **Peripheral Component Interconnect (PCI)** slots, though these offer limited bandwidth and are only used when PCIe or AGP options are unavailable.

Dedicated GPUs in Portable Systems

In portable devices such as laptops, dedicated GPUs often connect through proprietary, non-standard slots to save space and reduce weight. These interfaces may logically behave like PCIe or AGP but differ physically, making them incompatible with their desktop counterparts. Systems equipped with dedicated GPUs are sometimes referred to as **DIS systems**, in contrast to **UMA systems**, which rely on unified memory architecture and share memory resources with the CPU

Multi-GPU Technologies

Technologies like Nvidia's **SLI (Scalable Link Interface)** and **NVLink**, as well as AMD's **CrossFire**, have enabled the use of multiple GPUs to collaborate on rendering tasks for a single display. By distributing the workload, these setups significantly enhance graphics processing power. However, such configurations are increasingly rare in consumer systems due to the high costs and diminishing software support. Most modern games are not optimized to utilize multiple GPUs effectively, and the average user finds single-GPU systems sufficient for their needs.

Despite this decline in popularity for consumer applications, multi-GPU setups remain crucial in certain professional and industrial environments. They are widely used in:

- **Supercomputers:** For example, the Summit supercomputer employs multiple GPUs for high-performance computing.

- **Workstations:** Multi-GPU configurations accelerate tasks like video editing, 3D rendering, and visual effects (VFX).

- **GPGPU Workloads:** General-purpose computations on GPUs for scientific simulations or complex modeling tasks.

- **AI Training:** Multi-GPU setups significantly expedite the training of machine learning models, as seen in Nvidia's **DGX systems**, **Tesla GPUs**, and Intel's **Ponte Vecchio GPUs**

Dedicated GPUs are an essential component of modern computing, offering unparalleled performance for graphics-intensive tasks and computational workloads. While their prominence in consumer applications has shifted towards single-GPU systems, they continue to play a vital role in professional, scientific, and AI-driven domains, driving innovation and enabling advanced capabilities in various fields

Integrated Graphics Processing Units

An **integrated graphics processing unit (IGPU)**, also known as integrated graphics, shared graphics solutions, or integrated graphics processors (IGP), relies on a computer's system RAM for its operations rather than using dedicated video memory. Unlike discrete GPUs, which have their own dedicated memory, IGPs share the computer's main memory, making them cost-effective but often less powerful alternatives. Integrated GPUs can be built directly onto the motherboard as part of the **northbridge chipset** or integrated with the CPU itself, as seen in processors like **AMD APUs** and **Intel HD Graphics** series.

Memory Configuration and Performance

Some AMD motherboards include **sideport memory**, a block of high-performance memory exclusively reserved for the GPU's use, which enhances graphics performance. However, this is not a standard feature across all integrated GPUs. Integrated graphics typically share the computer's RAM, resulting in lower memory bandwidth compared to discrete GPUs. For example, integrated GPUs access memory bandwidths up to 128 GB/s, whereas dedicated graphics cards may achieve over 1000 GB/s between their GPU core and VRAM. This discrepancy can limit the performance of integrated graphics, particularly in memory-intensive tasks.

Despite this limitation, modern advancements in memory management, such as **multi-channel memory configurations**, have helped mitigate these constraints. Furthermore, newer integrated GPUs include features like hardware-based transform and lighting, which were absent in earlier models, significantly improving their capabilities.

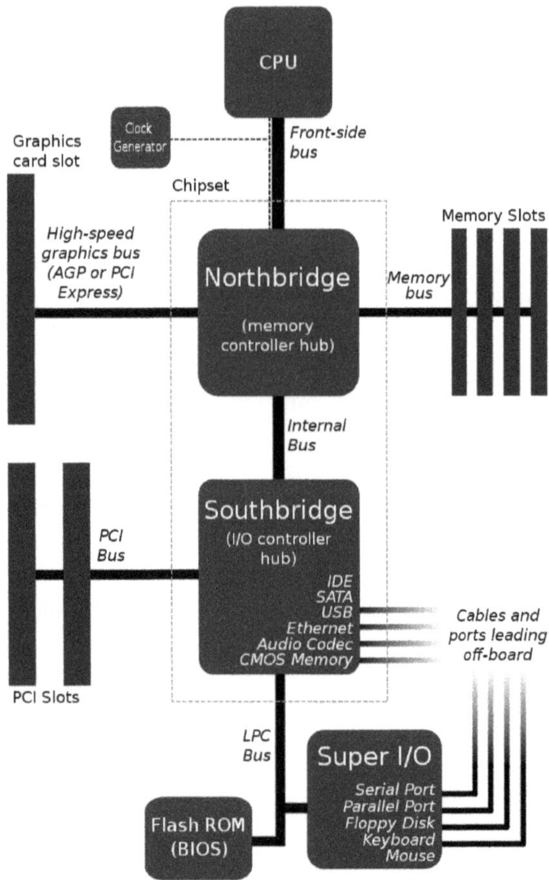

Figure 3.12: Position of an integrated GPU in a northbridge/southbridge system layout

Advancements in Integrated Graphics

Historically, integrated GPUs were seen as unsuitable for running 3D games or graphics-intensive applications. They were, however, sufficient for less demanding tasks such as running **Adobe Flash** or handling basic 2D graphics. Examples of these early IGPs include those produced by **SiS** and **VIA Technologies** around 2004. In contrast, modern integrated GPUs, such as AMD's **Accelerated Processing Units (APUs)** and Intel's **Graphics Technology** series (HD, UHD, Iris, Iris Pro, Iris Plus, and Xe-LP), can handle 2D graphics and even low-complexity 3D applications with ease.

Unified Memory Architecture (UMA)

In systems utilizing **Unified Memory Architecture (UMA)**, both the CPU cores and the GPU share the same pool of RAM and memory address space. This design is implemented in modern processors from **AMD** and **Intel**, as well as Apple's chips and gaming consoles like the **PlayStation 5** and **Xbox Series X/S**. UMA enables dynamic allocation of memory between the CPU and GPU based on current workload demands, eliminating the need for a fixed division of system memory.

Additionally, UMA employs **zero-copy transfers**, which streamline data sharing by avoiding the need to copy data between separate memory pools or address spaces. This results in a more efficient transfer of information and improved overall performance, particularly in applications requiring frequent data exchange between the CPU and GPU.

Integrated GPUs have come a long way from their humble beginnings. While traditionally seen as an economical solution for basic graphics tasks, modern advancements have enabled them to handle more complex workloads, blurring the lines between integrated and dedicated graphics. Thanks to technologies like **UMA** and **sideport memory**, as well as continual improvements in hardware design, integrated GPUs now offer a viable solution for many everyday computing tasks, providing a balanced mix of cost-efficiency and functionality

Hybrid Graphics Processing: Bridging Performance and Cost

Hybrid GPUs serve as a middle ground between integrated and dedicated graphics solutions, targeting the budget-conscious segment of desktop and notebook markets. Technologies like **ATI's HyperMemory** and **Nvidia's TurboCache** exemplify this category, blending aspects of both integrated and discrete graphics.

Cost-Effective Performance

While hybrid GPUs are slightly more expensive than integrated graphics, they remain significantly cheaper than dedicated graphics cards. This makes them an appealing option for users seeking enhanced graphics performance without the steep price tag of high-end GPUs. To balance cost and efficiency, hybrid GPUs share the system's memory resources while incorporating a small amount of dedicated memory cache. This cache helps offset the latency typically associated with using system RAM, improving overall performance.

Memory Sharing Capabilities

The integration of **PCI Express** technology enables hybrid GPUs to effectively utilize shared system memory alongside their dedicated cache. Marketing for these cards often highlights their ability to leverage up to **768 MB of memory**, a figure that includes the portion of system memory they can access in addition to their dedicated cache. While the actual dedicated memory is relatively small, the ability to tap into system RAM allows hybrid GPUs to deliver better performance than purely integrated graphics solutions, making them suitable for less demanding graphical tasks.

By combining elements of both integrated and dedicated GPUs, hybrid graphics cards offer a budget-friendly alternative for users who need modest performance enhancements. Their ability to share system memory while using dedicated cache ensures smoother operations than integrated graphics alone, striking a balance between affordability and capability

Stream Processing and General-Purpose GPUs (GPGPU)

Modern **general-purpose graphics processing units (GPGPUs)** are often repurposed as stream or vector processors, enabling them to run compute kernels efficiently. This adaptation leverages the immense computational power of the shader pipelines found in modern GPUs, transforming them into versatile tools for general-purpose computing. For tasks requiring extensive vector operations, GPGPUs can deliver performance that is several magnitudes higher than conventional CPUs. Both **AMD** and **Nvidia**, the leading designers of discrete GPUs, have embraced this technology for a wide array of applications.

Collaborative Applications in Science

A notable example of GPGPU utility is its contribution to the distributed computing project focused on protein folding, initiated in partnership with **Stanford University**. By employing GPU-based clients for these computations, processing speeds can be up to **40 times faster** compared to traditional CPU-based methods. This level of acceleration is particularly beneficial for scientific simulations and analyses requiring significant computational power.

Ideal Tasks for GPGPUs

GPGPUs excel in performing embarrassingly parallel tasks, such as **ray tracing** and other data-parallel operations. Their **Single Instruction, Multiple Data (SIMD)** architecture and wide vector widths make them ideal for high-throughput computations. These GPUs are also pivotal in **large-scale modeling** for various fields, with some of the world's most powerful supercomputers—three of the top ten—utilizing GPU acceleration to achieve remarkable performance levels.

Programming APIs and GPU Utilization

To facilitate GPGPU use, GPUs support **C language API extensions** like **OpenCL** and **OpenMP**, as well as proprietary APIs introduced by vendors such as **CUDA** from Nvidia and **AMD APP SDK**. These APIs enable compute kernels to operate on the GPU's stream processors, allowing programs to take advantage of the parallel processing capabilities of GPUs while using CPUs as needed. **CUDA**, in particular, was the first API to allow GPU resources to be accessed directly by CPU-based applications, without the constraints of traditional graphics APIs.

GPUs in Evolutionary Computation

Since 2005, there has been a growing interest in utilizing GPU performance for evolutionary computations, particularly in accelerating fitness evaluations for genetic programming. Typically, linear or tree programs are compiled on the host PC and transferred to the GPU for execution. Significant performance gains can be achieved by running single active programs across multiple parallel problem examples, leveraging the GPU's SIMD structure. Alternatively, interpreting these programs directly on the GPU allows further acceleration by running multiple programs or problem examples simultaneously, or a combination of both.

Unprecedented Parallelism

Modern GPUs are capable of simultaneously interpreting **hundreds of thousands** of small programs, underscoring their unparalleled potential for parallelism. This capability positions GPGPUs as indispensable tools for computational tasks across diverse fields, from scientific research to high-performance computing and artificial intelligence.

External GPU (eGPU)

An **external GPU (eGPU)** is a graphics processor housed outside a computer, resembling an oversized external hard drive. These devices are commonly used with laptops that possess ample RAM and powerful central processing units (CPUs) but lack robust graphics processors. Instead, such laptops often rely on energy-efficient onboard graphics chips, which may struggle with tasks like gaming, video editing, or 3D rendering.

To address this limitation, an eGPU can be connected via an external interface, enhancing the laptop's graphical capabilities. **PCI Express (PCIe)** is the primary bus used for this purpose, interfaced through various ports like **ExpressCard**, **mPCIe** (offering speeds of up to 5 Gbit/s or 2.5 Gbit/s, respectively), or **Thunderbolt** (versions 1, 2, and 3 support 10, 20, and 40 Gbit/s, respectively). Some systems may also use **OCuLink** ports for this connectivity. These ports, however, are not universally available and are typically limited to select notebook models.

Since powerful GPUs can draw significant power—often hundreds of watts—eGPU enclosures include dedicated power supplies (PSUs) to meet these requirements.

Growing Adoption of eGPUs

In recent years, official support for external GPUs has increased. A key development was Apple's introduction of eGPU compatibility with **MacOS High Sierra 10.13.4**, enabling more seamless integration. Hardware vendors such as **HP** and **Razer** have also launched **Thunderbolt 3 eGPU enclosures**, further fueling interest in these devices among technology enthusiasts.

Energy Efficiency in Modern GPUs

As GPUs continue to advance, their energy consumption has also risen, presenting challenges in maintaining efficient power usage. Unlike CPUs, which have recently prioritized performance-per-watt improvements, GPUs often draw significant power, necessitating intelligent energy management techniques. Metrics such as **3DMark2006 score per watt** can offer insights into GPU efficiency, although they may not fully reflect real-world usage, where systems frequently perform less demanding tasks.

Energy consumption directly impacts the computational potential of GPUs, as performance is fundamentally constrained by power consumption and heat dissipation limits. Consequently, the performance-per-watt metric is critical for determining the scalability and peak capabilities of GPU designs. Manufacturers have addressed these challenges by employing scalable architectures that allow multiple chips on a single video card or the use of multiple cards operating in parallel.

GPUs Beyond Graphics

Modern GPUs are not solely used for rendering graphics; their applications have expanded to general-purpose computations. When evaluating GPU performance for such tasks, metrics traditionally associated with CPUs, like **FLOPS per watt**, are often used. These measures provide a clearer understanding of how efficiently a GPU can perform computational tasks, bridging the gap between graphical and non-graphical processing.

By balancing power efficiency with performance, eGPUs and modern GPU architectures continue to drive innovation, enabling high-powered computational tasks on a wide range of systems.

3.5 Workstation-Based Architecture for Virtual Reality

Virtual reality (VR) is no longer confined to the realm of gaming; it has rapidly expanded into fields like architecture, engineering, and construction. As VR technology becomes increasingly accessible, professionals are discovering its transformative potential when utilized on purpose-built VR workstations.

Although VR has existed for years, its adoption in professional settings has grown due to advancements in the technology. Manufacturers like **Oculus** and **HTC** have introduced consumer-friendly VR headsets, broadening the scope of VR applications. These innovations have enabled immersive experiences that allow stakeholders to engage deeply with 3D models and presentations, enhancing their understanding of intricate details and designs. With VR's usability and versatility still evolving, adopting VR-ready workstations can position professionals at the forefront of this technological wave.

What is Workstation-Based VR Architecture?

Workstation-based VR architecture refers to setups where powerful workstations serve as the backbone for running VR applications, as opposed to standalone VR devices or cloud-based systems. This architecture is widely employed in professional domains such as:

- **Architectural Visualization**: Creating immersive virtual walkthroughs of buildings or spaces.

- **Product Design**: Prototyping and visualizing products in 3D environments.

- **Medical Simulation**: Training healthcare professionals in virtual scenarios.

- **Scientific Research**: Modelling and visualizing complex data sets in an interactive manner.

A breakdown of the key components and considerations for workstation-based VR architectures:

- **Hardware Components**:

    - **Workstation**: A high-performance computer equipped with a powerful CPU, GPU, and sufficient RAM to handle complex VR applications.

    - **Graphics Processing Unit (GPU)**: A powerful GPU is essential for rendering high-quality VR graphics in real-time. Professional-grade GPUs from NVIDIA (Quadro series) or AMD (Radeon Pro series) are often preferred for their optimized drivers and reliability.

    - **Memory (RAM)**: Sufficient RAM is required to handle the large datasets and textures associated with VR applications, ensuring smooth performance.

    - **Storage**: Fast SSD storage is preferred to minimize load times and ensure smooth data streaming during VR experiences.

    - **VR Headset**: High-quality VR headsets from manufacturers like Oculus, HTC, or Valve are used to provide immersive visual and audio experiences. These headsets typically connect to the workstation via USB and HDMI/DisplayPort.

- **Software Stack**:

    - **VR Development Platforms**: Unity3D, Unreal Engine, and Autodesk Stingray are popular game engines and development platforms used for creating VR applications. They provide tools for scene design, asset management, scripting, and optimization.

    - **Graphics Drivers and APIs**: Optimized graphics drivers and APIs (such as DirectX or Vulkan) ensure efficient communication between the VR application and the GPU, maximizing performance and visual fidelity.

    - **Operating System**: Workstation-based VR architectures often run on Windows or Linux operating systems, depending on the specific requirements of the VR application and hardware compatibility.

Workstation-based VR architectures are often integrated into existing design and development workflows. For example, architects may use VR to visualize building designs created in CAD software like Autodesk Revit or SketchUp. Seamless data transfer and compatibility between VR tools and existing software suites are essential for efficient workflow integration. Workstation-based VR architectures can support collaboration and remote access capabilities, allowing multiple users to experience and interact with VR environments simultaneously from different locations. Remote access solutions may involve streaming VR content over network connections, requiring robust network infrastructure and low-latency communication protocols.

Optimizing performance is crucial for delivering a smooth and immersive VR experience. This involves hardware upgrades, software optimization, and efficient asset management techniques to minimize rendering latency and maximize frame rates. Techniques such as level of detail (LOD) management, occlusion culling, and texture streaming can help optimize VR applications for workstation-based architectures. Workstation-based VR architectures provide a powerful platform for creating and experiencing immersive virtual environments in professional settings, leveraging the computational resources of high-performance workstations to deliver compelling VR experiences.

Unlocking the Potential of VR and CAD Applications

For professionals, combining virtual reality (VR) with CAD applications like Revit or 3ds Max offers an exciting frontier. These tools provide advanced modeling capabilities and richly detailed visuals, creating impressive outcomes. However, leveraging these technologies effectively requires an understanding of the ideal workstation setup to support their demanding workflows.

Understanding the Demands of CAD and VR

- **CAD Software**: Predominantly single-threaded, CAD applications prioritize core frequency over multiple cores for optimal performance. This means the CPU's clock speed is a critical factor for efficient processing.

- **VR Technology**: Unlike CAD, VR operates through game engine technology, relying heavily on high-end graphics performance to deliver smooth and immersive experiences.

Balancing Power for Both Worlds

For workflows that combine CAD and VR, a workstation tailored to meet the distinct demands of both technologies is essential. Options such as the **APEXX S3** and **APEXX A3** offer powerful configurations to ensure seamless performance:

1. **APEXX S3**

   - Performance-tuned Intel® Core™ i7 or i9 processors, delivering high-frequency performance for CAD applications.

   - Support for up to two NVIDIA RTX™ GPUs, providing exceptional graphics capabilities for VR.

   - Up to 128GB of memory, ensuring smooth multitasking and handling of complex models.

2. **APEXX A3**

   - Powered by AMD Ryzen™ processors, known for their balanced performance and efficiency.

   - Equipped with two professional graphics cards to handle demanding visuals.

   - Up to 128GB of RAM for handling large-scale projects.

With these VR-ready workstations, professionals can fully harness the power of both CAD and VR, unlocking possibilities for innovative designs and immersive virtual experiences.

3.6 Distributed VR Architectures

Distributed VR (Virtual Reality) architectures refer to the systems and software designs that allow multiple computers or devices to work together in order to create a shared, immersive virtual environment. In these types of systems, each computer or device typically takes on a specific role or set of responsibilities, such as rendering graphics, tracking user movements, or managing network communication.

One common approach to building distributed VR architectures is to use client-server model, where one or more powerful servers handle the heavy lifting for tasks like physics simulation and graphical rendering, while clients running on user's devices are responsible for handling input from controllers, headsets, and other peripherals. This allows for high levels of performance and realism, but can also introduce latency issues if not properly optimized.

Another approach is peer-to-peer architecture, where all devices connected to the network share responsibility for maintaining the virtual environment. This can result in lower overall performance compared to client-server models, but may offer better scalability and reduced reliance on centralized infrastructure.

Regardless of the specific implementation, key considerations for designing distributed VR architectures include:

- Low latency and fast response times to ensure smooth interactions within the virtual environment.

- Scalable design that can accommodate large numbers of concurrent users without sacrificing performance.

- Robust security measures to protect against unauthorized access and data breaches.

- Seamless integration with existing hardware and software platforms to enable easy deployment and maintenance

Multiview displays are increasingly common in various high-demand applications, including military command and control, mechanical engineering, and oil exploration. These systems cater to single users requiring enhanced visual perspectives. A distributed VR engine, which plays a vital role in these setups, leverages multiple rendering pipelines. These pipelines handle computations related to graphics or haptics and can be housed within a single machine, across multiple co-located systems, or spread across remote computers seamlessly integrated into a unified simulation environment

Synchronizing Multi-Pipeline Systems

In systems utilizing multiple graphics pipelines, whether within a single machine or across interconnected devices, synchronizing the resulting images is crucial. This is particularly critical for tiled displays, as desynchronization can result in unpleasant visual distortions. For instance, when side-by-side displays involve CRTs, unsynchronized vertical sweeps can lead to flickering caused by interference from magnetic fields. Proper synchronization also plays a significant role in reducing overall latency, maintaining consistent frame refresh rates, and minimizing the risk of simulation-related discomfort.

If one pipeline, say Pipeline 1, processes a lighter workload (fewer polygons, minimal overlap, or simpler textures), it will complete its task faster than Pipeline 2. Once its frame buffer is filled, Pipeline 1's image is ready to be displayed—or swapped—on the CRT. However, the system requires Pipeline 1 to wait until Pipeline 2 finishes filling its buffer before issuing a simultaneous swap command for both buffers. It's important to note that a buffer swap only occurs during the display's vertical blanking interval, the brief moment when the CRT's electron beam returns from the bottom of the screen to the top to prepare for a new frame. Without synchronization, one or both buffers must remain idle until their respective displays are ready to execute the swap.

An optimal solution involves implementing video synchronization across the monitors. This method designates one display as the master and the others as slaves. The master display's graphics card is interconnected with those of the slaves, ensuring that the slaves' vertical and horizontal retrace cycles are aligned with the master. This alignment is achieved by synchronizing the video logic circuitry of the slave displays to that of the master, creating a cohesive and artifact-free visual experience.

Exercise Questions

1. Explain Rendering in VR.

2. Draw and explain PC Graphics architecture.

3. Explain Haptic Rendering Pipeline with suitable diagram.

4. Give advantages of distributed VR architecture with examples.

5. What are three stages of an Open GL rendering pipe and how can their load be balanced?

6. What are the stages of haptic rendering pipeline?

7. Give an example of workstation based 3D graphics architecture.

8. Describe the X box architecture.

9. What is Distributed VR Architecture explain in detail?

10. Describe the Fire GL2 graphics board with suitable diagram.

11. Describe the Gloria III graphics board with suitable diagram.

12. Describe the graphics rendering modes with characteristics.

4. Introduction to Augmented Reality

This chapter introduces the fundamental concepts of Augmented Reality (AR), exploring its definition, working principles, and a range of applications such as remote collaboration, healthcare, gaming, education, and manufacturing. Additionally, it delves into the hardware, software, devices, and applications that power AR technology.

4.1 Defining Augmented Reality

Augmented Reality enables the real-time integration of virtual objects into physical environments, enhancing the real world with digital elements. For example, the IKEA AR app lets users visualize and design their ideal home by overlaying virtual furniture onto actual spaces.

In essence, AR is a technology that blends virtual 3D objects with real-world elements through specialized AR devices, creating meaningful interactions between the physical and virtual realms. Unlike Virtual Reality (VR), which immerses users entirely in a simulated environment, AR enriches the real world by incorporating computer-generated visuals, data, sounds, and more.

An AR device projects virtual images onto real-world objects by calculating their geometric relationships, including position and orientation. These combined visuals are then displayed on devices like smartphones, AR glasses, or tablets. Unlike VR headsets that isolate users in a digital realm, AR glasses allow users to view the real world while overlaying virtual elements, such as repair markers on machinery for maintenance tasks.

Initially used in military and television applications following the introduction of the term in 1990, AR has since expanded into gaming, education, training, and beyond. Modern AR is powered by mobile technologies like GPS, 4G, 5G, and remote sensing, making it accessible via apps on smartphones and computers.

Types of AR

AR can be categorized into four primary types: Marker-Based, Marker-Less, Projection-Based, and Superimposition-Based AR. Here's an overview of each

1) Marker-based AR

This type relies on specific visual markers, such as symbols or images, and a camera to trigger digital animations. The system calculates the marker's position and orientation to display 3D content effectively. *Example:* A furnishing app that uses a marker to place virtual furniture in a room.

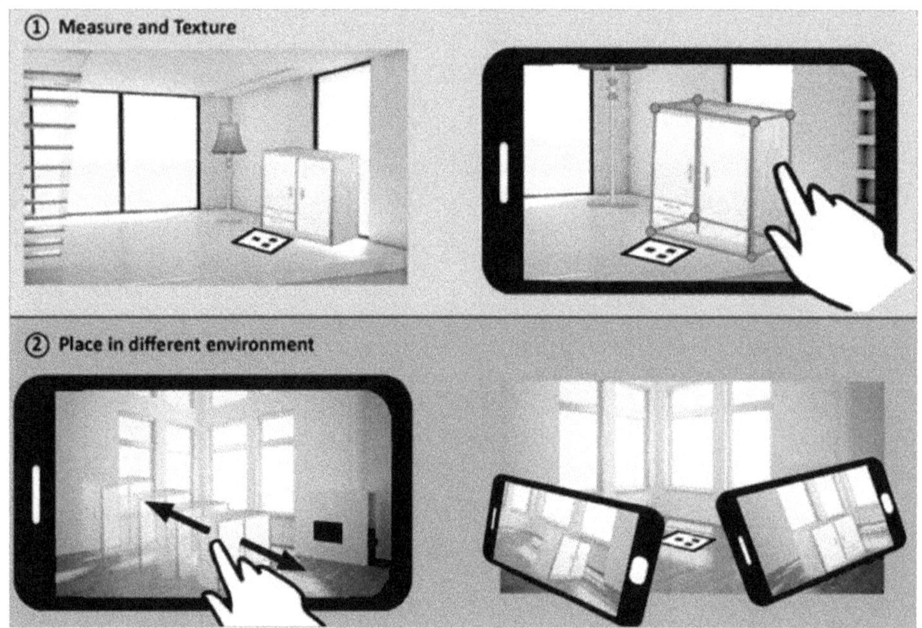

2) Marker-less AR

Unlike Marker-Based AR, this type doesn't require physical markers. It utilizes location-based data, such as GPS, gyroscopes, and accelerometers, to determine the placement of virtual objects in real-world spaces.

Example: Navigation or event apps using Marker-Less AR to provide location-specific content:

3) Projection-based AR

This AR type projects artificial light onto physical surfaces, allowing users to interact with the projected visuals. It's commonly seen in holographic technologies popularized by science fiction films like *Star Wars*.

Example: A projected virtual sword in an AR headset demonstration:

4) Superimposition-based AR

In this approach, physical objects are partially or fully replaced by augmented visuals. For instance, the IKEA Catalog app allows users to overlay virtual furniture onto room images, scaled accurately to fit the space.

Example: A virtual furniture overlay replacing the actual view of a room.

IKEA is an example of superimposition-based AR:

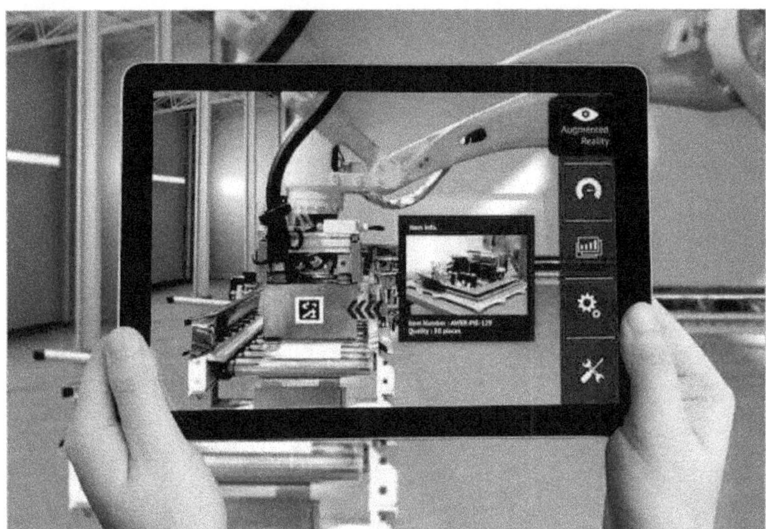

Location-based AR:

A subtype of Marker-Less AR, location-based AR uses GPS, accelerometers, and compasses to position virtual objects in physical spaces. This type adapts even when the display surface moves, offering a dynamic augmented experience:

Types of Location-Based AR:

1. **Surface-Based AR**: Displays augmented visuals on any surface by pointing the device camera at it.

2. **Area-Based AR**: Requires targeting specific areas to generate digital content.

Other AR Variants

- **Overlay AR**: Replaces real-world visuals with augmented ones, seamlessly integrating digital content to transform the perception of objects.

- **Contour-Based AR**: Employs a device camera to outline objects, particularly useful for identifying items in low-visibility conditions

4.2 How AR Functions: The Underlying Technology

The functionality of Augmented Reality (AR) involves three primary steps:

1. Capturing images of real-world environments.

2. Overlaying 3D digital objects onto these real-world images.

3. Enabling user interaction with the augmented environment.

AR content can be displayed on various platforms, including screens, smartphones, glasses, handheld devices, and head-mounted displays. Depending on the device, AR experiences may differ in immersion levels:

- **Mobile-based AR** and **web-based AR** are accessible and convenient but offer less immersion.

- **Head-mounted AR gear** provides a more engaging experience.

- **Smart glasses** are wearable devices offering a first-person AR view without full immersion.

- **Web-based AR** is particularly user-friendly as it doesn't require app downloads.

Configurations of AR Glasses:

AR glasses utilize advanced technologies like **Simultaneous Localization and Mapping (SLAM)** and **Depth Tracking** to calculate object distances using sensor data, alongside other supporting technologies.

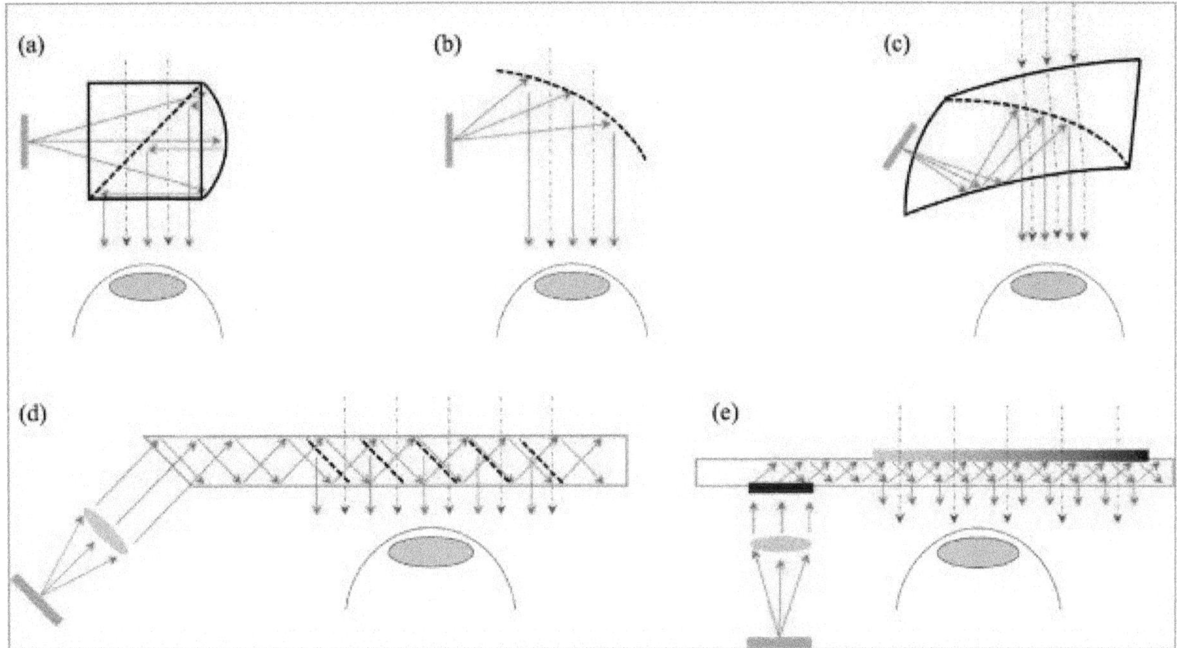

Core AR Technologies

AR technology enables real-time augmentation, integrating 3D models, animations, videos, and images into real-world environments under natural or artificial lighting.

Visual-Based SLAM

Simultaneous Localization and Mapping (SLAM) is a set of algorithms designed to address the challenges of mapping an environment while determining the device's position within it. SLAM facilitates AR experiences by:

- Using feature points to help applications interpret the physical world.

- Tracking and understanding 3D objects and scenes in real time.

- Overlaying digital simulations onto the physical world

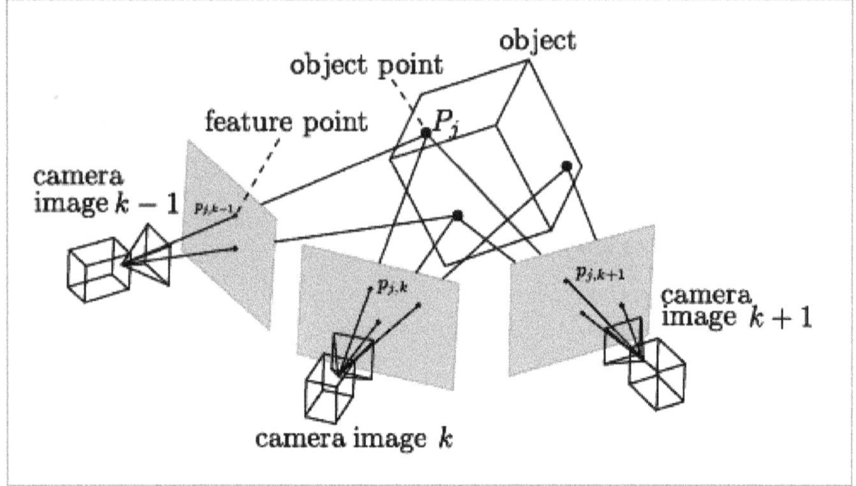

SLAM employs mobile device sensors to map the surroundings, identify the device's location, and track movement within the environment. This technology is not exclusive to AR but is also used in drones, autonomous vehicles, and robotic systems like robot vacuums. SLAM's effectiveness is enhanced by artificial intelligence and machine learning, enabling better spatial understanding.

SLAM gathers feature points from various perspectives using cameras and sensors, while triangulation estimates the 3D location of objects. In AR, this ensures virtual objects align seamlessly with physical objects, creating a cohesive augmented experience.

Recognition-Based AR

Recognition-based AR relies on cameras to detect and identify markers. Once a marker is recognized, the device calculates its position and orientation, replacing it with a 3D virtual version. Moving or rotating the marker adjusts the digital object accordingly, allowing for dynamic interaction.

Location-Based AR

This approach uses data from GPS, accelerometers, digital compasses, and velocity sensors to generate visualizations and simulations based on the user's geographic location. Commonly used in smartphones, it enables AR applications to deliver contextually relevant experiences in real-world environments.

Depth Tracking Technology

Depth tracking employs devices like depth-mapping cameras (e.g., Microsoft Kinect) to measure object distances in real-time. These systems generate depth maps, isolating specific objects for analysis. Depth algorithms allow features like hand tracking, enabling detailed interactions with virtual objects.

The below example is of hand tracking using depth algorithms:

Natural Feature Tracking

This method is used for tracking rigid objects in tasks like assembly or maintenance. Multi-stage tracking algorithms improve motion accuracy, while marker tracking and calibration techniques offer additional precision. This technology aligns virtual 3D objects with real-world counterparts based on their geometrical relationships.

Advanced depth-tracking cameras, such as the TrueDepth cameras on smartphones like the iPhone XR, enhance AR experiences by supporting extended face-tracking and improving object alignment.

Devices and Components of AR

Kinect AR Camera:

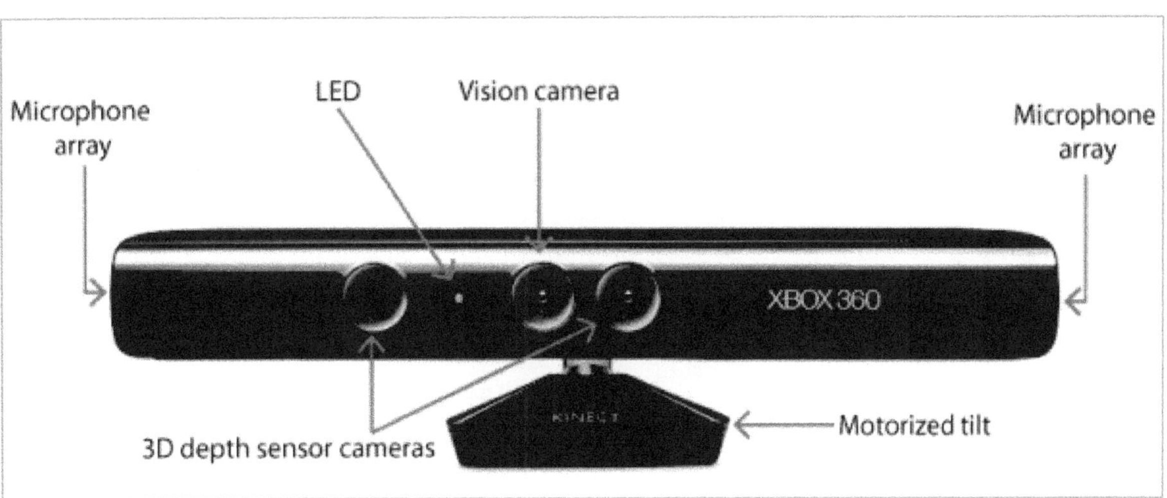

Cameras and Sensors: AR cameras, including those in smartphones, capture 3D images of real-world objects to process them further. Sensors collect information about the user's interaction with virtual objects and send this data for analysis and processing.

Processing Devices: Devices like AR-enabled smartphones, computers, and specialized hardware utilize components such as GPUs, CPUs, RAM, flash memory, Bluetooth, Wi-Fi, and GPS to process 3D images and sensor data. They analyse aspects like speed, orientation, angle, and direction to create immersive AR experiences.

Projectors: AR projectors display simulated visuals onto AR headset lenses or other surfaces. This is achieved using miniature projectors designed to project digital elements into the user's view.

Watch the first smartphone AR projector in action: (https://youtu.be/0hHtGglpvAM)

Reflectors: Reflectors, such as curved or double-sided mirrors, are key components in AR devices. They align and reflect light from the AR device to the user's eyes, ensuring the virtual visuals appear correctly positioned and realistic.

Mobile Devices: Modern smartphones are highly compatible with AR applications due to their advanced features like built-in GPS, cameras, accelerometers, gyroscopes, digital compasses, displays, and powerful processors. With AR apps, users can enjoy dynamic AR experiences right on their mobile devices.

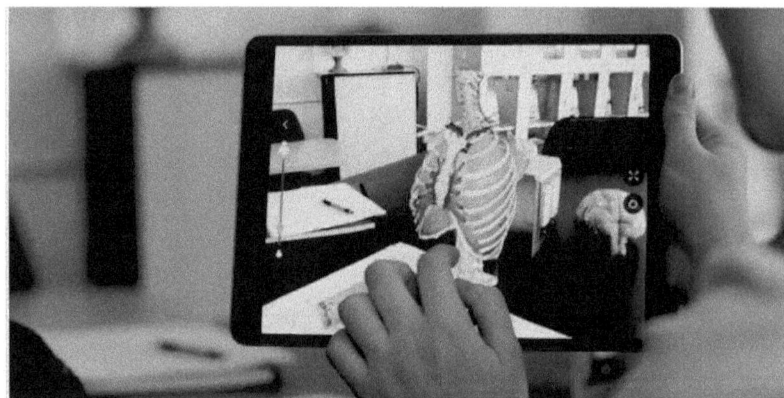

Example: *AR displayed on an iPhone X*

Head-Up Display (HUD): HUDs project AR content onto transparent screens, allowing users to view both virtual and real-world elements seamlessly. Originally designed for military training, HUDs are now widely used in aviation, automobiles, manufacturing, sports, and other industries.

AR Glasses (Smart Glasses): Smart glasses, such as Google Glass, Laforge AR eyewear, and Laster See-Thru, deliver notifications and AR content. These wearable devices extend smartphone functionalities by integrating virtual elements into the user's surroundings.

AR Contact Lenses (Smart Lenses): Designed to be worn directly on the eye, AR contact lenses are under development by companies like Sony. These lenses promise advanced features like capturing photos and storing data for later use.

Example: *Smart lenses worn in direct contact with the eye.*

Virtual Retinal Displays: These advanced displays project laser-generated images directly into the human retina, creating vibrant and immersive visuals that redefine the AR viewing experience.

Virtual Retinal Display

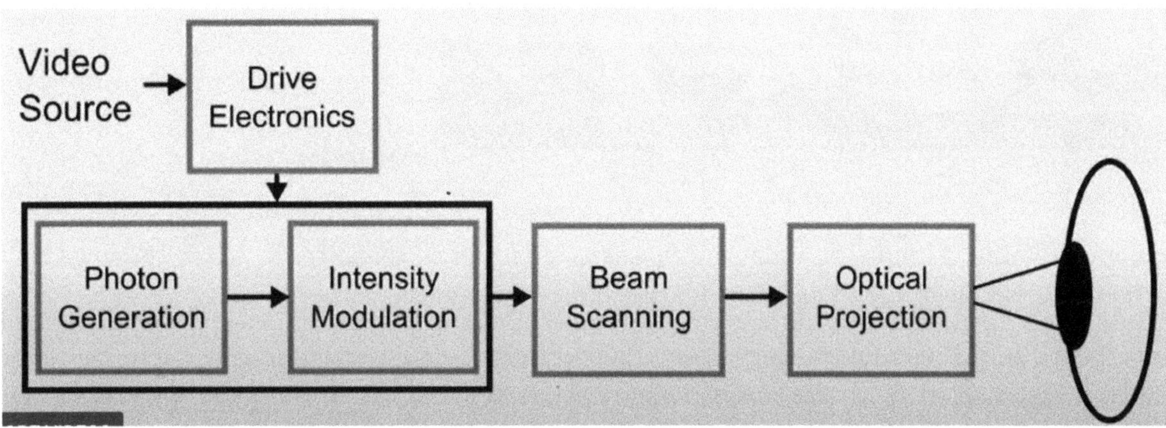

Benefits of Augmented Reality (AR)

Let's explore the advantages of AR and how it can be effectively integrated into various applications:

- **Tailored Integration:** The way AR is adopted largely depends on the specific use case or application. Businesses might use it to monitor production processes, conduct virtual walkthroughs for real estate, enhance product advertising, support remote design collaboration, or streamline maintenance operations.

- **Improved Shopping Experiences:** Virtual fitting rooms allow customers to visualize products, helping reduce return rates and enabling better purchase decisions.

- **Engaging Advertising:** Sales teams can create captivating AR-branded content, embedding advertisements to introduce products interactively. This approach enhances customer engagement and brand visibility.

- **Streamlined Manufacturing:** In manufacturing, AR markers can overlay crucial data onto equipment images, enabling project managers to oversee operations remotely. This minimizes reliance on physical maps or floor plans. For instance, AR can assess whether a machine fits within a designated space on-site.

- **Enhanced Learning Through Immersion:** AR simulations provide realistic, game-based training environments that enhance learning. Research shows these experiences boost empathy and offer psychological benefits, making them especially effective for educational purposes.

- **Medical Training Applications:** Medical students can perform virtual surgeries using AR and VR simulations, gaining hands-on experience without high costs or risks to patients. These simulations deliver immersive and practical training.

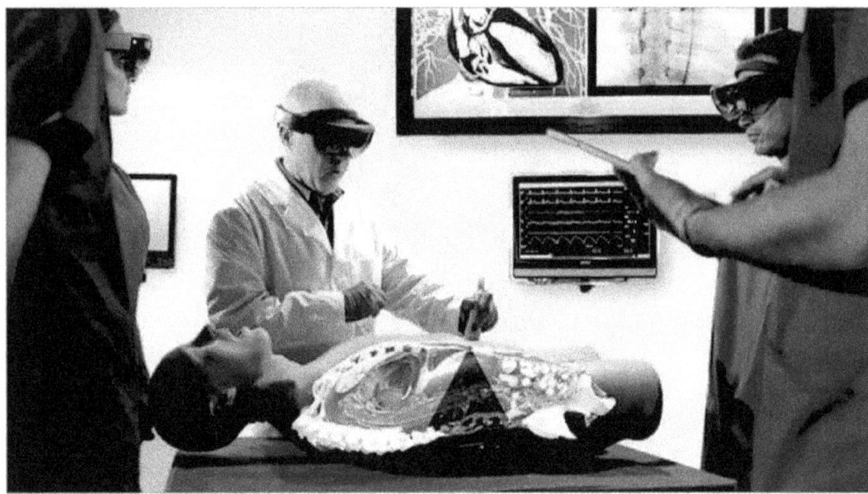

Example: *AR being utilized in surgical training.*

- **Astronaut Training:** AR provides aspiring astronauts with realistic simulations to prepare for upcoming space missions, offering a safe environment for practice and experimentation.

- **Virtual Tourism:** AR technology enables travellers to explore destinations virtually. Apps can offer directions, translate street signs, and provide information about attractions. For instance, GPS navigation apps use AR to enhance user experience, while museums can integrate AR to create enriched cultural exhibits.

- **Market Growth:** By 2020, the AR market was projected to grow to $150 billion, far surpassing virtual reality's $30 billion. With AR-enabled devices expected to reach 2.5 billion by 2023, the technology continues to expand rapidly.

- **Corporate Integration:** Companies are increasingly using branded AR apps to engage customers. Alternatives include placing ads on third-party AR platforms, purchasing software licenses, or renting virtual spaces for content promotion.

- **Developer Tools:** Platforms like ARKit and ARCore provide developers with the tools to create customized AR applications, making it easier to integrate AR into business processes and consumer experiences.

4.3 A Brief History of Augmented Reality (AR)

1968: Ivan Sutherland and Bob Sproull introduced the first-ever head-mounted display system, featuring basic computer-generated graphics. This groundbreaking device was famously dubbed *The Sword of Damocles*.

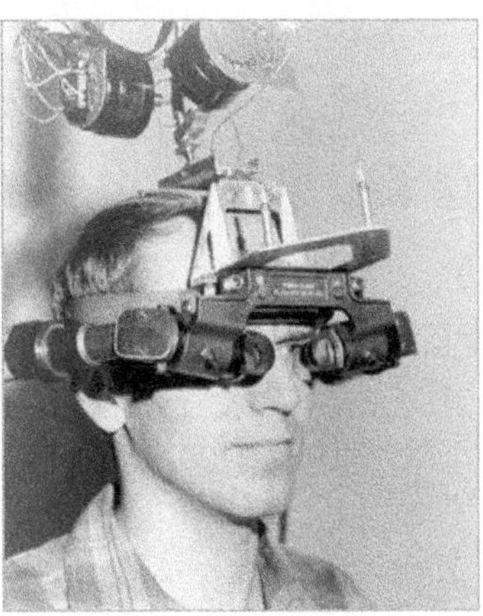

The Sword of Damocles

1975: Myron Krueger established *Videoplace*, an AR laboratory focused on enabling interaction between human movements and digital objects. This innovation later found applications in projectors, cameras, and on-screen silhouettes.

Myron Krueger

1980: Steve Mann created *EyeTap*, a wearable computer positioned in front of the eye. The device captured real-world images while overlaying additional graphics and allowed users to control it through head movements.

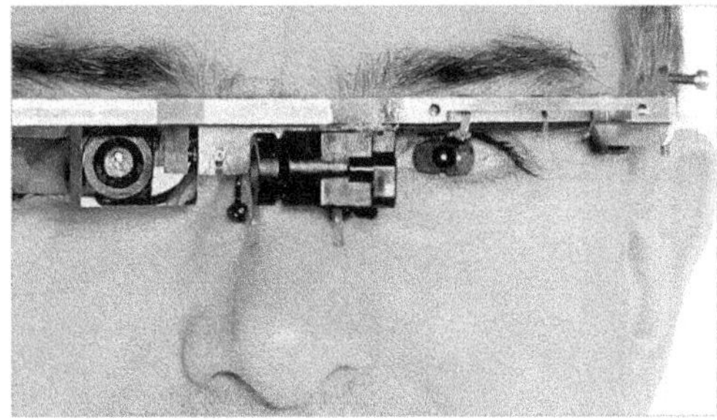

Steve Mann

1987: Douglas George and Robert Morris developed an early prototype of a Heads-Up Display (HUD) capable of overlaying astronomical data onto the real sky, paving the way for future HUD applications.

Automotive HUD

1990: The term *augmented reality* was introduced by Boeing researchers Thomas Caudell and David Mizell, giving a name to this emerging technology.

1992: The U.S. Air Force's Louise Rosenberg developed *Virtual Fixtures*; an AR system designed to enhance operational efficiency through immersive experiences.

Virtual Fixtures:

1999: Scientists Frank Delgado, Mike Abernathy, and their team created innovative navigation software capable of generating detailed runway and street visuals from helicopter video feeds.

2000: Hirokazu Kato, a Japanese scientist, launched *ARToolKit*, an open-source software development kit (SDK) for AR. The toolkit was later adapted for compatibility with Adobe platforms.

2004: Trimble Navigation unveiled an outdoor AR system that utilized helmet-mounted displays, offering an early glimpse into wearable AR solutions.

2008: Wikitude released an AR-based travel guide designed for Android mobile devices, showcasing how AR could enrich travel experiences.

2013 to Present:

- *Google Glass*: AR-enabled smart glasses featuring Bluetooth connectivity and internet access.
- *Microsoft HoloLens*: Advanced AR goggles equipped with sensors to display high-definition holograms.
- *Niantic's Pokémon Go*: A globally popular mobile game leveraging AR to create interactive gameplay experiences.

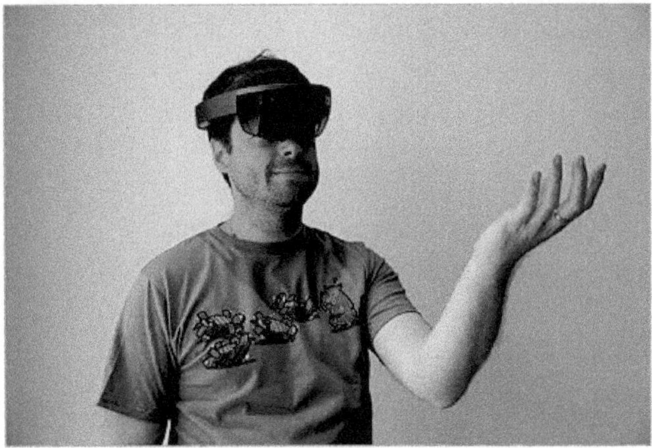

Smart Glasses:

4.4 Relationship between Augmented Reality and Other Technologies

Augmented Reality vs. Virtual Reality vs. Mixed Reality

Augmented reality shares similarities with virtual reality and mixed reality, as all three aim to create 3D virtual representations of real-world objects. Mixed reality, however, uniquely blends real and virtual elements, enabling interaction between the two.

In all these technologies, sensors and markers are used to track and map the positions of both real and virtual objects. Augmented reality specifically relies on these tools to identify the location of physical objects and align simulated elements accordingly. Once processed, AR generates and projects virtual images for the user to see.

Virtual reality, like AR, employs advanced mathematical algorithms to simulate environments that respond dynamically to the user's head and eye movements. However, VR completely isolates users from their physical surroundings, immersing them fully in a digitally constructed world. In contrast, AR integrates virtual elements into the real world, offering a partially immersive experience.

Applications of Augmented Reality (AR)

Application	Description/explanation
Gaming	AR enhances gaming experiences by shifting the gameplay from purely virtual environments to real-world interactions. Players can engage in physical activities as part of the game, creating more immersive and engaging experiences.
Retail and Advertisement	In retail, AR improves customer decision-making by offering 3D visualizations of products. Shoppers can take virtual tours of properties, such as real estate, or use AR to place 3D models of items like furniture within their own spaces to assess suitability in terms of size, shape, and colour. In advertising, companies can embed ads into AR content, boosting viewer engagement and brand awareness.

Manufacturing and Maintenance	AR supports technicians by enabling remote guidance from experts during repairs and maintenance tasks, eliminating the need for specialists to travel to challenging or inaccessible locations. This streamlines operations and enhances efficiency in remote areas.
Education	AR introduces interactive learning models, making training and education more engaging and effective by blending virtual simulations with real-world elements.
Military	The military uses AR for advanced navigation and real-time object identification, providing soldiers with enhanced situational awareness and decision-making tools.
Tourism	AR enriches tourism by offering features like virtual navigation, destination details, and sightseeing guidance. It can also be used to integrate advertisements, providing additional revenue streams while enhancing the traveller's experience.
Medicine/ Healthcare	AR facilitates remote training for healthcare professionals, supports health monitoring, and aids in patient diagnosis, offering innovative solutions to modern medical challenges.

Real-Life Examples of Augmented Reality (AR)

- **Elements 4D:** This AR-based chemistry learning app makes studying chemistry more interactive and enjoyable. Students use paper cubes resembling element blocks, which are scanned with an AR camera on their devices. The app displays virtual representations of the elements, including their names and atomic weights. By combining these cubes, students can observe potential chemical reactions and explore the behavior of different elements.

- **Google Expeditions:** Using Google Cardboard, this app enables students from around the globe to embark on virtual field trips. It enhances their understanding of history, geography, and religion by providing immersive learning experiences through virtual tours.

- **Human Anatomy Atlas:** This app offers a comprehensive exploration of human anatomy, featuring over 10,000 3D models of the human body in seven languages. It helps students visualize various body parts, understand their functions, and deepen their anatomical knowledge.

- **Touch Surgery:** Designed for medical training, this AR application simulates surgery scenarios, allowing students to practice procedures on virtual patients. In collaboration with DAQRI, an AR technology provider, medical institutions use this tool to enhance surgical training.

- **IKEA Mobile App:** Popular in real estate and interior design, this app allows users to virtually place furniture and home products within their spaces to assess fit and style. Similarly, AR gaming apps like Nintendo's *Pokémon Go* provide an engaging way to blend the digital and physical worlds

Developing and Designing for Augmented Reality (AR)

AR development platforms provide the tools needed to create AR applications. Popular platforms include ZapWorks, ARToolKit, MAXST (for Windows and smartphone AR), DAQRI, SmartReality, ARCore (Google), Windows Mixed Reality platform, Vuforia, and ARKit (Apple). These platforms cater to app development for various devices, including mobile phones, PCs, and other operating systems.

These platforms enable developers to incorporate diverse features into AR apps, such as integration with other platforms like Unity, 3D object tracking, text recognition, 3D mapping capabilities, cloud storage options, and compatibility with single or dual cameras, as well as smart glasses.

Some platforms support both marker-based and location-based app development. When choosing a platform, developers should consider factors like cost, platform compatibility, image and 3D object recognition capabilities, tracking accuracy, support for third-party platforms like Unity (enabling seamless import and export of projects), cloud or local storage options, GPS functionality, and SLAM (Simultaneous Localization and Mapping) support.

AR applications built using these platforms can incorporate a variety of features. They might enable content to be viewed using AR glasses, include pre-designed AR objects, provide reflection mapping for objects to display realistic reflections, offer real-time image tracking, and support both 2D and 3D object recognition.

Some software development kits (SDKs) simplify the app creation process with drag-and-drop tools, while others require programming expertise. Depending on the platform, users can design AR experiences from scratch, upload their own content, and make edits to create unique and customized AR applications.

Exercise Questions

1. Define AR. Explain types of AR

2. Compare Augmented Reality Vs Virtual Reality Vs Mixed Reality.

3. Give brief history of AR.

4. Elaborate various applications of AR.

5. Explain the technologies: GPS, GIS, Cyberspace

6. Where did Augmented Reality come from, explain are the historical perceptive of augmented reality?

7. Explain with example Mixed Reality.

8. How augmented reality is differ from virtual reality?

9. Explain in detail the key aspects of augmented reality.

10. Give a historical perspective on augmented reality (AR).Which major milestones have contributed to its evolution?

5. Augmented Reality Hardware and Software

Augmented reality (AR) delivers an immersive experience by merging elements of the real world with computer-generated content. This content can engage multiple senses, including sight, sound, touch, smell, and spatial awareness. AR systems are typically characterized by three key features: blending real and virtual worlds, enabling real-time interaction, and achieving precise 3D alignment between virtual and physical objects. The core value of AR lies in how seamlessly digital elements integrate into a person's perception of their physical surroundings, not merely as data overlays but as immersive components naturally embedded in the environment.

The hardware required for AR consists of processors, displays, sensors, and input devices. Alongside the hardware, five major software components drive AR experiences: artificial intelligence (AI), AR-specific software, and data processing tools.

The processor plays a central role by running the AR software and handling data captured by sensors. Displays showcase the augmented content to users, while sensors like cameras, accelerometers, and gyroscopes track movements and environmental changes. Input devices, such as controllers or touchscreens, provide users with a means to engage and interact with AR content.

Artificial intelligence enhances AR by recognizing objects and patterns in the physical world, enabling virtual elements to be accurately placed and rendered. The AR software is tasked with generating and visualizing this content, ensuring it blends naturally with the environment. Data processing, on the other hand, analyses and manipulates sensor input to create a coherent and responsive AR experience.

Processor

There isn't a dedicated processor exclusively for augmented reality (AR); however, a robust CPU is essential to seamlessly integrate with the hardware for optimal performance and real-time computation. ***For instance, Apple designs its hardware and software cohesively to deliver an exceptional AR experience.***

ARM's expertise in creating high-performance, energy-efficient processors makes it a leader in shaping the future of AR smart glasses. These specialized processors are expected to revolutionize daily life by enhancing immersive entertainment, gaming, navigation, and even real-time translation.

Google's ARCore, an AR platform developed by the company, is engineered to function on a wide range of Android devices running Android 7.0 (Nougat) or later, ensuring accessibility across various smartphones.

Display

AR displays come in various forms, ranging from compact devices like Google Glass to fully immersive systems like the HTC Vive. Head-mounted displays (HMDs) are a key component of AR and VR, and they typically feature two essential elements: ***optics and image display*** systems. Augmented reality displays can generally be divided into two categories: optical see-through and video see-through.

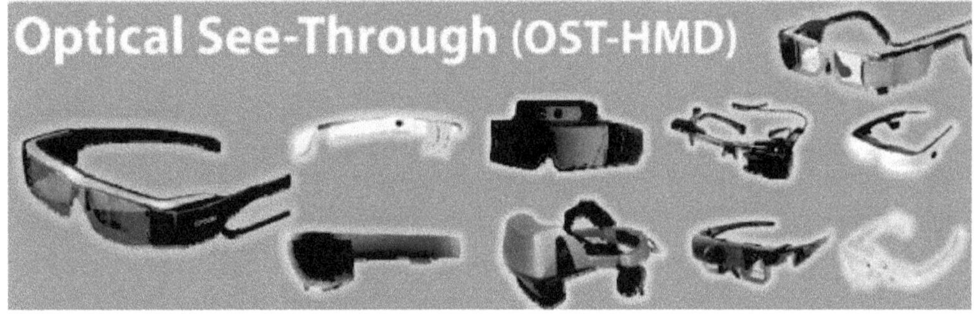

Optical see-through glasses allow users to view the real world directly through optical components, such as holographic waveguides. These systems enable virtual graphics to be overlaid seamlessly on top of the physical environment.

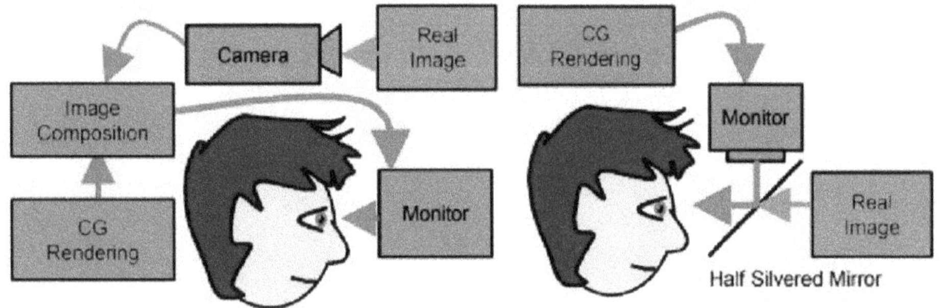

On the other hand, video see-through displays provide an augmented experience by using cameras embedded in the head-mounted device to capture video feeds of the surrounding environment. Smartphones often employ this approach for AR applications. This method proves especially valuable for scenarios that require remote engagement—such as controlling a robot to repair a leak in a chemical plant—or for virtual exploration of destinations you might be considering visiting. Additionally, video see-through is beneficial for image enhancement technologies, such as thermal imaging or night vision systems.

Sensors

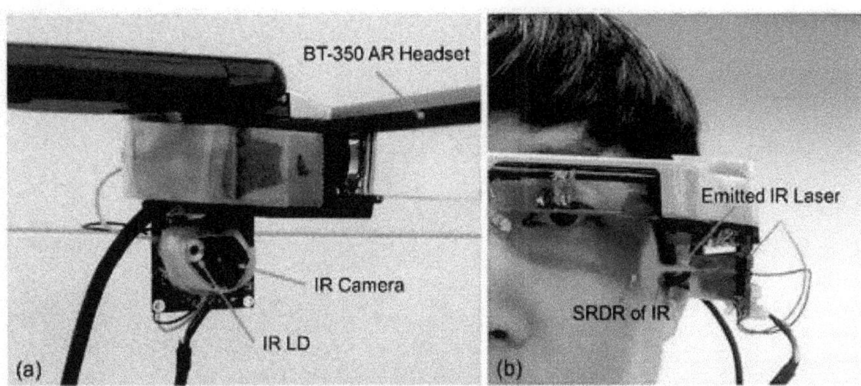

Augmented reality (AR) systems depend on a variety of sensor technologies to function effectively. Modern AR applications primarily focus on visual and auditory interfaces, utilizing motion tracking and voice recognition sensors. Since AR integrates virtual elements with the real world, it requires advanced sensing capabilities. These include basic components like an inertial measurement unit (IMU) as well as specialized technologies such as time-of-flight (ToF) sensors, heat mapping, and structured-light sensors.

Many AR headsets incorporate one or more specialized imaging sensors, including ToF cameras, LiDAR systems powered by vertical-cavity surface-emitting lasers (VCSELs), binocular depth sensing, or structured-light detection mechanisms. These sensors are crucial for accurately capturing and interpreting the surrounding environment.

Input Devices

Input devices in AR capture user interactions and environmental data through sensors. This data is then processed, potentially analyzed semantically, and integrated into the simulated world. A wide range of AR/VR input devices exists, and they can be categorized based on various criteria.

For instance, input devices may be classified by accuracy (fine or coarse) or operational range (e.g., close enough to be reached with an extended arm versus a broader area navigable by walking or looking around). Another distinction is between discrete input devices—those that produce singular events, such as a mouse click or a pinch glove with fingertip sensors—and continuous input devices, which provide ongoing data streams, such as the real-time position of a moving object.

5.1 The Core Process of Augmented Reality

The operation of Augmented Reality (AR) can be summarized in three primary steps (Craig, 2013):

- **Input:** Data is gathered from the real world using various sensors.

- **Processing:** The collected information is interpreted through hardware and software systems.

- **Output:** Virtual objects are displayed, blending seamlessly with the real-world environment to create an integrated experience.

Key Components of an AR System

An AR system comprises two main elements: hardware and software, as outlined by Craig (2013) and Chatzopoulos (2017).

Hardware

The hardware in an AR system is designed to collect, process, and present information effectively.

- **Input — Sensors:** Sensors gather essential data from the physical environment by responding to stimuli, whether physical or chemical, to enable the system's functionality.

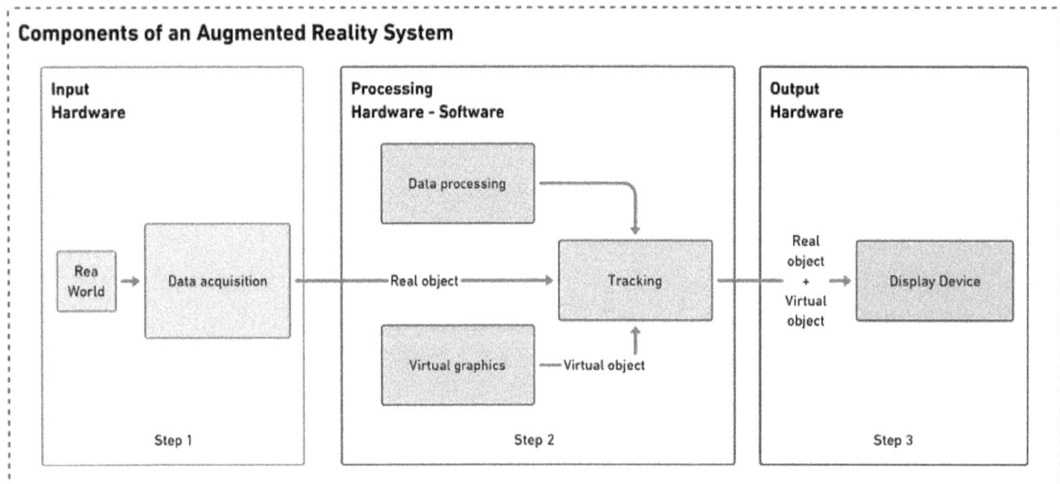

Examples of Input Hardware

AR input devices include cameras, GPS systems, gyroscopes, and accelerometers. These components capture environmental and user-related data.

Hardware	System	Type	Example
Input	Sensor	Optical	Cameras, Infra-red
		Magnetic	Compasses
		Inertial	Accelerometer, Gyroscope
		Others	GPS, Depth

- **Output — Display:** Display devices are categorized into wearable and non-wearable options. They can further be classified into optical, video, and projection-based systems.

Output hardware for Augmented Reality

Hardware	System	Type	Example
Output	Wearable	Optical	Helmets, Glasses
		Video	Head-Up Display
	Non-wearable		Smartphone, Tablets, PC
		Projection	Projectors

Types of AR Displays

1. **Optical See-Through Displays**

These displays project virtual content directly onto a transparent interface, allowing users to see the real world with overlaid virtual elements. Notable examples include devices like DAQRI, Microsoft HoloLens, and Epson Moverio.

Optical See-through display

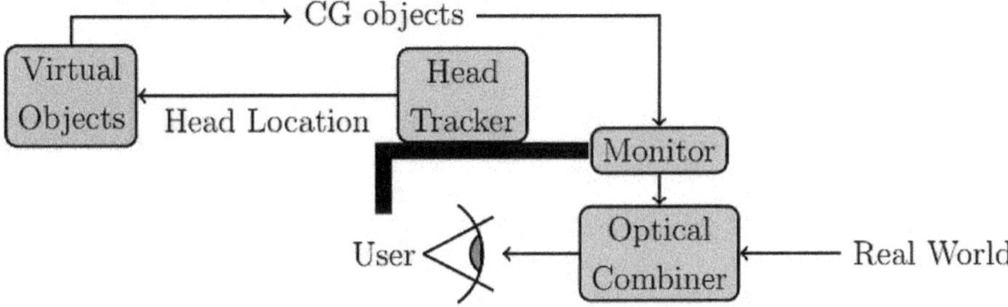

2. **Video See-Through Displays**

Video see-through technology operates in two modes. The first involves Head-Mounted Display (HMD) devices, while the second relies on cameras and screens in handheld gadgets such as smartphones and tablets. These displays offer a real-time feed of the environment augmented with virtual overlays.

Video See-through display

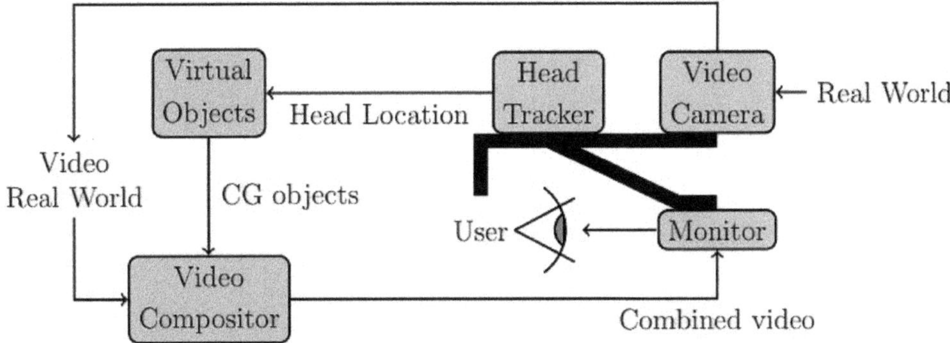

5.2 Software Components of Augmented Reality

The software components of an AR system primarily focus on interpreting and enhancing the data collected to create an enriched augmented experience.

- **High-level:** High-level components involve tools and platforms designed to simplify the development of AR applications. These tools, often referred to as Software Development Kits (SDKs), provide developers with pre-built functionalities. Popular SDKs include: Vuforia, ARKit, ARCore, Wikitude, ARToolKit, EasyAR, LayAR.

- **Low-level:** Low-level components encompass various domains that adapt based on the specific requirements of the application or developer. These include programming libraries, computer vision for object recognition, computer graphics (CG) for rendering visuals, image processing to enhance captured visuals, and human-computer interaction (HCI) for intuitive user engagement.

Augmented Reality (AR) systems are built on a foundation of multiple software components that seamlessly collaborate to deliver engaging and immersive experiences. Below are some of the essential elements:

- **Tracking:** This component is responsible for tracking the user's activities and the physical environment. It uses sensors such as cameras, gyroscopes, accelerometers, and sometimes external tracking devices like markers or beacons to determine the user's location and direction relative to the environment.

- **Computer Vision:** Computer vision algorithms process data from sensors to interpret and understand the user's surroundings. This may involve object recognition, scene understanding, feature detection, and matching techniques to identify objects and surfaces in the environment.

- **Rendering Engine:** The rendering engine generates the virtual objects and overlays them onto the real-world environment captured by the camera. It handles tasks such as 3D rendering, texture mapping, lighting, shading, and occlusion to make virtual objects appear realistic and seamlessly integrated with the real world.

- **Interaction Framework:** This component enables users to interact with virtual objects and the AR system. It includes gesture recognition, touch interfaces, voice commands, and other input modalities to manipulate virtual content and control the AR experience.

- **Content Management:** AR systems often require managing a large amount of digital content, including 3D models, textures, animations, and multimedia assets. Content management systems organize, store, and deliver this content efficiently to the rendering engine based on user interactions and environmental conditions.

- **Networking and Communication:** For collaborative AR experiences or remote assistance applications, networking capabilities are essential. This component facilitates communication between multiple devices, enabling real-time data sharing, synchronization, and collaboration among users in different locations.

- **Sensor Fusion:** Sensor fusion algorithms integrate data from various sensors to provide more accurate and robust tracking and environmental understanding. This may involve combining data from cameras, inertial sensors, GPS, and other sources to improve the overall AR experience.

- **Localization and Mapping (SLAM):** Simultaneous Localization and Mapping (SLAM) algorithms enable AR systems to create and update a map of the user's surroundings while simultaneously determining the user's position within that map. SLAM is crucial for anchoring virtual content to the real world and maintaining spatial consistency.

- **Performance Optimization:** Optimizing performance is critical for delivering a smooth and responsive AR experience, especially on resource-constrained devices like smartphones and AR glasses. Techniques such as level of detail (LOD) rendering, occlusion culling, and rendering optimizations help maintain high frame rates and minimize latency.

- **Integration with External Services:** AR systems often integrate with external services and APIs for additional functionality, such as geolocation services, social media sharing, e-commerce platforms, or data analytics tools. Integration enables developers to leverage existing services and extend the capabilities of their AR applications.

These software components work together to create immersive AR experiences across a variety of platforms and devices, ranging from smartphones and tablets to AR glasses and specialized headsets.

Several software tools are available for editing and creating 2D and 3D graphics in the context of augmented reality (AR). Here are some popular options:

- **Unity3D**: Unity is a widely used game engine that supports both 2D and 3D graphics development. It has robust tools for creating AR applications and supports various AR platforms like ARKit, ARCore, and Microsoft Mixed Reality. Unity offers a visual editor and scripting capabilities using C#.

- **Unreal Engine**: Unreal Engine is another powerful game engine suitable for AR development. It provides advanced graphics capabilities, including high-fidelity rendering, real-time global illumination, and cinematic effects. Unreal Engine supports AR development through plugins and integrations like ARKit and ARCore.

- **Adobe Creative Suite**: Adobe offers a suite of software tools tailored for graphic design and editing. Adobe Photoshop and Illustrator are commonly used for creating 2D graphics and textures, while Adobe Dimension allows for easy creation of 3D mockups and scenes. Adobe Aero is specifically designed for creating AR experiences.

- **Blender**: Blender is a free and open-source 3D modeling and animation software. It's widely used by artists and designers for creating 3D models, animations, and visual effects. Blender supports various export formats suitable for AR applications and has an active community contributing plugins and tutorials.

- **Maya**: Autodesk Maya is a leading software for 3D modeling, animation, and rendering, extensively utilized in the entertainment industries, including film, gaming, and television. It provides powerful features for crafting intricate 3D designs, character rigging, and scene animations. Additionally, Maya supports multiple file formats, making it highly compatible with AR development workflows.

- **SketchUp**: SketchUp is an intuitive 3D modelling tool ideal for architectural and product design projects. It provides user-friendly features for designing 3D structures, objects, and environments with ease. The software also allows exporting models in formats compatible with various AR platforms, enhancing its versatility.

- **Substance Painter**: Substance Painter is a texturing tool commonly used in the game development industry. It allows artists to create realistic textures and materials for 3D models using a non-destructive workflow. Substance Painter supports exporting textures in formats suitable for AR applications.

- **Vectary**: Vectary is an online 3D design tool that simplifies the process of creating 3D models for AR and other applications. It offers a user-friendly interface and a library of pre-made 3D assets. Vectary supports exporting models in formats compatible with AR platforms.

These software tools provide a range of features and capabilities for editing and creating 2D and 3D graphics in the context of augmented reality development. The choice of software depends on factors such as your specific requirements, skill level, budget, and preferred workflow.

There are many AR software tools available in the market, however, four of the most widely used and reputable ones are Unity, Unreal Engine, Sceneform, Vuforia, and ARKit. Unity is a cross-platform game engine that can be used to create both 2D and 3D AR applications and is suitable for both beginners and experts. It has a user-friendly interface, a rich asset store, and a powerful scripting language (C#). Unreal Engine is another cross-platform game engine that can create stunning 3D AR applications with its high-performance graphics engine, sophisticated animation system, and visual scripting language (Blueprints). Vuforia is a dedicated AR platform that specializes in marker-based AR and has a robust image recognition and tracking system. Finally, ARKit is an AR framework developed by Apple for iOS devices that uses markerless AR to detect and track the user's position and orientation. All of these tools offer great options for developers looking to create high-quality AR experiences.

To compare the different AR software tools, you need to weigh the pros and cons of each one according to your criteria. Cost is an important factor to consider; some AR software tools are free or have low-cost plans, while others may charge fees or royalties based on your usage or revenue. Additionally, ease of use should be taken into account; some AR software tools are more intuitive and user-friendly than others, and may have more tutorials, documentation, and support available. Furthermore, features and functionality should be assessed; some AR software tools have more features and functionality than others, and may offer more customization and integration options. Finally, you need to evaluate your own project requirements and goals to see which tool meets your expectations and standards.

When it comes to choosing the best AR software tool, there is no one-size-fits-all answer. However, you can do your research to explore the features, capabilities, limitations, and user feedback of each tool. Moreover, most AR software tools offer free trials or demos that you can use to experience the tool firsthand. Additionally, you can compare and contrast the different tools based on your criteria and factors. Furthermore, you can ask for opinions or advice from other developers or users who have used the tools before. By taking these steps, you will be able to make an informed decision and choose the best AR software tool for your project.

Exercise Questions

1. Explain in detail core components of augmented reality.

2. What are the primary categories of sensors used in Augmented Reality System?

3. What is the role of processor in augmented reality? Enlist the specification of processor.

4. What are the major software components of augmented reality?

5. How does Augmented reality work?

6. What are the major hardware components of augmented reality?

7. In augmented reality explain the audio display.

8. How visual contented are created in augmented reality?

6. Augmented Reality Applications

Rendering Mobile Augmented Reality (AR) refers to the integration of digital elements into the real world using mobile devices. By leveraging a smartphone or tablet's camera, computer-generated visuals and information are seamlessly layered over real-world objects. As users move their devices, the AR system dynamically adjusts, offering updated and contextually relevant data based on what the camera captures.

6.1 Introduction to Mobile Augmented Reality with its advantages and its disadvantages

At its core, mobile AR involves collecting data from the physical environment through the device's camera. This data might include text, objects, barcodes, IDs, or a mix of these elements. The system then processes this information to overlay pertinent digital content on the physical environment.

For instance, imagine standing in a store aisle and pointing your smartphone at a shelf of products. A mobile AR application could instantly identify barcodes or label details and present customized insights such as promotional offers, product reviews, or allergen information for each item.

This capability to deliver actionable, real-time data on products, machinery, or processes is transforming how businesses operate. It enables faster decision-making, improves efficiency, and enhances customer experiences—all while leveraging devices already available to most people.

Mobile AR stands apart from other AR systems by utilizing everyday devices like smartphones and tablets instead of relying on specialized headsets. While cutting-edge AR devices, such as Apple's Vision Pro, promise to merge augmented and virtual reality, the widespread adoption of mobile AR is driven by its accessibility. The prevalence of smartphones and tablets makes it an attractive solution for both personal and professional use.

Consider this: although the number of rugged wearable devices is projected to reach 3.6 million by 2026, this figure pales in comparison to the 50 million rugged mobile devices currently in use—and the nearly 5 billion global smartphone users.

Popular Use Cases of Mobile AR

One of the most iconic examples of mobile AR is *Pokémon Go*. This immensely popular mobile game enables players to explore their surroundings, using their phone cameras to "find" Pokémon characters that appear as though they exist in the real world. According to Niantic's CEO, John Hanke, mobile devices are key to AR's current success, although the company is also exploring opportunities with AR headsets.

The real power of mobile AR, however, extends far beyond entertainment. It holds significant potential in professional settings, where it can transform workflows and boost productivity just as effectively as it engages users in recreational activities.

The Role of Technology in AR Evolution

Technological advancements are shaping the rapid evolution of AR, with innovations designed to be faster, safer, and more efficient. One pivotal development is the advent of 5G connectivity, which has revolutionized internet speeds. Mobile AR, in particular, stands to gain significantly from this technology.

Previously, AR adoption was limited by hardware constraints, as delivering a high-quality AR experience often required expensive, head-mounted devices. However, with the rollout of 5G, AR applications are becoming more accessible and practical for everyday use. Consumers can now explore AR-driven solutions for activities like shopping, advertising, and beyond.

The combination of mobile AR and 5G connectivity is poised to unlock a world of possibilities, ensuring that AR is no longer a niche technology but a widespread tool for businesses and individuals alike.

Mind-Blowing AR Analytics

The rising number of mobile users in AR is one of the major growth drivers of the industry. Let's explore some amazing facts about the industry:

- A significant 73% of users engaging with mobile AR have expressed high levels of satisfaction with their experience.

- According to a report by ARtillery Intelligence, revenue generated from augmented reality is anticipated to skyrocket to $12.19 billion by 2024.

- By 2025, it's estimated that three-quarters of the global population will actively use augmented reality, as highlighted by Snap Inc.

- Deloitte Digital and Snap Inc. revealed that 200 million users interact with AR features on Snapchat every day. Recognized as the third-largest social media platform in the United States, Snapchat predicts that more than 75% of global shoppers will actively adopt AR technology by 2025, primarily through mobile apps.

- AR technology is already showing an increase in brand revenues. Herschel Supply Co reported a 152% increase in revenue per visit after a furniture visualization using Augmented Reality. Customers used L'Oreal make-up AR try-on feature and the company saw triple the conversions! These Apps are easily available on mobile devices.

App-based V/S Web-based Augmented Reality

We know what Augmented Reality is, but what is mobile augmented reality?

Mobile AR is using AR feature for social media, gaming, or even advertising through a mobile device. Mobile AR seamlessly operates in virtually any setting, enhancing environments with a tangible or tangible-like layer of information on demand. This technology has the potential to transform how information is delivered to the user via smartphones.

You can experience mobile Augmented Reality by two methods: App-based AR and Web-based AR.

App-based AR:

You must have used or heard of Ikea Place and Houzz applications that feature AR for Virtual Try-On. App-based AR means accessing immersive experience through downloadable apps. It is developed using tools that have depth, surface, object, and lighting recognition. This enables developers to create environments for multi-player gaming, indoor wayfinding, and more.

Developers use ARKit and ARCore to deploy app-based AR. These devkits allow extensive placement and tracking of objects even in detailed rendered environments. The biggest drawback is convincing users to download the application. Extensive QA and making apps compatible with different operating systems are other small hurdles that developers overcome on daily basis.

Web-based AR:

If you haven't already, check out these new web-based AR platforms- RPR & Microsoft's Holographic Retail Platform, Saatchi Art, and Jumanji the Next Level.

All you must do is use your explorer to access the platform for creating, engaging, and sharing! Although web-based AR is still under development and not all features are available as on the app-based AR. This is because of the data-light nature of the browsers and the supporting frameworks. You can feature uncomplicated animations, image target detection, video, and interactivity.

Even so, the demand is high from organizations looking for frictionless Augmented Reality options on mobile devices. Web-based AR is easy to log into as the user does not have to download any application specifically. It is a convenient and mobile-friendly AR alternative to app-based AR.

Advantages of mobile augmented reality

While entertainment applications often capture the spotlight when it comes to mobile augmented reality (AR), its most significant advantages and potential lie within various business sectors.

Many people have encountered mobile AR tools that allow them to visualize furniture in their own spaces. For instance, IKEA's app offers a feature that lets users see how a sofa would appear in their living room through their smartphone. Similarly, beauty brands like Arbelle have introduced AR tools enabling customers to virtually try on makeup products before purchasing.

Although these applications are engaging and innovative, they only represent a fraction of what mobile AR can accomplish. Its true potential emerges in industries that rely on mobile employees. According to VDC, the global mobile workforce includes approximately 1.8 billion individuals, making AR a transformative tool for roles that extend beyond desk-based or fully digital environments.

Unlike complex, graphics-intensive applications, enterprise AR solutions often rely on straightforward icons or pop-ups to provide users with immediate, intuitive instructions. These might include identifying the correct product, pinpointing a delivery location, or offering navigation assistance.

Practical Applications of Mobile AR

- Mobile AR is already proving its value across diverse sectors such as retail, logistics, civil engineering, emergency response, and field services. By offering instant access to organizational data, AR boosts productivity and simplifies reporting. Here are a few examples of its practical applications:

- Field Service Operations: Technicians can access plans and diagrams on the go, minimizing equipment or system downtime during maintenance.

- Retail and Inventory Management: Employees picking orders in-store can quickly locate specific products, even among similar items on shelves. With an AR scan, they can also view stock levels, delivery schedules, pricing, and expiration dates instantly.

- Logistics and Delivery Optimization: Drivers can scan packages to receive real-time guidance on the optimal loading sequence. Upon reaching their destination, AR overlays help them efficiently locate specific parcels.

- Warehouse Navigation: Distribution center staff can use AR to be directed precisely to storage locations. Similar benefits extend to roles such as emergency responders or traffic wardens, where quick, accurate navigation is crucial.

Transforming the Workplace

Mobile AR has the potential to fundamentally reshape work processes. Businesses collect vast amounts of data, but one of the biggest challenges lies in applying these insights in practical ways. AR bridges this gap by converting data—including inventory records, geographical information, and delivery timelines—into actionable guidance for employees in real time.

A key advantage of mobile AR is its ability to deliver critical information to staff precisely when and where they need it. Beyond empowering employees, AR can also serve as a feedback mechanism for companies. For example, AR can identify damaged items, report discrepancies in stock levels, and highlight worn-out equipment. By integrating these insights, AR enables organizations to streamline operations and improve visibility across both frontline and central office functions.

In conclusion, mobile AR stands to revolutionize various industries by enhancing efficiency, reducing downtime, and ensuring seamless communication between different organizational levels. As technology continues to evolve, its applications will only expand, offering businesses a powerful tool to stay competitive in an increasingly data-driven world.

Mobile AR is about changing the very core of everyday lifestyle, where augmented world meets real world. Let's walk through the benefits of mobile AR:

- **Pocket-sized immersion:** Mobile AR enables a pocket-sized immersive experience that lets you experience 3D easily from the comfort of any location, at any time. It is like the product is already in the customer's pocket. You can reach the customer without the dependency of them reaching out to you at a physical store.

- **Rich media:** With AR accessible so easily, the scope of content increases exponentially. 3D animation opens up a wide range of possibilities for social media and content. Using 3D elements users will engage in games, shopping, virtual social meets, sharing data, learning content, and so much more!

- **Improved buying experience:** Small businesses can directly benefit from Mobile AR. The products can be displayed through virtual try-on helping users make better purchasing decisions.

- **Interactive advertisements:** While image and video Ads are fine, AR Ads gives customers an opportunity to interact with the product and the brand. Ads where you point your phone towards an Advertisement on a bus stop which takes you to a web-based link to try the product on an avatar that looks like you. Sounds like a perfect way to gain attention and convert leads.

- **Boost retention rates:** For complex or new product-based companies, mobile AR is a great way to keep the customer engaged enough to be retained. AR can help make complex products seem easier and simpler through visual data which indirectly promotes spatial awareness for greater retention.

- **Personalization:** Personalizing the product with the customer makes the customer understand the desire or need of the product faster than leaving things to their imagination. With the right data, customers will not only buy the product but also spread the word.

- **Lesser returns:** Retail shopping means that there is a chance that the customer won't like the product once delivered. After trying the product virtually, the decision a firm one, and the products will be returned lesser number of times compared to image-based product shopping.

Challenges and Limitations of Mobile Augmented Reality

Mobile augmented reality (AR) leverages a device's camera to bridge the gap between the physical, three-dimensional world and the digital realm. However, applying traditional app design principles—intended for screen-based applications—to AR development can lead to issues. Developing for mobile AR demands a fresh perspective and specialized methodologies.

One of the most significant hurdles in mobile AR is achieving precise data capture. All forms of AR rely on accurately interpreting the physical environment. Without a clear and reliable understanding of what the device camera "sees," integrating digital elements into real-world settings in real time becomes unfeasible.

This demand for accuracy is even greater in enterprise contexts. While minor inaccuracies in consumer AR applications, such as a misplaced virtual character, might not matter, the stakes are much higher in business environments. For instance, in a warehouse or retail setting, selecting tightly packed products requires precision exceeding 95%.

For this reason, mobile AR is most effective for professional applications when paired with advanced data capture technologies, ensuring both accuracy and efficiency in demanding environments

6.2 Application Areas

Augmented Reality (AR) enhances how users perceive and interact with their surroundings. By overlaying virtual objects, it provides information that goes beyond what human senses can naturally detect. This additional data aids users in completing real-world tasks more efficiently. AR exemplifies the concept of Intelligence Amplification (IA), where computers serve as tools to simplify human tasks, a principle introduced by Fred Brooks.

Researchers have identified at least 12 distinct categories where AR can be applied. These include established fields such as healthcare, defence, manufacturing, entertainment, visualization, and robotics. Additionally, AR is making strides in emerging areas like education, marketing, geospatial analysis, navigation, tourism, urban development, and civil engineering.

The subsequent sections outline various research projects conducted within these domains. While these examples do not encompass every possible application of AR, they highlight significant advancements and ongoing exploration in the technology's capabilities

Healthcare

Augmented reality (AR) in healthcare focuses on integrating medical data with the physical presence of the patient, enabling real-time visualization of complex information in the same physical space. This approach aims to co-register and display diverse data types seamlessly, a goal pursued by many AR-driven medical solutions.

The foundation for AR in medicine dates back to 1968, when Sutherland introduced a head-mounted display designed to enable viewpoint-dependent visualization of virtual objects, marking a significant leap in human-computer interaction. Two decades later, Roberts and his team developed the first AR system specifically for medical applications.

One prominent use of AR in healthcare is ultrasound imaging. Using an optical see-through display, technicians can project a volumetric image of a fetus directly onto a pregnant woman's abdomen. The visualization aligns accurately with the user's perspective, making it appear as though the image exists within the body, and it adjusts dynamically as the user moves.

In addition to imaging, AR is making strides in guided surgery. For example, Blum et al. introduced early innovations toward X-ray-like vision using a brain-computer interface (BCI) and gaze-tracking technology, allowing users to control AR visualizations intuitively. Similarly, Wen et al. proposed a collaborative surgical system leveraging hand gestures and AR to create a system-assisted guidance mechanism. This approach combines visual AR cues, the expertise of the surgeon, and precise surgical assistance to enhance accuracy and efficiency.

Beyond healthcare, AR applications extend into diverse fields, including guided surgeries, product assembly processes, and urban navigation systems, showcasing its versatility and transformative potential

Applications of AR in (a) guided surgery; (b) product assembly; and (c) navigation in urban environments

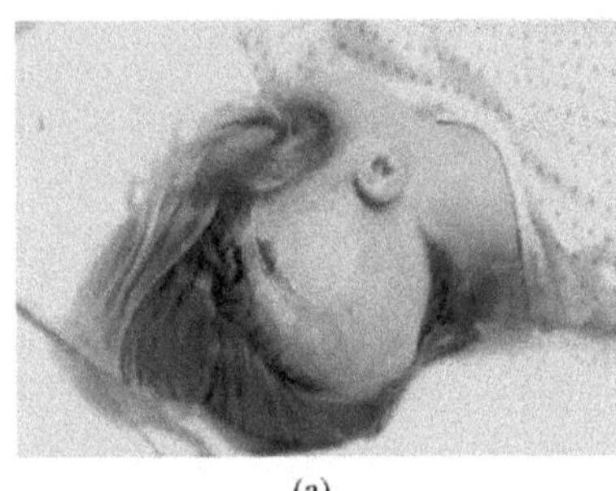
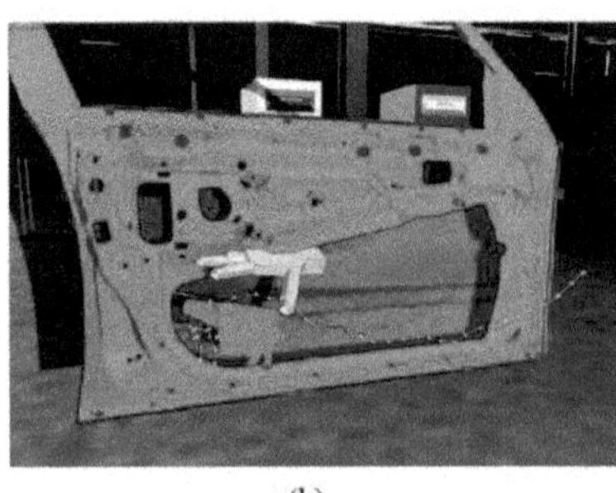

(a)   (b)   (c)

Defence

Augmented reality (AR) has transformative applications in the defense sector, offering enhanced situational awareness by overlaying real-time information on battlefield scenarios. For instance, Liteye developed head-mounted displays (HMDs) specifically for military use. These devices incorporate hybrid optical and inertial tracking systems utilizing miniature micro-electromechanical systems (MEMS) sensors, ensuring precise cockpit helmet tracking and augmented visualization.

AR technology has also been applied to military training and operational planning. Arcane, for example, created an AR-based system to display animated terrains for urban combat preparation and intervention strategy development. Similarly, Canada's Institute for Aerospace Research (NRC-IAR) engineered a night vision system for helicopters that uses AR to improve navigation in low-visibility conditions, expanding the capabilities of rotorcraft pilots.

In addition to hardware innovations, AR supports large-scale combat simulations and real-time enemy action scenarios. The Battlefield Augmented Reality System (BARS) exemplifies this, offering tools to integrate new 3D data into the environment that can be shared with other users. This capability allows for immersive training and advanced collaboration during missions.

Furthermore, portable information systems combined with HMDs provide military personnel with dynamic, real-time data visualization, streamlining mission planning and execution. By simulating realistic battlefield environments and enhancing tactical decision-making, AR is reshaping how defence forces prepare for and respond to complex challenges.

Manufacturing

The integration of augmented reality (AR) in manufacturing is rapidly advancing, offering transformative solutions to improve efficiency, reduce costs, and enhance product quality. The primary challenge lies in designing AR systems that seamlessly integrate with manufacturing processes to optimize workflows and accelerate product development. The overarching objective is to create systems that not only match real-world efficiency but exceed it through enhanced capabilities.

AR technology significantly improves how workers perceive and interact with their environment, making assembly tasks more intuitive and efficient. At the design stage, graphical instructions and animated sequences can be pre-programmed for various assembly procedures. These virtual guides are displayed on-demand, overlaid directly onto physical products on the assembly line. This real-time overlay ensures that instructions dynamically adapt to specific conditions or scenarios, providing precise guidance as needed.

Furthermore, these AR-driven systems can be continuously updated with the latest knowledge and practices from manufacturers. This dynamic adaptability minimizes the cognitive load on operators, reduces the need for extensive training, and ensures that workers are equipped with accurate, up-to-date information. By streamlining assembly processes, AR significantly shortens production timelines, thereby decreasing product lead times and boosting overall operational efficiency.

Visualization

Augmented reality (AR) serves as a powerful tool for visualization by blending computer-generated graphics with the physical world. Its ability to enhance perception has found applications across various fields. Vision-based AR systems have been introduced to facilitate interactive visualization, while specialized devices like GeoScope have been developed to support tasks such as city planning, landscape design, and architectural modeling.

In the medical domain, AR has been explored for applications like laparoscopic surgery, providing enhanced visual guidance for complex procedures. Beyond tangible applications, AR enables the representation of otherwise invisible phenomena by overlaying virtual objects or information onto real-world environments. This makes abstract concepts more comprehensible, benefiting educational and scientific endeavors.

For instance, AR systems can help students visualize intricate scientific principles or phenomena, such as airflow dynamics or magnetic fields, through virtual representations like molecules, vectors, or symbolic annotations. A notable example is Augmented Chemistry, which allows learners to select chemical elements, construct three-dimensional molecular models, and manipulate them for better understanding. These capabilities empower users to grasp abstract and unseen concepts more effectively, demonstrating the immense potential of AR in visualization.

Entertainment and Games

The entertainment industry has embraced augmented reality (AR) to transform gaming experiences and enhance live sports broadcasts. By incorporating AR, games become more immersive, and critical aspects of live sports are brought into sharper focus for audiences. With its ability to engage large audiences, AR also provides opportunities for advertisers to present virtual ads and product placements seamlessly within the broadcast.

Sports arenas, such as swimming pools, football fields, race tracks, and other controlled environments, are particularly suited for AR applications. Video see-through augmentation, powered by tracked camera feeds, enables precise overlays of digital information. For instance, the Fox-Trax system revolutionized hockey broadcasts by visually tracking and highlighting the puck as it sped across the ice, making it easier for viewers to follow the action.

Similarly, AR has been used to provide annotations for racing cars, predict snooker ball trajectories, and analyze swimmer performances. These applications benefit from predictable environments and techniques like chroma-keying, ensuring that digital overlays appear accurately on the field or track rather than on the players themselves. AR continues to redefine how audiences interact with entertainment and sports, making experiences more engaging and informative

Robotics

Augmented reality (AR) serves as an excellent medium for enhancing human-robot collaboration, offering innovative solutions across various domains. In medical robotics, AR has facilitated breakthroughs in image-guided surgeries, where predictive displays for telerobotics provide surgeons with real-time visualization and improved precision during operations. Research into AR-enabled remote manipulation has further expanded the scope of robotics, allowing operators to control robots from a distance while maintaining a sense of immersion and control.

AR also plays a pivotal role in simplifying the communication of complex robotic data to humans. Through visualization tools, AR can present intricate robot inputs, outputs, and states, enabling better understanding and interaction. This capability has been applied in robot development and experimentation, including the integration of AR with surgical robotics for procedures like head surgeries.

The use of AR in teleoperation systems has significantly improved operator performance by providing intuitive and immersive control interfaces. Additionally, AR has been explored to enhance robot programming in unstructured environments, making it more accessible and efficient. In the realm of robotics education and entertainment, AR-based learning and gaming applications have emerged as engaging platforms for users to interact with robots.

One noteworthy application is the use of 3D AR displays during robotic-assisted surgeries, such as Laparoscopic Partial Nephrectomy (LPN). These systems allow surgeons to view detailed anatomical structures in three dimensions, overlaid onto the patient's body, offering a "see-through" perspective that enhances precision and outcomes. Overall, AR continues to drive advancements in robotics, bridging the gap between human capabilities and machine potential.

Education

The integration of augmented reality (AR) into education has opened up unprecedented opportunities for teaching and learning, garnering attention from educational researchers worldwide. AR's ability to blend virtual objects with real-world settings allows learners to grasp intricate spatial relationships and comprehend abstract concepts that might otherwise remain elusive.

This technology enables students to experience phenomena that are impossible to observe directly in real-world conditions, offering a dynamic and immersive way to engage with both two-dimensional and three-dimensional synthetic objects within a mixed-reality environment. By doing so, AR fosters the development of essential skills and practices that are difficult to cultivate through other technology-driven learning methods.

The unique advantages provided by AR have positioned it as a transformative force in education, with its adoption expected to expand significantly in the next five years. As an emerging educational tool, AR is set to reshape how learners interact with information and develop their understanding of complex topics.

Marketing

The application of augmented reality (AR) in marketing initially gained traction in the automotive industry, where innovative campaigns used specialized flyers that, when recognized by webcams, displayed 3D models of advertised vehicles on-screen. This pioneering approach quickly expanded into diverse sectors, including gaming, entertainment, fashion, and home furnishings.

A simple example of AR in marketing is the use of QR codes, which transform basic black-and-white patterns into interactive content when scanned by a smartphone or other devices. More advanced implementations include virtual try-ons, such as footwear, where users don specific socks, walk past a camera, and see a virtual version of their chosen shoes overlaid on their image. With just a few clicks, users can adjust the style, color, and features of the footwear, creating a seamless and personalized shopping experience.

Beyond individual products, AR is utilized on a broader scale to augment objects and spaces, such as designing interactive surfaces on cups or shirts and enhancing urban environments. Marketers leverage this technology to deliver tailored promotions like virtual billboards, digital coupons for nearby pedestrians, and interactive prototypes. Given the wide-ranging applications of AR in advertising, platforms must incorporate filtering tools to help users manage and customize the displayed content effectively.

Navigation and Path Planning

Over the years, navigation within controlled environments has been extensively explored and refined. For instance, NaviCam was developed for indoor navigation, utilizing fiducial markers to track position by enhancing video streams captured through a handheld camera. For outdoor navigation, systems have been designed for pedestrians and vehicles, offering overlays of routes, highway exits, warnings, fuel prices, and even follow-me vehicle features. These technologies have been tested with prototypes, such as video see-through PDAs and mobile phones, while envisioning integration into heads-up displays on car windshields. Augmented reality (AR) has proven particularly effective in grabbing a driver's attention to highlight potential hazards. Additionally, conventional 2D navigation services can be transformed into immersive 3D experiences through GIS data for AR-based navigation. Studies confirm that augmented displays significantly reduce navigation errors and mitigate issues stemming from divided attention when compared to traditional display systems.

Tourism

The ARCHEOGUIDE project introduced an augmented reality (AR)-based guide designed to enrich visitor experiences at cultural heritage sites by providing archaeological insights. AR technology has also been utilized to create interactive visualization systems, enhancing cultural and historical tourism through mobile devices. One concept, "Augmented City," focused on using AR for information sharing and filtering, presenting a novel approach to tourist guidance. Guided tours, particularly those involving visits to cultural heritage locations, have been improved with AR interface designs developed through multimedia sketches. Additionally, an accessible and collaborative platform leveraging AR and mobile devices was proposed to enhance tourist guidance. By incorporating AR technology, tourists gain enriched experiences, including deeper knowledge exploration, improved museum exhibitions, mobile multimedia guides, and enhanced viewing opportunities in museum settings.

Geospatial

Technological advancements in hardware and software have enabled collaborative representation and interaction with geographic data through augmented reality (AR) interfaces. AR has been explored for applications such as urban terrain planning in military training. It has also been utilized to illustrate ecological barriers and pinpoint their locations within the landscape. A method combining AR and Geographic Information Systems (GIS) was proposed to create realistic visualizations of landscape changes in an immersive environment. AR interface designs have been developed to enhance urban navigation and location-based services, making wayfinding more intuitive. A Tangible Augmented Street Map (TASM) system was introduced to integrate AR for interactive map experiences. Additionally, a system using Mobile Augmented Reality (MAR) techniques was created to construct and present geographic information in an innovative manner.

Urban Planning and Civil Engineering

Augmented reality (AR) has emerged as a powerful tool for decision-making in architecture and interior design. A distributed AR system was introduced to facilitate collaborative design applications. The technology has been applied to analyze the relationship between perceived architectural spaces and structural systems. AR systems have also been utilized to enhance construction methods, inspection processes, and the renovation of architectural structures. Outdoor visualization of architectural designs using AR has provided new perspectives for urban environments.

A prototype system demonstrated the potential of AR in facility management and maintenance within architectural applications. Research has explored the use of tangible interfaces and projection-based AR tabletop systems, such as the luminous planning table, for urban simulation. AR-based systems with tangible interfaces have also been implemented for city planning tasks. Advanced user interaction techniques in AR now support the creation and capture of 3D models for large outdoor construction projects.

One notable system, A4D, was designed as a cooperative AR tool for architectural, engineering, and construction (AEC) industries, enabling human-computer interaction, AR visualization, and building simulations to engage effectively with architectural designs. AR has also been employed as a resource for visualizing building performance, managing construction processes, and accessing information on building equipment.

Furthermore, AR-based solutions have been developed to assist architects in making complex design and planning decisions. Simulated 3D animations of construction operations have been explored using AR, offering valuable insights into project workflows. Research has indicated that AR-enhanced spatial design environments can support urban planning and design initiatives. Discussions have also centered around integrating AR and GIS technologies in architecture to streamline construction management and improve overall design efficiency.

6.3 Future Trends in Augmented Reality

When augmented reality (AR) first emerged, it rapidly gained recognition as a medium for entertainment, popularized by phenomena such as Pokémon Go, Snapchat filters, and video games. However, AR has since evolved far beyond these initial applications, becoming a valuable tool across various industries.

TREND #1 — ARTIFICIAL INTELLIGENCE POWERS THE AR INNOVATION

The progression of artificial intelligence (AI) has been deeply intertwined with the advancement of augmented reality. AI excels in tasks like facial recognition and spatial scanning, outperforming traditional algorithmic methods. Today, AR is leveraging AI for more than just interpreting sensor data. Some key advancements include:

- **Creating Realistic 3D Models:** AI enables AR to go beyond identifying facial features, now reconstructing entire faces or objects into detailed 3D models. These models can be used as avatars or integrated into virtual environments.

- **Object Recognition and Augmentation:** Machine vision technologies identify and label real-world objects, allowing virtual elements to interact seamlessly with them, enhancing AR experiences.

- **Text Interpretation and Translation:** AI-powered tools allow users to point their device at text, instantly recognizing and translating it in real-time.

The rise of generative AI technologies, such as ChatGPT, holds significant potential for the future of AR. For instance, platforms like Spline already utilize natural language processing and generative AI to design and manipulate 3D objects. These advancements extend to creating textures, animations, and other assets, broadening the scope of AR's applications.

AI ENHANCING AR DEVICE SETUP AND TROUBLESHOOTING

At MobiDev, innovative solutions combining augmented reality (AR) and artificial intelligence (AI) have been explored to address modern business challenges. One notable example is a demonstration project designed to streamline the onboarding and troubleshooting of Wi-Fi routers. By utilizing a smartphone camera, users can access step-by-step 3D visual instructions in AR to set up their router or diagnose common issues.

This proof-of-concept application integrates AR and AI to automate several tasks, including:

- Router Detection: Automatically identifying the physical router.

- Cable Configuration: Assessing whether cables are correctly connected to the device.

- Status Analysis: Interpreting the router's indicator lights to determine its operational status.

While AR-based remote assistance tools can perform similar functions with live support, this approach eliminates the need for human interaction, relying solely on the user's actions and the intelligent system to achieve successful setup and troubleshooting.

TREND #2 — ADVANCING THE METAVERSE THROUGH AR TECHNOLOGIES

While the initial excitement surrounding the metaverse has diminished, its development and related technologies continue to progress. Early discussions about the metaverse often revolved around decentralization, cryptocurrencies, and blockchain. However, as enthusiasm for these elements fades, augmented reality (AR) has emerged as a more stable and promising technology in this domain.

AR frequently features in metaverse-related innovations due to its practical applications and longevity. A prime example of AR's future potential is Apple's Vision Pro headset, which demonstrates the strides being made to integrate AR seamlessly into the evolving metaverse landscape.

REALISTIC AVATARS: CONNECTING THE PHYSICAL AND VIRTUAL WORLDS

The evolution of social augmented reality (AR) is shifting from cartoon-style avatars to highly realistic representations. This transformation allows for more authentic and immersive AR experiences. For instance, Apple has showcased advancements in this area with the introduction of "Spatial Personas" in its Vision Pro announcements.

Spatial Personas leverage machine learning to capture detailed body language and facial expressions, significantly enhancing social interactions in AR and VR, such as during FaceTime calls.

Apple isn't alone in this pursuit. Meta is also developing "Codec Avatars," a technology powered by deep generative models to produce lifelike 3D faces. By automating the creation of realistic avatars, these tools make it easier for everyday users to access and utilize these advanced features.

TREND #3 — MOBILE AUGMENTED REALITY: FROM ENTERTAINMENT TO BUSINESS SOLUTIONS

Initially popularized as a source of entertainment, mobile augmented reality (AR) has grown into a powerful tool for solving real-world challenges. Beyond gaming, mobile AR is now widely used in business settings for tasks such as navigation, scene analysis, remote assistance, employee training, and product visualization.

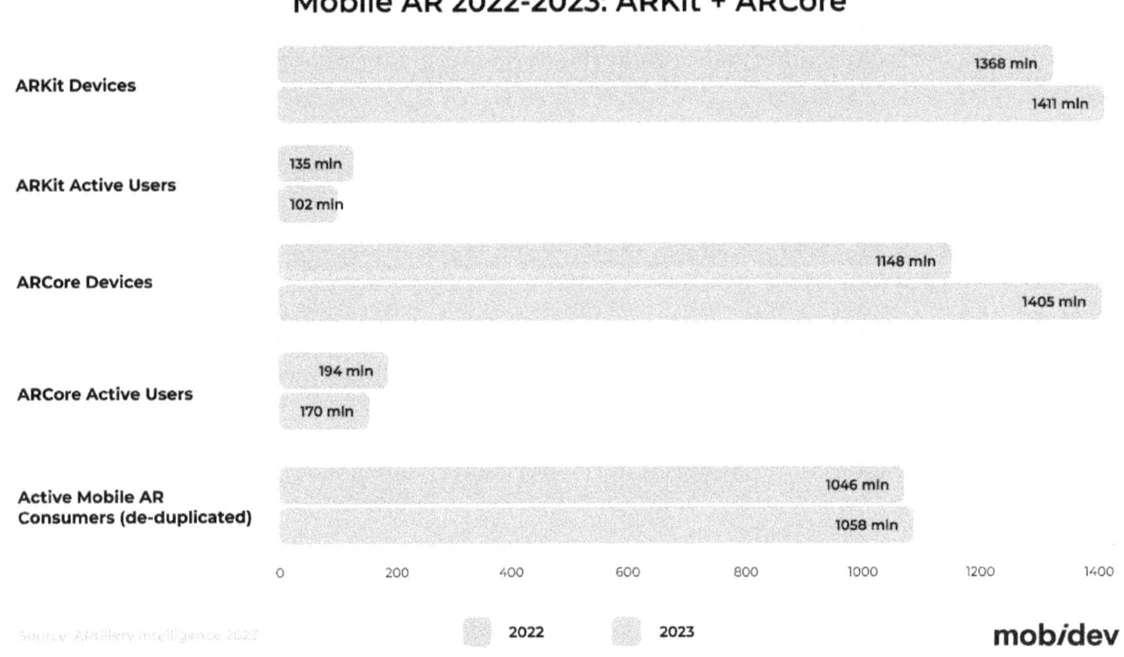

ADVANCEMENTS IN ARCORE FOR ANDROID

Google continues to refine its AR technology with updates to its ARCore platform. Building on the geospatial API introduced in 2022, the latest enhancements include a feature called Streetscape Geometry. This tool provides access to detailed geometric data of buildings and terrain within a 100-meter radius, enabling developers to create immersive AR applications that interact seamlessly with real-world structures.

Another notable addition is the introduction of rooftop anchors. This feature allows digital objects to be precisely placed on rooftops, using the building's actual dimensions and geometry as reference points. These innovations open new possibilities for AR experiences, blending digital and physical worlds in practical ways.

ARKIT 6: PUSHING THE BOUNDARIES OF AR ON IOS

Apple continues to refine its augmented reality platform, ARKit, to remain competitive with Google's ARCore. The latest iteration, ARKit 6, introduces a suite of advanced features designed to enhance AR experiences:

- **4K Video Recording:** Capture high-resolution video during AR sessions.

- **LiDAR Depth API:** Utilize the LiDAR scanner for precise depth mapping.

- **Instant AR:** Leverage plane detection powered by the LiDAR sensor for immediate AR experiences.

- **Motion and Pose Tracking:** Accurately capture body movements and poses.

- **Expanded Location Anchors:** Support for new global locations, including Montreal, Sydney, Singapore, and Tokyo.

One standout feature in ARKit 6 is the upgraded RoomPlan. By harnessing the capabilities of the LiDAR scanner on select iPhones and iPads, RoomPlan allows users to generate detailed floor plans of interior spaces quickly. This feature serves as the backbone for advanced AR measurement tools, offering practical applications for design, architecture, and beyond.

ARCORE VS ARKIT

The primary distinctions between ARCore and ARKit lie more in hardware variability than software functionality. While some Android devices can match the cutting-edge capabilities of LiDAR-equipped iPhones, these are exceptions rather than the rule. The vast diversity of hardware specifications across Android devices poses challenges in delivering consistent AR experiences.

Apple devices, despite their standardization, face a similar limitation. LiDAR scanners are exclusive to specific models, primarily the Pro versions of iPhones and select iPad Pro models. Devices without this advanced depth-sensing technology offer less precise AR interactions. As a result, high-fidelity AR experiences remain limited to devices equipped with LiDAR, regardless of the platform.

Comparison of ARKit and ARCore features in 2024

Feature	ARKit	ARCore
World Tracking	●	●
Image Tracking	●	●
Face Tracking	●	●
Geo Tracking	●	●
Body Tracking	●	●
Plane Detection	●	●
Scene Depth	●	●
Object Detection	●	●
Shared AR	●	●
Meshing (LiDAR)	●	●

● the feature is presented on the platform and is effective ● the feature is less effective or not available for developers ● the feature is not presented on the platform

TREND #4: WEBAR - CREATING ACCESSIBLE AR EXPERIENCES

Mobile AR has made significant strides, but its adoption is often hindered by hardware compatibility issues. Advanced AR applications remain inaccessible to many due to hardware limitations. WebAR, however, offers a more inclusive alternative, delivering simpler AR experiences directly through a web browser on devices with cameras.

While WebAR lacks the sophistication of native AR applications, its accessibility is its greatest advantage. WebAR enables users to apply face filters, change hair or object colors, replace backgrounds, and interact with simple 3D objects, all without relying on high-end hardware.

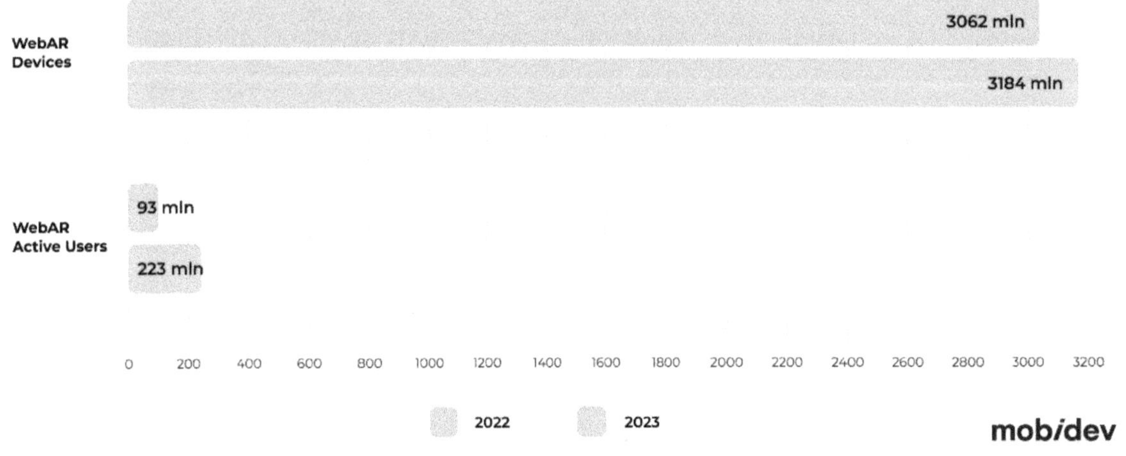

The future of WebAR is increasingly intertwined with AI. Platforms like **8th Wall** from Niantic are driving innovation by introducing tools for developers to create more immersive web-based AR applications. These

include features like sky replacement with images or textures, which can even be generated using AI models such as DALL-E or Stable Diffusion. Furthermore, WebAR enables shared AR experiences, making it a promising tool for collaborative and creative applications in augmented reality.

TREND #5 – CROSS-PLATFORM AUGMENTED REALITY APPLICATIONS

For companies focused on delivering augmented reality experiences, reaching the widest possible audience is a key objective. However, this goal is accompanied by significant challenges:

- **Platform Variability**: Different platforms come with unique constraints and capabilities, and users may access AR through a variety of devices.

- **Cost and Complexity**: Developing AR applications natively for each platform can be expensive and requires dedicated teams to maintain consistency.

- **Performance Trade-offs**: Cross-platform AR development tools, while convenient, often lack the power and quality of native applications.

Cross-platform development works best for relatively simple applications. For instance, an online store with a basic AR product preview feature, where most of the functionality doesn't rely on specific platform performance, is a good candidate for cross-platform solutions.

However, when the application demands high performance or includes platform-specific features—such as 3D scanning or precise AR navigation—native development is the superior choice. While cross-platform tools offer accessibility and reduced costs, projects requiring advanced capabilities will benefit more from tailored native approaches.

TREND #6: WEARABLE AUGMENTED REALITY EXPERIENCES

Recent advancements have significantly transformed the wearable AR industry, with notable progress driven by leading tech companies. Apple has introduced the Apple Vision Pro, a groundbreaking AR headset that, despite its premium pricing, sets a new benchmark for consumer-level augmented reality devices.

One key feature of wearable AR is the ability to create virtual screens, allowing users to access computer apps from virtually any location. Similarly, users can enjoy a cinematic experience by projecting movies onto a large virtual screen, anywhere in their home. These headsets usher in a new era of spatial computing, enabling more intuitive and natural interactions with digital interfaces.

Meta has also made strides with its Quest 3 and Quest Pro headsets, offering affordable AR functionality with full-color pass-through capabilities. One standout mixed-reality application for the Meta Quest 3 is PianoVision, a learning tool that displays either 3D notes or sheet music to guide users in playing the piano. For beginners, labeled keys further simplify the learning process. These developments highlight the growing potential and accessibility of wearable AR technology.

AUGMENTED REALITY AND APPLE VISION PRO

Apple's Vision Pro represents a significant leap forward in the AR/VR market, offering advanced features such as ultra-high-resolution displays, an array of sophisticated sensors, spatial audio, and precise eye and gesture tracking. These capabilities position it as a robust solution for various industries, particularly retail.

In the retail sector, the Vision Pro can transform the customer experience by enabling immersive 3D product showcases. Shoppers can interact with virtual product models, gaining a more comprehensive understanding before making purchasing decisions.

The Vision Pro development process is centered around the visionOS SDK, leveraging familiar Apple development tools like SwiftUI, RealityKit, and ARKit. Developers can create entirely new applications for the Vision Pro or adapt existing apps using the SDK. While much of the existing code can be reused, adjustments and rigorous testing are necessary to optimize app performance on this platform.

By integrating ARKit with visionOS, developers can unlock advanced features, including skeletal hand tracking and enhanced accessibility. Users can interact with AR environments using various inputs such as eye movements, voice commands, head motions, and hand gestures. For developers experienced in ARKit and iOS development, transitioning to Vision Pro app creation is a natural progression.

While the broader market for affordable mixed-reality headsets is still maturing, Apple's Vision Pro marks a major milestone in the evolution of augmented reality technology.

TREND #7 – EMERGING TREND: AUGMENTED REALITY IN MARKETING

Augmented Reality (AR) has become a transformative tool in the marketing sector, offering innovative ways for businesses to engage customers and stand out in competitive markets. Applications like AR-enhanced business cards, interactive user manuals, and dynamic product demonstrations create immersive and memorable experiences for consumers.

For example, AR business cards provide a unique platform for professionals to showcase additional information or creative content using ARKit or similar technologies. Similarly, AR-based user guides, such as one developed for a coffee machine, help customers understand product operation through visual and interactive instructions. These guides can be adapted for a variety of products and services, enhancing customer satisfaction and ease of use.

AR's ability to create engaging experiences is also a driver of financial growth for businesses. Industry forecasts, including those from AR Insider, project that global AR-related revenues could soar to $39.8 billion by 2027, underscoring the technology's potential to generate substantial economic impact.

As AR continues to evolve, its integration into marketing strategies will become a key differentiator, providing businesses with innovative tools to connect with their audiences more effectively.

TREND #8 – AUGMENTED REALITY IN INDOOR AND OUTDOOR NAVIGATION

Augmented Reality (AR) is revolutionizing navigation by providing immersive and interactive experiences for both indoor and outdoor environments. Unlike traditional navigation methods that rely on flat maps and screen-based directions, AR introduces 3D markers and guides that seamlessly integrate into a user's surroundings, enhancing awareness and engagement.

INDOOR NAVIGATION WITH AR

Indoor navigation remains challenging due to limitations in precise positioning. While AR can guide users to general locations, such as a specific department in a store, it is less capable of pinpointing exact items on a shelf. Current indoor AR navigation relies on three main approaches:

1. **Beacons**: Utilizing Bluetooth LE, Wi-Fi RTT, or UWB technologies for location tracking.

2. **Markers**: Visual markers that AR devices can identify and use for guidance.

3. **Visual Positioning Systems (VPS)**: Leveraging visual data to establish positional accuracy.

Marker-based AR navigation, for instance, has proven effective in corporate campuses by using ARKit, offering a cost-effective alternative to beacon systems. However, this approach may face issues such as marker obstructions or misconfigurations.

OUTDOOR NAVIGATION WITH AR

Outdoor navigation benefits from GPS, which provides high accuracy in most scenarios. However, two significant challenges exist:

1. **Rural Areas**: While GPS functions well, the demand for AR navigation is low due to straightforward routes and minimal turns. Additionally, driving regulations may limit the use of AR heads-up displays.

2. **Urban Areas**: Skyscrapers and dense infrastructure can interfere with GPS signals, reducing positioning accuracy. Despite higher demand for AR navigation in such areas, these obstacles remain a concern.

To address these challenges, platforms like Google and Apple have integrated VPS into their AR systems. By comparing real-world street view images, these systems determine user locations and provide AR-based directions. However, adverse conditions like fog or unclear whether can disrupt VPS functionality.

During favorable conditions, developers can use platform-specific tools to anchor 3D objects to geographic coordinates and structures. This creates a more engaging experience for users navigating or exploring outdoor environments.

As AR navigation technologies continue to evolve, they hold the potential to transform how we navigate and interact with both indoor and outdoor spaces.

TREND #9 – AUGMENTED REALITY IN HEALTHCARE

Augmented Reality (AR) is revolutionizing the healthcare sector by offering hands-free, real-time interfaces that enhance medical efficiency and accuracy. Devices like Microsoft's HoloLens are already enabling surgeons to access critical data, such as patient vitals, without diverting attention from their procedures. Despite uncertainties surrounding the HoloLens's future, competitors like Apple Vision Pro are poised to meet market demand with similarly advanced, competitively priced solutions.

Enhancing Surgical Precision

AR tools integrated into wearable displays provide surgeons with layered visual insights, improving decision-making and precision during operations. By overlaying crucial information directly within a surgeon's field of vision, these technologies reduce the need for physical documentation or screen-based references, streamlining workflows in operating rooms.

Disease Detection and Diagnostics

AR, when paired with machine learning, is proving to be an invaluable resource for disease detection. For instance, Google's AR microscope repository, accessible on GitHub, empowers developers and healthcare professionals to refine cancer detection methods. This innovation allows AR to magnify and identify anomalies in biological samples, improving diagnostic speed and accuracy.

The Future of AR in Medicine

The integration of AR in healthcare is not limited to surgery or diagnostics. Its potential spans productivity enhancements for medical practitioners and breakthroughs in medical research. From training simulations for medical students to advanced diagnostic tools for clinicians, AR is shaping a future where technology and medicine converge seamlessly.

As AR continues to evolve, it promises to redefine healthcare delivery, making it more efficient, accessible, and precise.

TREND #10 – RETAIL TRANSFORMATION THROUGH AUGMENTED REALITY SHOPPING

Augmented Reality (AR) is reshaping the retail landscape by introducing innovative shopping experiences that make online purchasing more interactive and personalized. One of the most impactful applications is virtual try-on technology, which has become a cornerstone of AR in retail.

Enhanced Online Shopping Experiences

Retailers are leveraging AR to create immersive shopping solutions, allowing customers to visualize products in real-world contexts. For example, furniture retailers like IKEA and Target enable users to view how items would look and fit within their living spaces using AR tools. This capability enhances confidence in purchasing decisions and reduces return rates.

Advancements in Virtual Fitting Rooms

The evolution of AR-powered virtual fitting rooms is transforming the way people shop for clothing online. Enhanced body measurement technologies now provide highly accurate and personalized experiences, enabling customers to find the perfect fit from the comfort of their homes.

FRED Jewelry Virtual Try-On Presented on Viva Tech 2022

Innovative Marketing Partnerships

Brands are also exploring creative ways to integrate AR into their marketing strategies. A standout example is the collaboration between e.l.f. Cosmetics and Google, which introduced an interactive YouTube ad. Viewers could engage with the ad to launch an AR experience, virtually testing how cosmetics would look on their faces in real-time.

A Glimpse into the Future

The use of AR in retail goes beyond convenience—it's about building deeper customer engagement and trust. As AR technologies continue to advance, the possibilities for retail innovation will expand, offering increasingly seamless and engaging shopping experiences that cater to diverse consumer needs.

TREND #11 – AUGMENTED REALITY IN MANUFACTURING

Augmented Reality (AR) is revolutionizing the manufacturing industry by enhancing efficiency, reducing costs, and improving worker skills. Its application in this sector extends across multiple areas, driving innovation and productivity.

Key Applications of AR in Manufacturing

1. **Worker Training:** AR enables immersive training experiences by using digital twins and simulated environments. These tools allow workers to gain hands-on experience and learn how to handle complex or hazardous situations in a safe, controlled setting.

2. **Simplified Maintenance:** AR assists technicians in routine maintenance by visually identifying machine components that require attention. With AR overlays, maintenance tasks are more intuitive and less time-consuming, reducing the margin for error.

3. **Remote Assistance:** One of the most transformative uses of AR in manufacturing is remote assistance. Through AR-enhanced video calls, off-site engineers can interact with users in real time, pointing out components and guiding them in 3D space. This approach minimizes the need for on-site visits, saving both time and resources.

The integration of AR in manufacturing is still evolving, but its potential to streamline operations and enhance workforce capabilities is undeniable. As technology advances, AR is set to become a cornerstone of modern manufacturing practices, offering unparalleled solutions to industry challenges

TREND #12 – AUGMENTED REALITY IN THE AUTOMOTIVE SECTOR

The automotive industry has embraced augmented reality (AR) innovations, unlocking new possibilities across various aspects of vehicle usage and management. Key applications of AR in this sector include:

- **Enhanced Car Sales**: Leveraging AR as a tool for immersive marketing experiences.

- **Remote Assistance**: Offering real-time guided diagnostics and support for drivers.

- **Smart Parking Solutions**: Identifying vacant parking spots in congested areas.

- **Driver Drowsiness Detection**: Utilizing facial recognition to identify signs of fatigue and helping drivers stay alert.

- **Heads-Up Displays (HUDs)**: Projecting navigation and safety information directly into the driver's field of view.

Advancements in Heads-Up Displays

The development of AR-based HUDs is a significant milestone in the automotive sector. Manufacturers like Mercedes-Benz are preparing to launch vehicles equipped with AR HUDs by 2024. These systems aim to project critical information onto the windshield, eliminating the need for headsets traditionally used for AR experiences.

Ensuring safety remains a top priority in AR HUD designs. Future innovations could focus on making these systems more reliable and user-friendly. By removing the dependency on headsets, drivers can maintain a clear line of sight and avoid risks associated with hardware malfunctions.

Combating Driver Fatigue

An exemplary innovation in AR technology for driver safety is the WakeUp app, created by MobiDev. The app employs ARKit facial recognition to monitor drivers' eyes and head movements. If it detects prolonged eye closure or head tilting, an alarm sounds to alert the driver.

Future advancements in this technology could include the integration of TrueDepth cameras for accurate head and eye tracking in low-light conditions. Additionally, artificial intelligence could analyze driver behavior to predict drowsiness, enabling preventive alerts before fatigue becomes critical.

As AR continues to evolve, its applications in the automotive industry will likely expand, enhancing both safety and convenience for drivers worldwide.

THE FUTURE OF AUGMENTED REALITY TECHNOLOGY

In 2020, augmented and virtual reality technologies had an estimated market value of $15.3 billion. Projections suggest this figure will surge to $198 billion by 2025 (Statista). A report from ISACA indicates that 70% of consumers recognize the potential benefits of AR, motivating businesses to drive innovation and expand the augmented reality market.

Augmented reality's growth is increasingly intertwined with advancements in artificial intelligence. While the initial excitement around AI remains robust, its long-term integration into AR is poised to enhance user experiences even as interest in AI normalizes over time. This synergy underscores AR's evolution from a gaming and entertainment tool into a powerful asset for businesses across industries.

Collaborating with skilled AR developers can be the key to unlocking your vision of success. If you're ready to explore the potential of this transformative technology, connect with us today to discuss how we can bring your ideas to life.

Exercise Questions

1. What is mobile augmented reality?

2. Explore various field where AR technology is being applied and provide examples of its use in each field

3. What is content in augmented reality?

4. What is interaction?

5. What are the trends of Augmented reality?

6. In augmented reality how visual contents are created?

7. Explain advantages and disadvantages of mobile augmented reality.

Epilogue

As we reach the conclusion of *Exploring the Virtual Frontier: An Introductory Guide to Virtual and Augmented Realities*, we find ourselves standing at the threshold of boundless possibilities. Virtual Reality (VR) and Augmented Reality (AR) are not just technological advancements—they are transformative mediums that challenge our understanding of reality, enabling us to imagine, innovate, and connect in ways previously unthinkable.

Throughout this journey, we have explored the principles, devices, and architectures that underpin VR, the rich history and evolving technology of AR, and their profound applications across industries. From immersive virtual worlds to augmented overlays that enhance our perception of the physical realm, these technologies are shaping how we live, work, and interact.

But this is just the beginning. The fields of VR and AR are still in their infancy, with countless opportunities for growth and innovation. As computing power increases, devices become more accessible, and user experiences become more intuitive, these technologies will weave themselves even more deeply into the fabric of our daily lives.

The true potential of VR and AR lies not merely in their ability to simulate or augment, but in their capacity to empower. They allow us to visualize the invisible, to immerse ourselves in environments that defy the limits of geography and physics, and to communicate ideas and emotions in profound new ways. They challenge us to think creatively, solve problems innovatively, and approach the world with a renewed sense of curiosity and wonder.

As readers, whether you are researchers, developers, educators, or enthusiasts, you hold the key to the future of these technologies. Your curiosity, passion, and ingenuity will shape the next wave of advancements and applications. Let this book serve as a foundation for your journey—a stepping stone toward exploration, innovation, and discovery.

The virtual frontier is vast, uncharted, and full of promise. Let us continue to push boundaries, question assumptions, and create a future where VR and AR enrich the human experience in extraordinary ways.